DARIO FO

DARIO FO

Stage, Text, and Tradition

EDITED BY

JOSEPH FARRELL

and

ANTONIO SCUDERI

Southern Illinois University Press ▪ *Carbondale and Edwardsville*

Library of Congress Cataloging-in-Publication Data
Dario Fo : stage, text, and tradition / edited by Joseph Farrell and Antonio Scuderi.
   p. cm.
   Includes bibliographical references and index.
   1. Fo, Dario—Stage history. 2. Fo, Dario—Criticism and interpretation. 3. Theater—Italy—History—20th century. I. Farrell, Joseph. II. Scuderi, Antonio, 1956–

PQ4866.O2 Z63 2000
852′.914—dc21   00-038785
ISBN 0-8093-2335-4

Title page illustration: Sketch for *Gli arcangeli non giocano a flipper*
(Archangels Don't Play Pinball) by Dario Fo. Courtesy C.T.F.R.

Contents

Illustrations

Editors' Preface

Although any attempt to standardize references to English-language translations of the plays of Dario Fo and Franca Rame will ultimately fail—there is no "official" Fo translator—the editors have tried, wherever possible, to include mention of published translations or better-known English-language productions, in addition to the "original" Italian titles (some of which also change over time). In many instances it is possible to find several different translations of the same text, some of which correspond to successive drafts of the original, while others reflect the dissatisfaction of directors with previous translations. There are even disputes over exactly how many versions of *Accidental Death of an Anarchist* exist in English. For other plays, different titles are in use in different English-speaking countries, and some early Fo pieces have not yet been translated into English. In this book, most of the translations have been done by the authors of the individual articles. It is our conviction that anyone interested in Dario Fo will be at home with the great variety—the harlequinade—of these writings.

The editors would like to express their gratitude to Dario Fo for permission to use his original artwork. We are grateful also to Walter Valeri and the C.T.F.R. for permission to retranslate and use copyrighted material and for permission to reprint photos of, and drawings by, Dario Fo. Michael Imison of Alan Brodie Representation was kind enough to provide a list of titles of Fo's works in English.

■
Joseph
Farrell
and
Antonio
Scuderi

established in the post–1968 period. Never before or since those heady days when discussions on the new order of politics and culture would last from curtain down until dawn has he been so reliant on quotations and categories from Lenin, Mao, and Gramsci. That, however, is no excuse for critics today to lazily turn back to those debates and discuss his work in terms of "struggle," of the imminent disappearance of a historically spent bourgeoisie, or of the coming to power of a newly empowered proletariat. Anyone looking for such analysis in this volume will be disappointed. It is time to turn the page. The most urgent task of Fo criticism today is to establish an appropriate language in which to conduct debate about his theater. Much of what was written about him in the 1970s and 1980s is couched in sub-Marxist jargon, now as inaccessible as the jargon of twelfth-century Scholastic philosophers, and representative of a worldview once widespread among the intelligentsia but now gone beyond recall. The biographical-critical works of Lanfranco Binni, however indispensable they will remain as sourcebooks penned by someone who was there, reflect a culture that collapsed with the Marxist dream.

The task is not to erase the political dimension of Fo's theater and thereby neuter him, as has been achieved, too successfully, with Shelley and as is being attempted with Brecht. The author of *Queen Mab* and *Prometheus Unbound* has been presented to generations of schoolchildren as the bloodless Romantic given to composing odes on the winds of England or the landscape and flora of northern Italy, while Brecht, if certain directors have their way, is liable to be converted into the author who dramatizes, in *Galileo*, engrossing historical dilemmas or, in *Mother Courage*, the clash of interests between titanic individuals. Already, various directors of works by Fo, finding it impossible to identify an acting and directing style that would respect both the knockabout humor and the political passion of, for example, the 1970 *Morte accidentale di un anarchico (Accidental Death of an Anarchist)* or the 1974 *Non si paga! Non si paga! (Can't Pay! Won't Pay!)*, have settled for the madcap farce alone. Others have opted for the sobriety they believe politics requires. Others again have approached Fo with a set of idées fixes over what a Fo play should be and have written all kinds of irrelevant but supposedly hilarious slapstick stage business into later plays like the 1986 *Una giornata qualunque (An Ordinary Day)*, so as to ensure that the laughter occurs with the regularity their notion of farce imposes. *Una giornata qualunque* is a decidedly poignant comedy, with passages of grotesque and wild humor, but to play it as though it were grotesque throughout is to risk breaking its fragile spine. The adaptor of the British version of *Il papa e la strega (The Pope and the Witch)* distorted the play because of his, perhaps unwitting, conviction that it was not funny enough to be a farce. To ensure an acceptable decibellage of hilarity, he stooped to devices such as giving the cardinals in the Papal Curia the names of the Italian soccer team players who had just won the World Cup and having them use four-letter words with the abandon of infantrymen on leave in a foreign capital. Perhaps he could have examined more closely his own preconceptions about Fo or could even have subjected the original play itself to more rigorous scrutiny.

As the editors of this volume, we have set ourselves the task of beginning a reexamination of Fo's work and of identifying the core that will be of lasting value. This task has many aspects. It involves locating Fo in history, underlining the nature of his development through successive phases, incorporating his politics into a wider framework of radical dissent, and setting his theatrical achievements in a context and a tradition. In a wider sense, it involves establishing what could reasonably be called the "poetics of Dario Fo." Fo himself never fought shy of employing this somewhat grandiloquent terminology, often in a deliberately paradoxical or provocative context. In his essay on the Neapolitan comic actor Totò, *Totò, manuale dell'attore comico* (Totò, the comic actor's manual), he wrote that a comic actor could only be understood and appreciated if he operated within an identifiable poetic (1991a:9). In Fo's own case, the poetics are rich and complex but paradoxically at odds with the politics. If Fo was a revolutionary in politics, he reveals himself an intransigent conservative in poetics. His theatrical credo requires abstracting from the many interviews, workshops, and laboratories he gave over the years, some later collected in *Manuale minimo dell'attore* (Actor's mini-manual, published in English as *Tricks of the Trade*). Even so, Fo will never rival Stanislavsky or Brecht as a theorist of the stage. All his theorizing dwindles into nontheory at the point when his urge to demonstrate, to practice, and to perform takes over, but he is not a purely instinctive performer, for there is behind him a richer tradition and a deeper culture than has been admitted by both admirers and opponents. The clichéd image of Fo the militant playwright is not misguided, but it is inadequate.

It might be valuable at this stage to outline briefly the career and development of Fo. Unlike Franca Rame, his wife and collaborator, Fo was not part of a theatrical family. Born in 1926 in a small community on the shores of Lake Maggiore in northern Italy, he trained first as an architect and seems to have gravitated toward performance as the natural outlet for his innate creativity and exuberance of character. Rame was born in 1929 to a family of strolling players who could trace their theatrical pedigree back to the eighteenth century. Fo made his theatrical debut in the early 1950s with *Poer nano* (Poor wretch), a series of comic monologues he wrote for performance onstage and for broadcast on radio. Fo and Rame met while performing in the same show in Milan, and Rame relishes telling how it was she who took the initiative with the gangling, awkward youth who was plainly captivated by her but was too shy to make the first approach. After their marriage in 1954, the pair founded their own company, the Compagnia Fo-Rame, whose first initiative was to stage two quartets of one-act farces written by Fo. The second set of these plays, the 1958 *Comica finale* (Comic finale), is of special interest, since it highlights tendencies that were to be characteristic of the man and his theater at every stage of his life. The four constituent pieces were adaptations of works that had been part of the repertoire of the Rame family. Although he later elaborated complex views on what constitutes "popular theater," he stumbled onto it at the beginning of his career since it was a style of theater the Rame family had practiced before the term became current. Similarly, the tendency to find inspiration in the past, to be a respecter of theatrical tradition and not an anarchic iconoclast, a conservative rather than an experimentalist, was to be a constant in Fo's career. Fo's debt to Rame is enormous.

The span of years from 1959 to 1968 was a period later tagged Fo's "bourgeois" period. This vogue for periodization is generally a critic's game, but since Fo does not deny that he made a fresh start in 1968, the term has some value in denoting a stage in his evolution. However, in this volume, Bent Holm subjects that period to trenchant reexamination, questioning whether, in the light of the mordant satire Fo expresses in an age when censorship was rigidly enforced, the "bourgeois" tag remains appropriate. It is tempting to follow the categorization used of Pablo Picasso and dub Fo's successive phases by appropriate colors. The "bourgeois" years could be labeled the "blue period," when Fo and Rame performed with enormous success in the established theaters of the great cities of Italy. Italy was experiencing its "economic miracle," and although Fo and Rame took a sufficiently jaundiced, satirical view of developments in the country to provoke the censors, their general stance was no more adversarial than is conventionally expected of writers in Western society today. Their critique of society could be compared with that advanced by, for example, Norman Mailer in the United States. All of that changed with Fo's "red period," the years following the student revolts of 1968, when opposition to the Vietnam War provided the focus for the radicalization of a generation and when a wider if imprecise discontent with the tedium of affluence and materialism took hold of sections of youthful society. For the self-proclaimed revolutionaries of those years, it seemed that a new civilization, to be created in accordance with the teachings of Karl Marx, mediated by Herbert Marcuse, Antonio Gramsci, and Jean Paul Sartre and tempered by Groucho Marx (as a famous graffiti on a wall in Paris had it), was in the making. In this climate, Fo, by then indisputably the most successful playwright in Italy, broke with "bourgeois theater" to forge a new style of popular theater and to establish an "alternative circuit" of spaces far removed from established commercial venues. In the first years, 1968–70, with the company called Nuova Scena, he played in spaces managed by a cultural and recreational circle linked to the Communist Party. But he moved further to the left, grew dissatisfied with the caution of the Communists, and established another company, La Comune, which had its own venue in Milan, Il Capannone, but toured widely and performed in improvised venues managed by members of the group.

It is to this arc of years that his best-known plays belong. This is Fo the revolutionary, who attacked American involvement in Vietnam in plays such as the 1967 *La signora è da buttare (Toss the Lady Out)*; who ridiculed the church, the army, and big business in the 1968 *Grande pantomima con bandiere e pupazzi piccoli e medi* (Grand pantomime with flags and small and medium-sized puppets); who slammed the Italian Communist Party for their feeble compromise with capitalism in the 1969 *Legami pure che tanto io spacco tutto lo stesso* (Tie me up but I'll still smash everything); who mocked the church, if not Christian belief, in the 1969 *Mistero buffo* (Comic mystery); who denounced the connivance between the police, politicians, and neo-Fascist terrorists in the 1970 *Morte accidentale*; who supported Palestinian militants in the 1971 *Fedayn* (Fedayeen); who advocated what was then termed "proletarian expropriation" and what lawyers call shoplifting in the 1974 *Non si paga!*; and who denounced the power of industrial bosses in works such as the 1981 *Clacson, trombette e pernacchi (Trumpets and Raspberries)*. It is not possible, in other words, to take the politics out of Fo or to present him as a mild liberal. When President Reagan's administration refused Fo a visa to perform in America on the grounds that he was a "subversive," they chose the wrong grounds. There was nothing subversive, or at least nothing covert, about Fo's aims. He was as openly revolutionary as any man could be.

Fo was the singer of the new revolutionary forces, but his voice faltered when some worshipers of the new dawn decided to hurry the process of history by taking up the gun. Neither Fo nor Rame had any sympathy with violence, and while their allegiance to the extreme left was of the solidity of iron, they represented a beacon of decency in those dark days. They spoke against the "opposing extremisms," as the phrase was, condemning the violence of the Left to which they belonged and fulminating against the unpunished violence of the Right. This latter, composed of genteel elements inside ministries and sinister wolf packs in cellars, was permitted, or even encouraged, to commit acts of mass slaughter, like blowing up railway stations and setting off bombs in banks and piazzas. The same grim forces were responsible for the kidnapping and rape of Rame in 1973. The subsequent phase, when the political passion deriving from 1968 was spent and the frustrated revolutionaries retired to dig their gardens and cultivate private or social concerns, was also a fertile period in Fo's career, but with the withering of the post-1968, extraparliamentary movement, Fo had no longer the same appeal for mass audiences. Fo and Rame themselves never betrayed their principles. In later years, Rame wrote with bitter irony of her surprise and dismay on seeing the faces of erstwhile rebels on television.

> Incredible! We know that lawyer, he was in Red Aid, his generous heart and intelligence at the service of the class struggle! And that other one used to teach law at the university. He gave us lectures on the tricks of bourgeois justice and its phoney liberties. And now both (for a fee, obviously) defend the most famous sleaze-merchants, the ones that counted their bribes in the billions. (Fo 1998:204)

Around 1977, the "red" period of militant piazza politics gave way for Fo and Rame to a "rose" mood with *Tutta casa, letto e chiesa (All Bed, Board, and Church)*, the first of a series of strongly feminist pieces. With these and subsequent monologues and plays, Rame became a feminist icon in Italy and abroad, but as Sharon Wood discusses, her

brand of feminism was more idiosyncratic than was realized at the time.
It is at this point that it became common to refer to the theater of Fo
and Rame, rather than of Fo alone. In terms of actual writing, little
changed. He remained, for the most part, the writer and she the only
trusted critic. Her influence in the shaping and modifying of their theater had always been considerable and now received more generous notice on the covers of the printed versions. It could be said that if the plays
began as his, they ended as hers. A Fo, or a Fo/Rame, script undergoes
endless modifications during rehearsal, during the run, and during debates to test audience reaction. Rame is obviously in a position to comment from the first, and she intervenes substantially from the beginning
of rehearsals. It is also she who administers the companies and prepares
the changing versions of the script into something that could be distributed to the company and later delivered for publication. Some works
were wholly hers, most notably the heart-wrenching one-act monologue, *Lo stupro (The Rape),* based on her own appalling experiences.

If the popularity of Fo inside Italy went into temporary decline in
the 1980s, he continued to be invited to perform in the world's most
prestigious theaters, and his work continued to be staged in all five con-
tinents. The highest recognition of his achievements came with the
award in 1997 of the Nobel Prize for Literature. The citation issued by
the Swedish Academy, even if inevitably couched in the kind of language that could be inscribed on marble, is a marvel of concision and
precision. The actor and playwright was recognized for having "in the
tradition of the medieval players castigated power and restored dignity
to the oppressed" (1997).

The words highlight the dissonance between the poetics and the
politics, between the revolutionary and the traditionalist. The revolutionary having been debated ad infinitum elsewhere, it is time to focus
on "the actor and playwright" and to put flesh on the poetics. Fo inhabits
tradition. He has had no truck with the avant-garde, ever. His distaste
for any semblance of experimentalism lay behind one of the more bizarre incidents in his career. In 1953, he set up, with Giustino Durano
and Franco Parenti, a company that staged the "leftist" review, *Il dito
nell'occhio (A Finger in the Eye),* written mainly by him and performed
by all three. The group met with public and critical acclaim, but the company broke up when on the crest of a wave. In all subsequent statements,

including those given decades later, Fo explained the split by reference to Parenti's ambition to stage Ionesco. In an interview with *Drama Review*, he said:

> Then came the parting of the ways between Parenti and myself. It occurred mainly for political reasons. He wanted to stage a socially inclined type of theater, but not one directly involved with politics as that I had in mind. In fact he ended up doing Ionesco. I could not possibly bring myself to agree with his choices. (1978:77)

Other groups might have been able to disagree over Ionesco and find a modus operandi, but for Fo, there was a principle involved. There was a political dimension to the separation but also a disagreement over theater. Popular theater was Fo's chosen option. The avant-garde he left to others.

In the 1960s and 1970s, Fo did not disdain agit-prop when called on to lend support to specific factory occupations or strikes, but his finest works transcend that category. The underlying tension in his most important political plays concerns culture, when culture is seen in the terms defined by Antonio Gramsci. Any attempt to put flesh on the theatrical poetics of Fo has to begin with the thought of Gramsci (1891–1937). Gramsci, probably the most original theorist in the Marxist tradition after Marx himself, had been imprisoned under Mussolini in a vain attempt, as the prosecutor said at his trial, to stop that brain working for a generation. His *Prison Notebooks* became available in Italy in the immediate postwar period, when Fo was a student in Milan, and their main contribution was to switch the emphasis of Marxist theory away from economic-based thought to culture itself. In classical Marxism, cultural activities are no more than a projection on a "superstructure" of tensions and contradictions that exist on the basic, that is, economic, substructure of society. Gramsci was concerned with an analysis of power structures in society and included culture in that analysis on the grounds that it was a pillar of that structure—a means by which privileged elites maintained their hegemony. Since it was not the case that the subaltern classes in society were in continual revolt against a system that was oppressive, unjust, and exploitative, nor were they held down by police or military activity, what kept them in a state of willing subjection? Gramsci found the answer in his notion of culture—a prerational complex of ideas, values, and assumptions. The human creature inhabits a dimension that is unknown to other animals but that shapes his being as powerfully as any physical force. The seventeenth-century philosopher Blaise Pascal spoke of human beings inhabiting an area between the brute animals and the angels, where the life of the spirit had the same importance as sensual cravings. We take it that much of what thinkers of other times saw as "spirit" is now conveyed by the term "culture." Culture determines action, because culture conditions and determines expectations. For Gramsci, the primacy of culture meant that people were cowed by what they had been conditioned to believe was right and proper or was their allotted portion of life. The revolution of society had to be preceded by a liberation of that sphere of the individual that was not amenable to public action. Fo saw cultural change, which could be worked by theater, as a tool for the decolonization of the mind, of the will, and of the imagination. He was not alone. The American writer Sam Shepard, in an astonishing but amazingly little-known work, *Angel City*, dramatized the international power of Hollywood, questioning the willingness of people to hand over the dream dimension of their lives to such an evidently crass and self-serving machine as the film industry.

Crucially, Gramsci held that side by side with the high, aesthetic culture of the patrician and educated classes there was a popular culture that had been systematically debased. Fo's political radicalism would be principally cultural radicalism but not of the sort advocated by avant-garde playwrights, who performed to consenting adults in private. Under Gramsci's influence, Fo adopted a style of popular theater, with its roots in tradition. Fo has always been the Gramscian word made flesh. Theater, in Fo's eyes, that is, comic theater, satirical theater, the theater that flayed abuses with the severity Aristophanes, Plautus, Ruzzante, and Molière had displayed, could perform a revolutionary function. When Fo chose to use theater for that end, he turned to a modern philosophy—Marxism—and to theatrical devices of the past—those used by the *giullare*. He was simultaneously, and disconcertingly, an innovator and a reactionary. It could be added that while the failure of Italian intellectuals to appreciate Fo is itself incomprehensible to outsiders, their inability to see him in a Gramscian perspective is downright perverse. Cultural problems identified by Gramsci became the common currency of debate in leftist intellectual circles, and, indeed, the absence of a genuine popular language was routinely trotted out by critics to explain the catastrophic state of Italian theater and the failure of the country to produce playwrights in the numbers they appeared in other cultures. But it is always easier to spend days and nights pining for a regretted absentee than to recognize a figure in flesh and blood who promises to fill that absence.

Fo combined past culture and future aspirations with his famous explanation of his change of direction in 1968. He was tired, he said, of being the "*giullare* of the bourgeoisie and wished to be the *giullare* of the proletariat." The decision to turn away from "bourgeois" to socialist theater was justified, in other words, by a reference to a figure from Italian theatrical history. The translation of the word *giullare* is tricky. The *giullare* was a performer in medieval Europe, a one-man actor-writer who played in the streets and piazzas. The word is linked with the English word "juggler," but the *giullare* has more in common with the minstrel, the clown, the Shakespearean fool, and even the modern busker. In Fo's eyes, the *giullare* was the quintessentially popular entertainer who expressed in satirical, comic form the feelings — be they resentments, anger, joy, or passion — of ordinary people. This is disputed by experts who point out that there were purely conventional *giullari* who played for the captains and kings, but here we can ignore the scholarly debates. At the point when he was at his most radical, Fo felt the need to base himself on a figure from the theatrical past of Italy. It is extraordinary that if the matter of his plays is taken from the headlines of the day, Fo the man of theater is in many ways outside history. He could have acted, clowned, juggled, joked, sang, tumbled, performed handstands or acrobatics at any period of the past. His work involves a dialectic between the past and the present. In theatrical practice, in his poetics, Fo is the reverse of an iconoclast. His break with commercial — or bourgeois — theater was *also* an attempt to link up with other predecessors from other times. The niches in his personal pantheon are filled with statues of writers such as Molière, Ruzzante, perhaps Shakespeare, with representatives of the various Harlequins, *giullari*, and vaudevillians. There would be scarcely a contemporary among them.

Other dominant influences in the formation of his poetics also come from outside the world of theater. Fo has always spoken of the impact of the *fabulatori*, or storytellers, whom he had known in his boyhood on Lake Maggiore. In his Nobel Prize speech in Stockholm, he still harked back to the influence of the glassblowers and fishermen of his native place who told tales as they worked, making use of grotesque irony, of wild exaggeration, of ribald wit, interweaving into their tales episodes of unrestrained fantasy and of what they would not have known to call surreal humor but never losing sight of the narrative momentum that held the attention of listeners. Fo's is a storyteller's theater in the sense that plot always takes precedence over character. (Indeed, character scarcely exists.) Fo the storyteller is most evident in his one-man pieces, whether the early radio monologues of the *Poer nano* series, or the later bravura pieces, such as *Mistero buffo* or *Storia della tigre (The Tale of the Tiger)*. Political or satirical it may be, but there is always a tale to be told. His drama is founded on the momentum of endlessly changing situations, or on a whirligig of comings and goings, in which well-grounded, plausible situations are twisted and stretched to the verge of the surreal, only to be brought back to some semblance not of order but of the chaos that is political reality. The absurdity of the situation is never whimsical fantasy as an end in itself but an invitation to the audience to impose order, their order, a new order, on a political status quo that has been revealed as nonsensical.

The type of acting Fo advocates is a consequence of his storyteller's theater. He has spoken, lectured, supervised, advised, and performed at numerous workshops and laboratories around the world on acting techniques, but his fundamental belief was succinctly expressed in the course of the lessons he gave in the Teatro Ateneo in Rome in 1986 (recorded on video by the Department of Drama at the University of Rome): "The great actors I have known do not perform but recount. In writing, the actor must find the story not the character. Characters exist in function of the story" (Fo 1986). The insistence on the need for actors to concentrate on telling the story, not on finding character, puts him at the opposite end of the specter from Stanislavsky, whom he abominates. The construction of a theater with an imaginary fourth wall dividing the stage from the stalls, with the audience reduced to the status of voyeur, was anathema to Fo. Stanislavsky became a *bête noire*, the incarnation of bourgeois theater, the theorist of acting as self-regarding sport.

However, if it is true that the two great schools of acting produced this century have been the Brechtian and the Stanislavskyan, Fo was not precisely a Brechtian either. His relations with Brecht have always been ambiguous. He has enormous respect for the pioneering work of Piscator and Brecht, but he found the Brechtian notion of "third person" acting, or the requirement imposed by the "alienation principle" that the actor maintain some form of critical distance from the emotional life of the character he was playing, simply confusing. In an interview with *Cahiers du cinema*, the famous French film magazine, he said of Brecht:

When people talk of epic theater, they always think of Brecht, who does explain his own views well, but they are hard to understand. He says that you have to perform in the third person, come out of yourself, get away from your egoism, from your individualism, to become a kind of chucker out, someone who is on the outside and who presents the characters in a choral setting. So the actor has to destroy the character and then put him back together so as to show him to the spectators. It's all a bit hard to understand, especially for the poor actor, because to "be inside without being inside," "to be a mirror," . . . the poor actor risks going mad and thinks he will go off and change occupation. . . . Whereas to really understand epic theater, all you have to do is to look at the people. Who always represent an ideology different from that of the bourgeoisie. Who have in themselves a collective dimension. (1974:33)

Fo believed he had a found an workaday equivalent of Brecht's epic theater in the traditions of popular theater, whether the styles of the *giullare* or of modern music hall or vaudeville, in which the performer simply overrode the gulf between stage and stalls by addressing the audience directly whenever necessary or advantageous. Even the "aside," eliminated by naturalism, was reintroduced by Fo as a helpful narrative device. He required actors to enter into a dialogue with the audience, not to display themselves in front of it.

The actor, not the writer and certainly not the director, is the central figure in Fo's theater. Fo relished quoting Molière's statement that he was first an actor and saw himself in similar terms. When he was awarded the Nobel Prize, he described it as a vindication of the actor. One of the reasons for his admiration for *commedia dell'arte* was that it represented the primacy of the actor. The *capocomico*, literally the head actor, was the linchpin in this tradition. Fo saw this performance style in action when he met up with the Rame family. His principal collection of what could be called instructional rather than theoretical pieces was given the title *Manuale minimo dell'attore* (The actor's mini-manual), although the impact of this is lost in the English title, *Tricks of the Trade*. Initially, he planned to give it a title such as "Antiparadosso dell'attore" (Antiparadox of the actor) to enter into direct conflict with what he considered to be antiactor views expressed by the eighteenth-century thinker Denis Diderot, but his publisher warned him that the reference would be too erudite and obscure for most readers.

Fo's scripts are not elaborate literary or verbal constructs but texts

at the service of performance. He distinguishes between theater and
dramatic literature, in which the second was very certainly not for him.
This distaste for the page as against the stage even led him to express
some ironic uncertainty about Shakespeare, of whom his views are idiosyncratic but, in general, respectful. Fo was enchanted by a view Brecht
had once expressed on Shakespeare, to the effect that his only defect
was that his works were "too beautiful on the page" (1991b:183). A genuine work of theater should require being husbanded by the actor so as to
release all its force and energy. The same grounds go some way to explain Fo's lifelong dispute with Pier Paolo Pasolini. Pasolini chose the
moment when Fo was at his most vulnerable—after his arrest in Sassari
in 1973 for allegedly failing to allow the police access to the theater
where he was performing—to issue his most notorious attack. "Dario
Fo," said Pasolini then, "is a plague for Italian theater" (1973:57).

Fo did not reply, but the intellectual differences between the two
over questions of poetics are more profound than this episode of name-
calling might imply. Pasolini drew up his own *Manifesto for a New
Theater* in the aftermath of the May 1968 riots but dismissed the possibility of attracting a mass or popular audience. Instead, he aimed his
theater at "the progressive groups of the bourgeoisie." His new theater
was to be essentially a "theater of the word," or a literary theater.

> Come to the performances of the "theater of the word" with the
> idea of listening more than seeing (this is a necessary constraint in
> order to understand better the words you will hear, *and therefore
> the ideas, which are the real characters of this theater*). (Pasolini
> 1996:181; emphasis in the original)

For Fo, it was essential to see as well as listen, to enjoy the spectacle
as much as to hear ideas. The aridity of intellectual debating theater,
including Pasolini's, was not for him. It left no scope to the actor and
little, or inappropriate, challenge to the spectator. Fo's preference was
for "theater of situation," in which situation is "the basic structure that
allows the progress of the narrative to be constructed in such a way as
to involve the audience in the tension and make it participate fully in
the unfolding of the plot" (1991b:89). Situation is essential to farce,
Fo's chosen genre, and one that, in his poetics, is no longer a form of
despised, theatrical lowlife but a style of theater whose dignity was un-
apparent only to patrician snobs. His aim is to subvert the hierarchy

established by the Greeks that sets tragedy as the highest dramatic form, comedy as acceptable, and farce as a condescension to the bestial. Fo's preference is invariably for those types of theater that were previously regarded as marginal—clown shows, farce, acrobatic displays, *pochades* (one-act farces), stand-up comedy, and the medieval jester's routines— provided they were imbued with satirical fire against the oppressive powers that be and not merely decorated with pricks and prods that allowed the authorities to appear to tolerate ridicule without risking anything. Fo's satire on those who wield power in society falls like a lash on a naked back yet arouses the hilarity of a clown on stilts. The combination of satire and farce has produced a wholly new style of theater. The fact that *Morte accidentale* is so funny and so traditional in form has sheltered people from recognizing his boldness in employing farce to deal with the murder of an innocent man in police custody. A comparison with the open rage expressed in works by Athol Fugard or other South African writers on similar crimes under apartheid would be instructive.

The image of Fo in most countries has been shaped by a few plays and by attention devoted to his politics, to the detriment of his stagecraft. Some of these plays are reconsidered in this volume; others, most notably *Non si paga!*, are neglected. This decision was made because the stagecraft questions are debated in relation to other plays, and the politics of the piece reflect a particular moment of rampant inflation in Italian society, when a particular course of direct action—the removal of goods from shop shelves—was advocated. The omission is not to be taken as a judgment on the work itself.

The essays and artwork in this volume make it clear that Fo cannot even be restricted to the theater. He trained as a painter and is an artist of high talent, as is demonstrated by the original pieces he so generously provided for this volume. All throughout his life, he has written lyrics and music for songs. Perhaps a study of music might provide a new key for the interpretation of Fo. Although little of his musical theater is available in English, music has been a vital ingredient in all phases of his theater. A sensitive study might reveal that the development of his plots have something of the rhythm of music. In any case, he has shown himself to be, as Tony Mitchell reveals, a *chansonnier* of the highest order. His grainy voice is no more or less musical than that of, say, Charles Aznavour, but he has often written for, among others, Enzo Jannacci, a close friend and a singer-songwriter. Fo's songs from the 1950s not only are in keeping with *chansons* composed and sung in the bistros of Paris

by Juliette Greco in those days when existentialism, surrealism, and he-
donism went hand in hand but also offer an uncanny foretaste of the
themes he would develop in his major theater.

Although Fo's artistic activities cannot be restricted to theater, it is
in theater that he has made his name. Ron Jenkins and Walter Valeri
have each worked with Fo both onstage and offstage, so their contribu-
tions here offer a unique perspective on Fo the writer and Fo the actor.
Valeri has collaborated with Fo in many fields—as his agent in Italy
and America and as critical exponent of Fo's and Rame's views of theater
as a whole or of specific plays. Recently he has become champion of
Rame's right to consideration as an independent artist, rather than being
thought of as an appendage of her husband. It was Valeri more than
any other who defended Rame when, in 1995, *Sesso? Grazie, tanto per
gradire* (Sex? Yes, much obliged)—her one-woman play, based on a satirical work by the couple's son Jacopo, lamenting the primitive state of
sex education in Italy—earned the disapproval of the censors. His essay
on Fo the actor-author is based on deep knowledge of theater history
and firsthand acquaintance with Fo's way of thinking.

Ron Jenkins, the clown-turned-academic, has translated Fo's texts
and has worked with Fo during his visits to America. Jenkins has performed the demanding and dangerous task of interpreting Fo onstage as
he launches into his improvised prologues and has acted as assistant
while Fo was in rehearsal with American actors in Boston for a performance of *Gli arcangeli non giocano a flipper* (*Archangels Don't Play
Pinball*). His own experience of performance, his knowledge of theater
from Bali to Boston, and his familiarity with Fo's techniques put him in
a unique position to discuss Fo's view from the stage.

If he made a late arrival in the United States, having been refused a
visa by successive American administrations, Fo has acquired an unparalleled international reputation. The description of Fo as the "most performed playwright in the world today" now trips lightly off the tongue.
Perhaps there is a distinct mask of Fo for each country in which he is
produced. Certainly he represented a distinct challenge for each society.
The old Soviet Union found him as unpalatable as did the Vatican, but
the Soviet censors had the power to ban him, whereas the Vatican had
only the power to remonstrate and protest. It would be worth analyzing
the separate masks Fo donned, or had imposed on him, from Turkey to
Japan and to find out why he has attained such popularity in such disparate cultures as those of Brazil and Scandinavia. Jennifer Lorch makes

a start on this project with a consideration of the impact of one play, *Morte accidentale*, in English-speaking countries and a study of the exact form in which that play was presented. The other work of Fo's that could be put on the same level of popularity is *Mistero buffo*, examined critically by Costantino Maeder, whose essay addresses the concept of "text." For Fo, the text is never conceived as a fixed, written document but rather as a fluid ensemble of ideas, constantly in flux. Maeder's analysis of various manifestations of *Mistero buffo* enhances recognition of Fo's dedication to the craft of playwriting.

Joseph Farrell and Antonio Scuderi attempt in their essays to elucidate the extent and nature of Fo's technical and intellectual dialectic with the theater of the past. As he himself never tires of telling people, Fo is an inheritor, who lays claim to possessions, titles, and wealth accumulated by his ancestors. Perhaps Fo is a treasure hunter. He pleads proudly guilty to charges of plagiarism and plunder from the scripts of his predecessors, but he has been fulsome in his praise of those from whom he has stolen or, in less sensational terms, learned. He filched the idea for twins or doubles (as Shakespeare did) from Plautus for both the 1960 *Aveva due pistole con gli occhi bianchi e neri (He Had Two Pistols with White and Black Eyes)* and the 1981 *Clacson* and, though more debatably, the inspiration for the intrusion of a *faux-naif* outsider in *Morte accidentale* from Gogol's *Government Inspector*. There is nothing different here from the multiple echoes that resound in the works of poets like T. S. Eliot and Ezra Pound. The influence of writers such as Ruzzante and Molière is of a different order, and one of the characteristics of Fo's activity in the 1980s and 1990s has been his dedication to paying debts. He has produced Molière at the Comédie Française and Ruzzante at Spoleto. He edited an edition of Mayakovsky, and his 1984 play, *Quasi per caso una donna, Elisabetta (Elizabeth: Almost by Chance a Woman)*, may be regarded as, among other things, an act of homage to Shakespeare.

The best of his critics—and none surpasses Paolo Puppa—have already begun the important work of reevaluation. In his 1978 *Il teatro di Dario Fo* (1978), Puppa sought to move beyond idolatry and to undertake a balanced study of Fo's contribution to theater. It has to be said that Fo was not grateful for this effort (he did not agree with all of Puppa's conclusions), but hagiography is not a critical tool. As Massimo Bontempelli wrote of Pirandello, "the best criticism is always adversarial" (1945:33). Paolo Puppa continues his own highly personal encounter

with Fo in his essay in this volume. Puppa sets aside facile talk of "tradition," with its implication that any historical dynamic could be reduced to one linear development, and establishes Fo's relations with
some of the various traditions that constitute the Italian theatrical heritage. As has now been authoritatively acknowledged by the award of the
Nobel Prize for Literature, Fo has enriched that heritage. This volume
aims to clarify the nature, and limits, of that process of enrichment.

All translations are by the authors.

References

Bontempelli, Massimo. 1945. *Introduzioni e discorsi.* Milan: Mondadori.

Fo, Dario. 1974. "Culture populaire et travail militant: Dario Fo et le collectif La Comune." Interview. *Cahiers du cinema* 250:11–25.

———. 1978. Interview. *Drama Review* (March).

———. 1986. Video of workshops for the Department of Drama, University of Rome.

———. 1991a. *Totò, manuale dell'attor comico.* Ed. Liborio Termine. Torino: Adelph.

———. 1991b. *The Tricks of the Trade (Manuale minimo dell'attore).* Tr. Joseph Farrell.
Ed. Stuart Hood. New York: Routledge.

———. 1998. *Le commedie di Dario Fo.* Vol 13. Turin: Einaudi.

Pasolini, Pier Paolo. 1973. *Panorama* (November).

———. 1996. *Manifesto for a New Theater.* Cranbury, N.J.: Associated UPs.

Puppa, Paolo. 1978. *Il teatro di Dario Fo: Dalla scena alla piazza.* Venice: Marsili.

Swedish Academy. 1997. Official press release.

CHAPTER 1

An Actor's Theater

WALTER VALERI

From its origins, Italian theater developed within a strong dialectic between two seemingly contradictory currents. The literary
tradition, in which the performance event is based on a scripted
text, includes writers such as Seneca, Tasso, Alfieri, and, more recently,
Pasolini and his *Theater of Words*. On the other hand, there is a popular
comic theater, steeped in an oral tradition and enriched by the vast expressive resources of Italian regional dialects. Within this fertile contradiction, this dialectic of opposites, is the theatrical experience of Dario
Fo, actor and playwright with roots in popular oral culture, whose theatrical activities are the source of debates and conflicts, both old and new.

Fo's professional activities encompass all aspects of theatrical production. Besides being an accomplished playwright and performer, he
is also a director, choreographer, set designer, costume designer, and
songwriter. By pursuing these various interests simultaneously, he caused
an uproar in the Italian theater community, which back in the 1960s was
divided into separate professional associations: "Authors refuse to accept
me as an author and actors refuse to accept me as an actor. Authors say
I am an actor trying to be an author, while actors say I am an author
trying to be an actor. Nobody wants me in their camp. Only the set
designers tolerate me" (1992:21).

There is a sense of irony in this, for in Italy there has been a long tradition of an actor's dramaturgy, or an "actor's theater," with many notable examples throughout history. The tradition can be traced all the way back to the second century B.C.E., to Plautus, who was an actor, playwright, and producer. It continued with illustrious examples, from the extraordinary Renaissance actor Ruzzante (Angelo Beolco) to Raffaele Viviani and Eduardo De Filippo, twentieth-century masters of the Neapolitan stage. All of these figures may be viewed as either predecessors or descendants of the great Italian tradition of the actor's theater that culminated in the sixteenth century. The *commedia dell'arte*, or *all'italiana*—praised and criticized, exalted and derided—was a form of European theater in which the actor was without question at the center of the performance event, involved with and in control of all the aspects of the business. On many occasions, Fo has expressed his preference for a theater based on actors, in which "the actor is the author, manager, storyteller, director" (1987:14). He asserts that the theatrical phenomenon works best when in their hands.

Having written nearly eighty theatrical pieces and having directed close to twenty works by Molière, John Gay, Achard, Stravinsky, Rossini, and Adrien de la Vigne, Fo had established himself as a leading figure in European theater and literary culture long before receiving the Nobel Prize. He is part of a tradition of satire that includes writers such as Plautus, Rabelais, Molière, and Swift. Fo's satirical theater does not shun the farce, as can be noted, for example, in the 1963 *Isabella, tre caravelle e un cacciaballe* (*Isabella, Three Sailing Ships, and a Con Man*), the 1967 *La signora è da buttare* (*Toss the Lady Out*), the 1981 *L'opera dello sghignazzo* (*The Opera of the Sneering Laugh*), or the 1993 *Mamma! I sanculotti!* (Oh mommy! The San-culottes!). In the best Western tradition, his comedies often unfold amidst tragic events and aim at confronting and unmasking the abuse of power. However, the central figure and creative force in all of this remains the actor. In fact, Fo's abilities as an actor and a writer developed in tandem, that is, he learned how to write for the theater as he learned how to interpret roles. His emphasis on performance over text, which is closer to the oral rather than to the literary tradition, causes difficulty for critics assessing Fo as a playwright. His texts are a result of continual modifications based on audience reaction, often to his improvisations. This approach to theater exalts a performance tradition that is historically more akin to popular cultures over the literary tradition of official, dominant cultures (see Scuderi 1998).

Franca Rame

When discussing the theater of Fo, the name of Franca Rame should be mentioned. With the exception of the earliest years, Fo's entire career was affected greatly by their collaboration. In an interview in 1973, Fo discussed her extraordinary theatrical abilities:

> While studying architecture in Milan, I learned more from master masons than from books, and Rame has an innate knowledge of theater and a precision akin to that of a master craftsman. She has a keen sense of timing and rhythm. She can spot banality a mile away and at a first reading of a piece she can detect those literary qualities that have no place in theater. She rejects *literature* immediately like a painter might reject picturesqueness or a sculptor might reject classicism. (1973:48)

Rame, in turn, speaking of Fo and his contribution to *Tutta casa, letto e chiesa (All Bed, Board, and Church)*, stated:

> Dario is truly extraordinary. He has an incredible ability to empathize and actually think like me, like a woman. That is, he can intuit how something can be seen or felt from a feminine point of view. When writing he succeeds in detaching himself completely from his own subjectivity. I have never seen anyone able to do this quite like him. And when things are not going right theatrically, I simply point it out to him and he knows what to do. Sometimes I'll see a play where the female roles are weak because the playwright does not know how to handle them. That's not the case with Dario. (1992:23)

Both have profited immensely from each other's theatrical abilities, and their synergetic collaboration is unparalleled in twentieth-century European theater. It may even be argued that their collaboration has no equal historically in all of European theater, for even the great Andreini family of the sixteenth century, with the stellar presence of Isabella, lacked a collaboration that produced an equivalently vast corpus. In addition to the coauthorship of *Tutta casa*, Rame's participation in the revision and publication of Fo's comedies is evident in her introductions to his plays and in her translations of his dialect pieces into standard

Italian. Many of these dialect monologues were developed by Fo primarily in performance, in an oral context, subsequently transcribed by Rame. She should be credited as well for many of the notes and stage directions to some of his most important works.

Under the tutelage of Fo, Rame has become one of the most important Italian actress-playwrights. But even before meeting Fo, she was already a *figlia d'arte* (daughter of the métier), born to a family of itinerant players. *Figli d'arte* such as Rame were born to actresses who, very often, during pregnancy, played as long as they possibly could and returned to the stage as soon as possible after giving birth. Their children often made their stage debut as babies and literally grew up in the theater. Amongst the Italian family troupes, the Rame family has one of the longest theatrical heritages. Growing up in the family troupe, she naturally acquired the principles of performance, as she has explained on many occasions:

> I learned the art naturally like learning table manners. Being on stage for me coincided with being with my parents, my brother and sisters but in the presence of a paying public. Before learning how to read and write, as children do in schools, I learned how to be on stage. (1992:23)

In reference to Rame's talent, Fo explains why she is unique: "The audience is surprised and fascinated because it is clear that they never saw a woman perform with so much ease and detachment . . . yet, at the same time, succeeding in engaging them so much" (1997:23). Of course, Rame's success cannot be attributed solely to her links with the Italian theatrical tradition. It is also a matter of the choice of the themes and social commentary that have made her an original interpreter of innovative female roles in Italian theater, now performed by many actresses around the world. Beginning with Casellante, the character she played in a brief television sketch in 1962, to the semiautobiographical, solo role she portrayed in the 1995 *Sesso? Grazie, tanto per gradire* (Sex? Yes, much obliged), during her forty-year collaboration with Fo she has assumed a preeminent profile internationally as an actress. In discussing *Tutta casa* and the progression of Rame's roles over time, Marga Cottino-Jones writes:

> What this progression ultimately shows is the significant place that in the last decades this particular discourse, the feminist discourse,

has taken in Fo and Rame's theater. Just like their theater, this discourse is meant as resistance to authoritarian control. And there is no doubt that this particular place in their work is due to Franca Rame's invaluable collaboration as writer and performer. (1995:338)

Popular Elements and the Monologue

What causes difficulty for critics assessing Fo as a playwright is his emphasis on performance over text, which is closer to the oral rather than to the literary tradition. As mentioned above, his texts are a result of continual modifications based on audience reaction, often to his improvisations. This approach to theater exalts a performance tradition that is historically more akin to popular cultures over the literary tradition of official, dominant cultures. His use of popular techniques and his genius as a performer are evident above all in his monologues.

In the course of forty years, Fo has produced an impressive number of monologues, the most famous being *Mistero buffo* (Comic mystery), *Storia della tigre* (*The Tale of the Tiger*), *Fabulazzo osceno* (*Obscene Fables*), and *Johan Padan a la descoverta de le Americhe* (*Johan Padan — The Discovery of the Americas*). In this style of performance, Fo is the undisputed champion. In it, he demonstrates his extraordinary talents as a performer and his incredible ability for theatrical communication through language and mime. The language of his monologues is based on dialect rather than on standard Italian. He attributes this use of dialectal structures to the performances of the *fabulatori* of his childhood (1990:22). His distinctive style of mime is descendant from the French school, that of Marcel Marceau and Etienne Decroux. He learned it primarily from Jacques Lecoq, mime master, who in the 1950s collaborated with Fo, Franco Parenti, and Giustino Durano in *Il dito nell'occhio* (*A Finger in the Eye*).

In reference to Fo's solo performances, Bernard Dort writes:

Fo is able to play on the timing and the astonishment of metamorphosis. . . . His gestures are abruptly suspended. He observes them, comments on them, laughs at them, repeats them or extends them. Through his incomplete gestures, suspended as it were between past and present, and his words, which call up these gestures but are never completely resolved in them, Fo not only appeals to the spectators' imaginations; he activates the spectators. He obliges them to *accommodate* him continually, to multiply their perspectives and points of view. He engages them in debate. (1977:211)

Actor Versus Player

In an attempt to define the actor Fo, Louis Jouvet's distinction between what he refers to as the "actor" and the "player" *(comédien)* comes to mind. This distinction—which, even according to Jouvet, is never absolute—states that "while the player can interpret all of his roles while wearing the clothes of the various characters and hiding behind them (be they tragic or comic), the actor cannot. The actor remains simply an individual, markedly in possession of his distinct personality" (1947:19). He continues to explain that "the principal difference between the player and the actor is to be found in this mimicry of which the actor is not capable or at least not to the degree of the player" (1947:19).

Fo the actor is defined by his lack of this mimetic ability. It is a lack caused by an excess of personality that impedes a complete mimicry. The social function taken on by the actor Fo is molded by his response to the audience, based on content and a "dramatic" social significance involving the story's collective vision and sense of historical destiny. It is important to reiterate that Fo is working in an oral culture that is participatory. The actor working in this tradition can present a detached and objective performance that invites a total and immediate participation on the part of the audience.

Fo perfectly embodies the actor who is in control of his performance, without disappearing into the semblance of the character. He embodies the definition of the actor whose personality does not dissolve into the character he is playing. For an actor, there are no ultimatums on the stage, but there is the risk of sinking into oblivion during the course of a performance, an oblivion marked by the failure to make the principal impression that is intrinsic to the integrity of the entire performance.

Fo's talent as an actor is defined by his personal and moral integrity, for his histrionic qualities are firmly rooted in his political ideology. If an actor does not run the blockade of anonymity, he/she does not go beyond functioning simply as an executor and fails to convey a system of original ideas and messages identifiable as his/her own. The performance of such an actor is devoid of any effort to dramaturgically influence the audience, not an audience of voyeurs but an audience that collaborates actively in the dynamics that constitute a performance.

Fo opens each performance with an introductory presentation. It is a technique from the old *fabulatori*, the storytellers of his childhood, and a characteristic of all performances that involve direct address. On many occasions, Fo has asserted that this technique allows rhythms that are more eloquent and more spontaneous than an abrupt opening.

More than a simple prologue, this is an introductory monologue that runs from fifteen to twenty minutes. It is a digression that serves to establish a dramatic dialectic, distinguished from other forms of theater by its stylistic choices. By forming a dramatic field, the performer gets a preview of his/her audience. This is especially important for the oral actor who improvises in an agonistic tone. During his opening monologue, Fo takes note of an impressive number of facts concerning his audience, that is, he zeros in on what may be defined as the morphology of collective antagonism. He utilizes this information in order to create a rapport with the audience through his improvisation, at which he is extremely talented. It is a type of resurrection of the primordial genesis of the actor-protagonist, from the moment he distinguished himself from the chorus for his wisdom and capabilities.

The Epic Actor

Working within this intimate performer-audience dynamic, chosen to define his dramatic field, Fo is the quintessential epic actor. Over the years, he has developed his ideas on what should be the desired qualities, modes of expression, and function of the epic actor. With regard to this, he often refers to historical and cross-cultural models, maintaining that the Greek actors, for example, did not transform themselves into their characters but rather made it clear that there was an actor present. Fo maintains that the rejection of the actor's identification with the role is present in great theater of all times, including Japanese theater and puppet theater. A great actor does not identify with the character he is portraying but rather presents the character and tells his tale. In maintaining his/her personality, the actor should develop what Fo refers to as "poetics," a distinctive and unmistakable, personal imprint. With reference to the great Neapolitan comic actor Totò (Antonio De Curtis), Fo writes:

> A historical, critical analysis of an actor's technique is impossible if the actor does not have poetics, that is, a code of themes that gives depth and meaning to the actor's personal style. Totò has

poetics that are rich in themes and motifs that weave and dovetail, presenting a whole and complex vision that is always identifiable as being Totò's. (1995:7)

Fo's concept of poetics, as an artist's means of developing distinctive and original form and content, is in accord with a similar concept we find in the works of one of the major Italian aesthetic philosophers, Luciano Anceschi: "Poetics represents the reflection that artists and poets exercise on their creations, indicating their technical systems, their operative norms, their morality, and their ideal" (1976:348).

An actor cannot and must not avoid revealing himself/herself in every moment of performance. He/she must assume an aesthetic and social function within the greatest cultural sphere possible. The actor is the consciousness of all that takes place on stage, under pressure of the historical reality outside the theater. This is a difficult position that requires autonomy and that does not coincide with vision of the actor-interpreter or with the instrumentalist vision (often iterated by European, Stalinistic ideology), which is overtly political, that would have the actor subordinated to the party's sense of purpose and function as an instrument of propaganda.

The Actor as an Instrument for Social Change

Fo remains in a constant state of conflict with institutional power, the consequences of which have at times been severe, resulting in censorship, personal attacks, and violence. The worst of these incidents was the abduction of Rame by right-wing extremists in 1973. Fo has been put on trial, alienated and attacked by much of the Italian press, under the influence of the political establishment, and dominated by what was called the Christian Democracy (today, practically nonexistent, as a result of corruption and scandal).

They branded me a diabolical genius who brings moral contamination and chaos. This was written in *Il popolo*, a Catholic newspaper in Lausanne. What does this mean? It means my theater is an effective instrument with historical roots in our country. It is a means for involving public opinion and bringing it to a state of awareness. There is a price however. In the course of five years, twenty-five charges were filed against me and I have endured various trials. (1992:39)

Theater companies who put on his works in other countries have been targeted as well. Under the rule of Franco, members of the Spanish troupe were arrested for staging *Morte accidentale di un anarchico (Accidental Death of an Anarchist)* in Barcelona. His plays have been censored in South Africa, Israel, Chile, and in almost all the nations of the former Soviet bloc. He and Rame were denied entry into the United States. In Buenos Aires, a bomb blast welcomed Fo and Rame's troupe, which had traveled there to perform *Tutta casa*. Fo and Rame's conflict with authority can be viewed as a continuation of the conflicts that go back to the Middle Ages, that culminated with the torture and execution of defiant jongleurs who dared to criticize the power of church and state.

When the actor-playwright serves as a spokesperson for social change, it becomes necessary to temporarily transcend the state of subordination and question the dominant powers. Then theater becomes a historical phenomenon, an expression of social development. At the same time, it is inherently conflictive, and the actor embodies this conflictive nature. Fo's theater simultaneously defends subordinate peoples while defying dominant ideology.

The postindustrial world is engulfing all of society in its consumerism and dissolving the myth of the individual who dreams of freedom and collective justice, for whom Fo's theater is spokesperson. Even traditional leftist ideology—expressed by Fo in various plays, as, for example, in the 1968 *Grande pantomima con bandiere e pupazzi piccoli e medi* (Grand pantomime with flags and small and medium-sized puppets), the 1973 *La guerra del popolo in Cile* (The people's war in Chile), the 1974 *Non si paga! Non si paga! (Can't Pay! Won't Pay!)*, the 1979 *Storia della tigre*, and the 1981 *Clacson, trombette e pernacchi (Trumpets and Raspberries)*—is absorbing concepts and values derived from postindustrial, bourgeois society. The individual is no longer the keeper of those values that linked him to a utopian dream of freedom, expressed by his class of origin. He has become a pessimist, highly hedonistic, enchanted by lure of material wealth. As Franco Fortini foresaw back in 1965, the mechanics of the "new prince" consist in "rendering the power of capital almost invisible, introjecting the ethos of industrialization, of producer and consumer, completely into society, while giving it all the semblance of being natural" (1965:xxii).

In Fo's theater, the notion of the individual purely as consumer is refuted vehemently. His plays express the necessity for a total liberation from consumerism. There is also the assertion that the individual needs to exist as part of a collective experience that strives for a constant redefinition and radicalization of political conflict, always in the dimension of imagination, in adventure, and self-awareness. Watching Fo in performance, it becomes clear that above all his theater serves as a means for self-assessment as it gathers, utilizes, and projects the reaction of the audience back to the audience. It is a mask of a social ritual of dialectic and potential expression that ultimately remains in the possession of the audience, which oscillates between closeness and distance to the character without ever reaching complete identification.

Working with the Audience

By observing the audience during a performance by Fo (which is greatly facilitated by studying videotapes), the reaction of individual members at a given moment—their facial expressions and body language—makes it clear that there is another performance in progress. This secondary performance by the audience is activated by Fo via a process of empathy. In order to reach this dynamic interplay between performer and audience, it is necessary that the text be open, that there be space for variation. Although some theater companies believe they have discovered collective works, in the sense of cowritten or codirected, for Fo this does not change much of anything because the true advancement in the quality of a performance is attained when the performer learns how to cowrite and codirect with the audience, the people for whom the show is conceived in the first place.

This is to say that the spectator is no longer someone who arrives at the theater, consumes, and goes home. The spectator collaborates with the performer and becomes the force that drives the performance with his/her reactions and suggestions. This process produces a unique aesthetic, which is not based on content and style but on its profound links with the essential function of the "theatrical system," rendering it much more effective and powerful than the type of theater Fo has termed as "literary." Hence, Fo's plays often change with each performance, and his theater may be viewed as existing in a state of perpetual flux. It is incumbent upon those who interpret Fo's works to apply to the best of their ability these principles that define his theater, lest it should stagnate into a state of textual fixity, defying its original fluid vitality, the spirit of Dario Fo.

Translated from Italian by Antonio Scuderi.

References

Anceschi, Luciano. 1976. In *Enciclopedia Feltrinelli-Fischer: letteratura*. Ed. Gabriele Scaramuzza, 348. Vol 2. Milan: Feltrinelli.

Cottino-Jones, Marga. 1995. "Franca Rame on Stage." *Italica* 72.2:323–39.

Dort, Bernard. 1977. *Teatre en jeu*. Paris: Editions du Seuil.

Fo, Dario. 1973. Interview (Milan). *L'Europeo* (14 October).

——. 1987. *Manuale minimo dell'attore*. Ed. Franca Rame. Turin: Einaudi.

——. 1990. *Dialogo provocatorio sul comico, il tragico, la follia e la ragione*. Interview by Luigi Allegri. Rome: Laterza.

——. 1992. *Fabulazzo*. Ed. Lorenzo Ruggiero and Walter Valeri. Milan: Kaos.

——. 1995. *Totò: manuale dell'attore comico*. Firenze: Vallechi.

——. 1997. Interview (Rome). *Il manifesto* (7 December).

Fortini, Franco. 1965. *Profezie e realtà del nostro secolo*. Bari: Laterza.

Jouvet, Louis. 1947. "Attore e Commediante." In *L'attore*. Turin: Il Dramma.

Rame, Franca. 1992. Interview (Milan). *Sipario* (November).

Scuderi, Antonio. 1998. *Dario Fo and Popular Performance*. Ottawa: Legas.

CHAPTER 2

The Rhythms of Resurrection
Onstage with Fo

RON JENKINS

It's a question of balance, of equilibrium, and dynamics. So that when you climb up with your knee, you have to give it a good little push. And then wait for it to come back before you put up the second one. Look how it goes up. You shift your weight with your hands. You take a breath. Wait for the swing. Stretch yourself out. And there you go! Stretch out your leg. Wait for the swing. A breath. Change hands. Reverse position. Stretch out. Change hands. Open your legs. One on this side. One on that side. And you're there! It's all in the dynamics.

—Dario Fo, *Johan Padan a la descoverta de le Americhe*

This passage from an early version of Dario Fo's play *Johan Padan—The Discovery of the Americas* describes a clown's attempt to climb into a hammock. I translated the text while watching Fo perform it in the living room of his summer home on Italy's Adriatic coast. The precision of the language was matched by the precision of his gestures, rhythms, and intonations as he brought the scene to life. His arms would swirl and swing in complex cadences that caught the pulses of each phrase as the sounds swelled and faded in the air around him. Mesmerized by Fo's performance, I tried to capture his

movement in the language and realized that, coincidentally, his words
were also describing the act of translation in which we were engaged. If
one were to substitute syllables for body parts, the clown's struggle with
gravity and the hammock could be seen as strikingly similar to the translator's wrestling with meaning and syntax.

Both endeavors can be reduced to "a question of balance, of equilibrium, and dynamics." I am particularly sensitive to the fragility of the
translation process because of my experiences as an onstage interpreter
for Fo during his performances. In those situations, the kinesthetic music of the language was crucial. I spoke the English version of Fo's text
immediately after he spoke the Italian, and any deficiencies in the translation would become apparent immediately in the responses of the audiences. Fo knew the curves and angles of every sentence. He knew where
the gasps were. He knew where the laughs were. And if he didn't get the
appropriate feedback from the crowd at the appropriate moment, he
knew it was my fault.

Initially, I approached my task as interpreter with the tentative awk-
wardness of the clown attempting to mount the hammock. "Never get
on a hammock with your butt first," advises Johan Padan in Fo's fable.
"It's the first rule. You have to go in on your knees." Interpreting for Fo's
performances of *Mistero buffo* (Comic mystery) in New York, Cambridge, and Washington in 1986, I was, in fact, humbled by a string of
what might be considered "butt-first" mistakes and quickly shifted to
"going in on my knees," carefully choosing phrases I hoped would pack
the proper rhythmic punch. I used a nuanced vocal delivery to "give it
a good little push," paused for Fo's next phrase, which inevitably came
surfing on the crest of the audience's response to the previous line, and
tried again, always mindful to "wait for it to come back before you put
up the second one." Since Fo constantly changes and improvises his text
onstage, all my linguistic choices had to be made instantaneously.

Eventually, the word choices of the translation came to me as instinctively as the gymnastic choices of the clown faced with the swinging hammock. I sensed that phrases had to be succinct and muscular,
particularly the punch lines. The rhythms of the English had to rise and
fall as seductively as the rhythms of Fo's Italian. The audience had to be
respected. Its responses were sculpted into the text, not just their laughter but also their silences, time to wonder, to think. Fo's monologues
were, in fact, dialogues, shaped through countless improvisations in

Dario Fo performing in *Johan Padan*.
(Courtesy C.T.F.R.).

front of audiences throughout the world. The actor's words and the audience's impulses were like the inhalation and exhalation of a single breath. To translate the text without acknowledging the common breath of the actor and his public would undermine the slyly cumulative rhythms of the narrative.

During the nightly performances of *Mistero buffo*, while on Fo's American tour, I worked feverishly to stay true to the music of his texts, making split-second translation decisions that would enable me to squeeze the literal meaning of his words into English phrases that matched the rhythmic patterns of his sentences. For example, in the prologue to his piece about the medieval Pope Boniface, Fo describes an airport arrival of Pope John Paul II. He sets the scene as if it were being depicted in a documentary newscast, cutting back and forth between the crowd's anticipation and the trajectory of the pope's airplane, until the montage climaxes with the appearance of the pontiff at the door of the aircraft. The pace of Fo's speech builds slowly into a staccato delivery of the details of the pope's appearance. "Silver hair. Blue eyes. Big smile. Neck of a bull. Pectoral muscles bulging. Abdominal muscles prominent. A belt around his waist. And above all a red cloak down to his feet. SUPERMAN!"

I discovered through trial and error that the "Superman" punch line doesn't get a laugh unless the phrases that precede it are short and punchy. The words "pectoral" and "abdominal" have to be placed at the opening of their respective phrases to provide an aural momentum to the gestural portrait Fo is making of the pope as we speak. The sequential rhythm of the two languages is essential, and Fo uses the beats of my translation to punctuate his description with gestures that pantomime the traits being recalled. "Capelli d'argento." "Silver hair." "Occhi cerulli." "Blue eyes." "Grande sorriso." "Big smile." Italian. English. Italian. English . . . ba da da boom . . . "SUPERMAN!" The effect was similar to the famous television and radio introduction, "It's a bird . . . It's a plane . . . it's Superman!" The anticipation and bravado need to be translated along with the meaning of the words.

Fo spoke quickly, with a pulsing rhythmic drive that made no allowances for a translator's hemming and hawing over individual word choices. The phrases had to be there on my tongue at the right moment, or the beat would be lost. Fo played with language as if it were Johan Padan's swinging hammock. He responded to the pushes and pulls of the audience like a verbal acrobat, ready to launch into double or triple back flips when the momentum built up to a climax. I had to gauge each swing of his performance so that I could duplicate his verbal acrobatics in English without disrupting the dynamic equilibrium that propelled the performance forward. "Look how it goes up," says Padan. "Shift your weight . . . take a breath . . . wait for the swing . . . It's all in the dynamics."

Language and gesture intertwine in Fo's performances. Words dance in the air, propelling the performer's body through space the way music dictates the choreography of a ballet. As an interpreter, I entered this pas de deux with wary reserve but ended up feeling Fo's rhythms as palpable forces that had to be obeyed. Like a trance dancer, speaking in tongues, I was possessed by the kinesthetic power of Fo's music. On a good night, I would participate almost without thinking, simply shifting my weight, taking a breath, waiting for the swing, and speaking words that caught the cadences of Fo's texts successfully enough to bring the audience into his world of transformations, politics, and laughter. But it was impossible to stay in that rarefied atmosphere indefinitely. There were inevitable errors and temporary losses of equilibrium that paralleled the misadventures of Fo's overzealous hammock rider. Padan tried a few too many flips while making love one night in his hammock and ended up hanging from the tangled ropes by his testicles. I felt similarly exposed when my phrases failed to elicit the laughter that Fo had been building up to in a particular scene. Usually the error could be traced back to a literally correct translation that derailed the momentum of a comic scene.

My most humbling mistake occurred during a New York performance of the prologue to "Boniface VIII," shortly after the "Superman" sequence. Fo continued to build on the absurdity of the superhero analogy, depicting a scene in which the fanatic followers of the pope imagine him flying through the air like the man of steel. Again, Fo created a sequence in which the rising tempo of the text's delivery is crucial to the illusion being portrayed. The language builds with an increasing rhythmic intensity that takes flight along with the fantastical pontiff. Fo imitates the pope's flight path as he speaks, and it was my job as the interpreter to keep the phrasing aloft. "The pope is going to fly. They could already see him in their imaginations: His gowns blowing in the wind. A trail of smoke, yellow and white, coming out of his clothes, writing in the sky . . . God is with us! And he's Polish!"

That's the way I should have translated it. But one night in New York

I lost the rhythm of the last phrase. Up until then the audience was laughing at every phrase, and Fo was incorporating the music of their laughter into the absurd comedy of his scenario. The intricate choreography of Italian, English, pantomime, and audience response was balanced perfectly until the last moment, when I derailed the momentum by translating the punch line with leaden literalness. Instead of rendering the pope's skywriting as "God is with us. And he's Polish," I said, "God is with us. And he is a God of Poland." The meaning was the same, but the phrasing killed the rhythm of the sequence and sent the punch line crashing to earth with a laughless thud.

Surprised at the lack of response to a joke that he had performed successfully for years, Fo looked at me accusingly and teasingly chastised me with a hand gesture that the audience didn't notice. (It was one of the many surreptitious signals he gave me during a performance to direct the pacing of my interpretation, like a musical conductor orchestrating the English version of his text as he simultaneously performed it in Italian.) As the murderer of a stillborn laugh, I felt awful, but Fo continued cheerfully with his story: "And then a Bishop came along who ruined everything. He was distracted." Fo was talking about a bishop in the scenario who accidentally stepped on the pope's cloak and caused him to trip down the stairway from the plane, but I couldn't help but feel that there was a veiled reference to the "distracted" interpreter who had "ruined" the gag.

Miraculously, Fo would often find a way to incorporate my translation mistakes into the performance, creating a new set of rhythmic patterns that acknowledged the presence of the onstage translator as part of the narrative rhythm. Unlike many speakers and performers who perform as if the problem of translation did not exist, Fo refused to ignore its mechanisms and treated the potentially awkward necessity as an added dimension of theatricality that provided new opportunities for audience interaction. Although he speaks no English, Fo sensed from my rhythms and the audience's response whenever a mistake had been made, and he would often speak directly to me or comment to the audience about me. I would, of course, translate his remarks, creating a new three-way dynamic between Fo, myself, and the audience or consciously referring to the dynamic that already existed. For example, Fo might explain the meaning of a particular word directly to me and then quip to the audience that he had stayed up all night looking in the dictionary for difficult words that would throw the interpreter off balance. Other times he would stop to compliment me on a word that he liked ("pope-mobile" for the Vatican limousine was one of his favorites) and laughingly suggest that I begin performing the show directly in English while he translated for Italians in the corner. In Fo's hands, the act of translation became a Brechtian device of defamiliarization that engaged the audience to participate more fully in the event than they might without the translation.

Whether the onstage interpretation was working smoothly or calling attention to itself through its inevitable imperfections, translation of Fo's monologues became a conscious act of performance. Working with Fo in this context made me confront the fact that to write translations of Fo's (or any other writer's) texts is an equally self-conscious act of performance that should ideally incorporate the rhythms of the reader or theater audience into the phrasing of the language. The translator is always part of a three-way conversation, whose work is most satisfying when it is invisible. (My most gratifying comments from the audience came from non-Italian speakers who told me they forgot they were listening to a translation.) But the goal of invisibility cannot disguise the fact that every translation is a performance that can never perfectly duplicate the original.

I am more fortunate than most translators in having had the experience of assimilating Fo's performance rhythms by working onstage with him. Now, whenever I translate one of his texts for publication, I instinctively incorporate the cadences of stage gestures and audience response, which are integral to Fo's theatrical language. For instance, in a passage from *Storia della tigre (The Tale of the Tiger)* that I translated for the American actor Thomas Derrah, the hero contemplates the possibility that he might not survive. "Moro, moro, moro, vai morire," Fo says in Italian dialect. Literally, I might have translated this as "I'm dying. I'm dying. I'm dying. I'm going to die." Instead, I recalled Fo's performance of the lines, which incorporates a startling and comic shift after the third "moro." He shifts direction from morose self-pity to spunky determination, as if "vai morire" were a phrase full of joy and good fortune. To give the actor a sense of this shift in the phrasing of the translation, I chose, "I'm dying, dying, dying. I'm going to die." The subtle difference creates a stronger contrast between the last statement and the three references to death that precede it. The repetition "dying, dying, dying" gives more of the sense of falling and fading that Fo achieves with "moro, moro, moro" than would have been possible if the spaces between the word "dying" had been interrupted with the first-person pronoun between each repetition. The difference might seem negligible in reading the text, but for an actor, changes such as these are significant. Derrah captured the irony and contradiction in the passage with great precision and elicited laughter from the audience at the same moment that Fo had planned for it to arrive.

This passage demonstrates the intimate link between performance and translation that is necessary to bring Fo's texts to life in another language. The kinesthetic images and the presence of the public should reside as implicitly in the English text as they do in the Italian, and a good actor should be able to decode these subliminal dimensions of the text during the interpretation process of rehearsals. Because Fo is such a virtuoso performer, it is naïve to expect that nothing will be lost or altered in the translation, but ideally, each translated performance can exploit its distance from the original to inject the texts with something unique, the way Fo transforms the disadvantage of an onstage translator into an asset for developing an added bond with the audience.

A less tangible advantage in translating Fo's texts comes from the privilege of having occasionally watched Fo cook dinner at home in Italy. He is as deeply committed to his cooking as he is to his theater, and watching him stir multiple pots for a dinner of pasta and fresh clam sauce, one cannot help but be reminded of "The Hunger of the Zanni," his sketch about the hungry peasant who dreams that he is preparing a feast in a giant's kitchen of huge cooking vessels. One night, while sampling his seafood broth from a large wooden ladle, he sighed with a wave of contentment that traveled from his nostrils to his knees. "I don't know why it never comes out this deliciously when somebody else cooks it," Fo wondered aloud in terms that couldn't help but remind me of my efforts to cook our translation into the appropriately tasty stew of English phrases. "Maybe they just don't love it the way I do." No translator could argue with a pronouncement so simple and true. One can only attempt to leap onto the swinging hammock of Fo's texts and try keeping true to their rhythms without ending up dangling from tangled phrases by one's extremities. Like gourmet cooking, translating Fo's plays is all "a question of balance, of equilibrium, and dynamics."

All translations are by the author.

CHAPTER 3

Updating Antiquity

ANTONIO SCUDERI

One of the most significant elements that defines the unique performance art of Dario Fo is his ability to draw, both consciously and intuitively, from the rich tradition of Western comedy and to adapt principles and techniques of ancient and medieval spectacle to a contemporary context. Historically, the Italian comic tradition, with its roots in Roman Saturnalian forms and the extensive influence of the *commedia dell'arte*, is germinal to the development of European comedy as a whole. Fo, as one of the most important figures in twentieth-century theater, represents a continuation of the Italian influence on the European comic tradition. So many performers, writers, and directors of the dramatic arts, as well as millions of spectators, have been touched by his artistry that his legacy will surely continue throughout the twenty-first century.

The purpose of the present study is to investigate certain elements of ancient and medieval performance traditions that stem both directly and indirectly from Roman roots and continue today in the theater of Fo. The first part will concentrate on the Roman Saturnalian celebrations and related medieval traditions. The spirit of the Saturnalian sub-/inversion of the power hierarchy was encoded in the Roman *palliata* comedies; in related medieval forms, such as the *sotie*; and in the

were characterized by *licentia* and *libertas*, expressed in a ritualistic inversion of the Roman social hierarchy and serving as a release from the tensions of the rigid paternalistic social order and its oppressive restrictions. The *palliata* mirrored the Saturnalian sub/inversion onstage, where sons bettered their fathers, slaves outwitted their masters, and the gods were blasphemed. "In sum, the very foundation of Roman morality is attacked in word and deed. . . . Nothing is sacred in the world of Plautus; irreverence is endemic" (Segal 1968:31).

The spirit of pagan Saturnalian revelry survived in the European carnival tradition, and the staging of Saturnalian social inversion was alive in medieval popular spectacle of sacred and secular parody, such as the *festa stultorum* (feast of fools), the *risus paschalis* (Easter laughter), the *sermons joyeux* (joyful sermons), and the *sotie* (fool's play). In these satirical spectacles, amateur and professional performers of the lower classes portrayed and parodied authority figures of the nobility and the clergy, such as the King of Fools, the Bishop of Fools, and even the Pope of Fools. And modeled on the Roman *palliata*, some plays of the *commedia dell'arte* continued the social inversion and the brazen destruction of social conventions, with subversive servants replacing subversive slaves.

In the *soties*, satirical farces of medieval French theater, everyone, from peasant to king, was portrayed as a fool or *sot*. The *sot*'s license for satire lay in his being a fool, "for the *sot* is allowed to speak the truth if he covers it with the mask of his madness" (Arden 1980:67). Appropriately, Fo refers to a *sot* character as *un matto* (fool or madman; 1987:156), and this is the name given to the subversive clown at the center of his most famous farce, *Morte accidentale di un anarchico* (*Accidental Death of an Anarchist*), based on the circumstances surrounding the death of Giuseppe Pinelli, who "fell" out of a window while in police custody. Pinelli was being interrogated about the 1969 bombings in Milan at the railway station and at the Banca Nazionale dell'Agricoltura in Piazza Fontana (see Mitchell 1999:101–15). The Matto, originally played by Fo, infiltrates police headquarters in Milan and, through his zany antics, unmasks for the audience the absurdity of the official account of the anarchist's demise. The attributes that define this character are derived from the subversive clowns of earlier comic forms.

The quality that gives Fo's Matto intense comic electricity and allows him to cover an extensive area with carnivalesque zaniness and satirical bite has much in common with the *servus callidus* (clever slave) of the *palliata*. The extant plays by Plautus provide us with an illustrious "who's who" of cunning *servi*, including Palaestrio in *Miles Gloriosus* and Pseudolus in the eponymous play. The extent of the clever slave's trickery is illustrated in *Mostellaria*, by Tranio, who, in order to keep the elderly Theopropides out of his own house while his son and company are partying within, convinces him that the house is haunted and that his son has purchased the one next door. Key to the Plautine slave's ability to manipulate the plot and the other characters is his power of self-transformation, the quality known as *versipellis* (skin-changing).[4] "The powers of the clever slave are supernatural. Through his self-transformations he controls those around him; he is invested with magic" (Slater 1985:104).

Many attributes of the *servi callidi* resurfaced in the *zanni*, the servants of the *commedia dell'arte*, and the power of *versipellis* became a defining attribute of Arlecchino, who, as Fo explains, "can transform himself into anything: a stupid or clever servant, a judge, a woman, a donkey, a cat" (1986:35).[5] As Ron Jenkins puts it, "Fo's conception of Harlequin is central to the comic impulses of all of his plays, including farces with modern settings" (1986:11). The Matto of *Morte accidentale* brings together the Saturnalian properties of the *servus versipellis*, the *sot*, and Arlecchino.

The quality that gives the Matto Saturnalian license and the power to sub/invert at will is based on the principle of paradox, which includes a self-conscious and calculated lunacy. Metatheatrical self-consciousness is a prominent quality of both the Plautine *servus* and Arlecchino.[6] In the context of *commedia* plays, Arlecchino's behavior is typically highly incongruous, and as Fo puts it, "his morality always derives from paradox" (1986:35). This exaggerated paradoxical quality of Arlecchino never makes it clear as to whether he is truly a raving lunatic or he is putting everyone on. Carlo Goldoni alludes to this in his most famous *arlecchinata, Servant of Two Masters*:[7] In their attempt to figure out Arlecchino, who appears suddenly and inexplicably on the scene, Pantalone comments confidentially to the Dottore, "I think this fellow is an idiot." The Dottore answers, "He seems to me, instead, to be a trickster" (1983:10).[8] The same sense of uncertainty as to whether the character is truly a *sciocco* (dolt) or, in actuality, a *finto tonto* (fake idiot) is inherent in the antics of the Neapolitan *zanni* Pulcinella (Scafoglio and Satriani 1992:135).

The Matto in *Morte accidentale* is also a paradoxical lunatic and a

Pantalone by Dario Fo. (Courtesy C.T.F.R.).

trickster. The play begins with the Matto being interrogated by Police
Commissioner Bertozzo. He has been arrested for impersonating a university professor, and the interrogator discovers that he has previously
been arrested eleven other times for passing himself off as other profes-
sionals, ranging from a surgeon to a bishop. After trying to reason with
the madman, the exasperated Bertozzo exclaims, "Cut the crap! I'm

beginning to believe that you really do have a mania for role-playing, but that you're also playing at being mad when instead you're saner than me, I bet!" (1988:10), suggesting that he is in fact a *finto tonto*.

It is determined that the Matto is a mentally unstable individual, suffering from a form of multiple personalities or "histriomania" (7), which, in the context of the play, allows him to take on various roles at will. During the course of the play, the madman proves to be a true *versipellis*, changing from one role to another. This role playing is very much in *sotie* mode, for in succession, he transforms himself into three authority figures. He first leads a second commissioner and the chief of police to believe that he is a judge who has been assigned to conduct an inquiry into the anarchist's death. With a newspaper reporter about to arrive, he convinces them that they should play along in pretending that he is a police captain from Rome. He then "reveals" to the reporter that he is actually a "bishop in plainclothes" (68). In each case, the role-playing allows the Matto to wreak Saturnalian havoc right in police headquarters.

The Matto's subversive inclinations are signaled from the very beginning. Before assuming any of the three roles, while being questioned by Commissioner Bertozzo, he expresses his desire—sarcastically, his disdain—for power: "I don't like to defend, that is a passive art. I prefer to judge, to condemn, to oppress, to persecute! I am one of you, dear Commissioner!" (10–11). He goes on to deliver an ironic praise of judges and why he would love to play that role. He explains the peculiar qualities of the profession, for judges begin their careers at the age when most everyone else is expected to retire. A Marxist notion of class privilege is evident:

> In fact, at the very moment that an ordinary person, any ol' laborer, at fifty or sixty, is ready to be chucked aside because he begins getting a little senile, a little slow in his reflexes, the judge, on the other hand, begins the prime of his career. . . . "Go home, clear out, you're old and senile!" For the judge instead it's just the opposite: the older they are, the more worn out, the more they're elected to high positions and entrusted with important tasks. (11)

He continues by "praising" the extraordinary power that judges exercise over the lives of the accused: "Fifty years for you . . . thirty for you . . . for you, only twenty because you look like a nice guy!" (11; ellipses in the original). Later when Bertozzo is called out of the office, the madman, who had just been thrown out, reenters, tears up his criminal report, and begins reading the other reports on the desk. Frivolously deciding which reports he should tear up, he satirizes and subverts judges' authority by portraying a fickle, subjective, and idiosyncratic decision-making process:

> And who is this accusation for? *(He reads.)* "Aggravated robbery." In a pharmacy? . . . it's understandable . . . nothing, nothing, you're free. *(He tears it as well.)* And what did you do? *(He reads.)* "Embezzlement . . . slander . . . "* Rubbish, rubbish . . . Go my boy, you're free! *(He tears it up.)* Everybody's free! *(He stops to consider one page in particular.)* Oh no, not you! You are a scoundrel . . . you stay . . . you're in. . . . (15–16; ellipses in the original)

The iconoclastic irreverence continues as the Matto prepares to pass himself off as the judge sent from Rome to investigate the anarchist incident. He begins by attempting to imitate a judge's manner of walking, and he tries out several ways, including "arthritic but with dignity! Like this, with neck slightly crooked, like a retired circus horse" (16).

By having the second commissioner and the chief of police believe he is in fact the judge-investigator, he is able to pull off a Saturnalian inversion of the power hierarchy. In this position of mock authority, he reveals the absurdity of their logic:

> *Police Chief:* However, we had our suspicions. Since the suspect was the only railroad employee in Milan who was an anarchist, it was easy to conclude that it was him.
> *Matto:* Of course, of course, it's obvious. So if it's clear that the bomb in a train station was planted by a railroad worker, we can conclude then that those famous bombs at the courthouse in Rome were planted by a judge, and at the military monument they were planted by the captain of the guard. . . . *(He suddenly becomes enraged.)* Come now gentlemen, I am here to conduct a serious investigation, not to waste time with idiotic syllogisms! (26)

The inversions get more sophisticated and involved. After finding out that the police had lied to the anarchist about evidence and about the confession of a close friend—with the explanation that this is simply a common police practice for coercing the suspect to confess—the Matto leads the second commissioner and the chief to believe that they are done for. He explains that all the evidence in the case points to their murdering the anarchist and that the government and the national law enforcement authorities have decided to make them the sacrificial lambs in order to lay the matter to rest. His advice to them at this point is to jump out the window and be done with it. When they are finally convinced that they have been completely abandoned by the higher-ups and that there is no hope of avoiding prosecution, he reveals that it was all his invention and explains: "Baloney? No! It's simply one of those little 'snares' that even we magistrates resort to, in order to demonstrate to the police just how barbaric, not to mention criminal, these methods are" (32).

The *sot* disguises himself as a police captain of forensics. An eye patch, a wooden arm, and a wooden leg create opportunities for various *lazzi* (gags) and carnivalesque mockery of the authority figure: A congratulatory slap on the back knocks out his glass eye and costs the second commissioner a pratfall, and his wooden arm comes out in a handshake and is replaced by that of a female mannequin, "in such a way as to oppose or contradict every dramatic action that could be constitutive of social, political, or psychological stability and order" (Wing 1990:145).

All of these gags take place while the journalist conducts her interview. In this new authoritative role as police captain, the Matto suggests to the journalist the possible motives behind the police's behavior as being part of a larger right-wing conspiracy. However, the paradox behind the Matto's behavior and that which offers him credibility with the real police is his tone of sarcastic indignation:

> Matto (intervening ironically): Just what on earth do you expect to gain by your blatant provocations, young lady? Do you expect us to admit that instead of chasing that handful of rag-tag anarchists, we should have seriously pursued more viable avenues, such as fascist and parliamentary-backed organizations, financed by industrialists, directed by Greek and neighboring militants, that perhaps we would get to the bottom of all this mess? (65)

At this point, the chief of police is convinced that the Matto is on their side, and he assures the incredulous Bertozzo confidentially that the Matto is about to turn the argument on its head: "Don't worry! Now he'll flip the whole omelette" (65). This Italian expression conveys the sense of the paradoxical inversion in which the Matto engages, except that the real authority figures are convinced that it is somehow working in their favor.

The Pope of Fools

The aforementioned *licentia* and *libertas* that permitted the Saturnalian mockery and sub/inversion of rigid social order during the Roman *ludi* in Plautus's time extended to the severity of Roman religion as well. This institution was also fair game for Plautine comedies, in which there are many examples of blasphemy and irreverence toward the gods (Segal 1968:29–31). Later, the Catholic Church and members of the clergy, including popes, were the targets of the Saturnalian-carnivalesque spectacles of the Middle Ages. We find, for example, in the *sotie* entitled *Le Jeu du Prince des Sotz* "that the object of the satire—Pope Julius II—is both precise and clearly designated" (Arden 1980:63). Fo takes these ancient traditions and adapts them to a contemporary context by playing the role of powerful clergymen and denouncing the present-day Catholic Church as a corrupt and powerful bureaucratic institution, out of touch with the lives of the downtrodden it professes to serve. His satire is an attempt to unmask what he believes to be the pretense of the church. Heather Arden explains that *pretense*, the root of the satirical conflict of the *sotie*, "is found when a class or individual appears to fulfill the role allotted to it, while in reality betraying that role or usurping the role of another" (1980:127).

In *Morte accidentale*, when the Matto transforms himself into a clergyman, he begins a criticism of the Catholic Church's meddling in political affairs and power plays. The implication that the church, as a major economic and political institution in Italy, shares common interests with other major institutions, such as the police, is signaled immediately in the Matto's new role as "a bishop in plainclothes," and in his "assignment": "With your permission, Father Augusto Bernier, commissioned by the Holy See as Observer of Church-Police Relations." Bertozzo exclaims incredulously: "Oh no! Oh no! This is too much! Now he's a bishop-policeman!" (69). The Saturnalian inversion is rubbed in as the police authorities are obliged to kiss the Matto-bishop's ring, a traditional act of submission toward high-ranking clergy.

In the tradition of the *festa stultorum* and the *soties*, Fo played the role of a pope in two of his plays, *Mistero buffo* (Comic mystery) and *Il papa e la strega* (*The Pope and the Witch*). In his most famous one-man performance, *Mistero buffo*, he played a historical pope, Boniface

VIII (c. 1235–1303), in an eponymous sketch. In the extended prologue (1977:105–11), Fo gives background to the monstrous deeds of Pope Boniface, for whom Dante reserved a place in hell among the simoniacs (*Inferno* 19). In it, he focuses on Boniface's repression and cruelty toward reformist monks with sympathies for the peasants. In the sketch, Fo is primarily holding the church to some form of historical responsibility, yet much of the criticism can apply to the present day.

The general principle that the church became part of the power mechanism of official culture, detached in every way from the poor and downtrodden with whom Christ associated, is embodied in the pompous and cruel personage of Boniface as he dresses himself in finery in preparation for a procession. The pope is so removed from the original principles of Christ's teaching that he forgets who Christ is when he encounters him in person: "Who is that? Who? Who's the guy with the cross? Jesus? Of course! Christ! Jesus Christ!" (1977:116). Christ berates him for his evil ways, and a climactic kick in the seat removes the mask of false humility, the *pretense*, with which Boniface attempted to win Christ's favor.

Similar to the satire directed at the Catholic Church in *Morte accidentale*, in the farce *Il papa e la strega*, Fo criticizes the church's role as a player in the Italian and international scene (see Scuderi 1996a; 1998:38–40, 95–98). The two main points of criticism in the play are the Catholic Church's stance on birth control and illegal drugs. There is once again the implication that the Catholic Church shares interests with other powerful institutions. In this case, the focus is on organized crime, which benefits by keeping drugs illegal. Besides the satire directed at these two issues, there are many other allusions to the church's *pretense*. When the pope is outraged in discovering that the witch (originally played by Franca Rame) works in an abortion clinic, she scolds him for his hypocrisy: "You're disgusted at the thought of having touched my hands, but you had no problem in shaking the truly filthy hands of Pinochet, Marcos and other heads of state, such as the those of El Salvador" (1994:258).

While serving as a target for the criticism leveled by the witch character, often in a sober register, the pope *fou* concurrently performs the zany Saturnalian rites of the subversive clown. There are many sarcastic and cutting remarks by the pope directed at politicians and powerful members of the Roman Catholic clergy, with whom Italian audiences would have been familiar from their activities reported in the news. As part of the sub/inversion of the clergy's power, the pope *fou* delights in targeting his personal secretary, the Cardinal. After shooting a blunted arrow at the poor flabbergasted Cardinal, he explains: "Forgive me, but beneath these robes beats the heart of an actor who has always been anti-clerical. I cannot control myself in the presence of a Cardinal." This metatheatrical signal reminds the audience that behind the mask of the pope is a subversive *sot*. Then before his next line, the stage directions read: "He gets back into character" (240). The change in and out of character accompanied by the metatheatrical wink to the audience evinces both the *versipellis* and the paradoxical *finto tonto* qualities that underlie the clown's subversive power. It also attests Fo's epic approach to the *maschera* (mask/stock character) of the *commedia* tradition, as he explained to me in an interview:

> It's the ability to remain detached from the play: I am an actor who narrates something. I am not a pedestrian imitation, but rather he who tells about a character that's not me. The *maschera* means that inside I am a man. The *maschera* is something external, it's fake. Don't you see that I am not a real person? I'm fake. What is real is inside that which I narrate to you. (1993)

Fo's view of the Western comic tradition can be defined as a continuum whereby principles and techniques of comic performance are passed down from generation to generation, a point of view he develops in his 1987 *Manuale minimo dell'attore* (The actor's mini-manual, published in English as *Tricks of the Trade*). This mind-set, by which he views himself as an inheritor of an ancient tradition, facilitates his ability to draw from earlier forms, for he is aware that the principles and techniques of comic performance have survived while mutating to adapt to the various cultural and historical contexts. In particular, the Saturnalian tradition suits his needs in his chosen role and function as subversive clown, forever challenging the power structure in an attempt to unmask the hoax of hypocrisy, the *pretense* of those who have the responsibility inherent in the privilege of power.

Fo and the *Giullare*

The *giullarata,* Fo's unique style of one-man show, represents the most fascinating and innovative aspect of his multifaceted theatrical achievements. Bringing together his talents as a writer and performer, he has projected his personality through his storytelling to countless audiences in Italy and around the world. By using a special performance language based on northern Italian dialects and on *grammelot* (defined below), accompanied by a intricate system of gestures and mime, he has presented the elaborate narratives of his four major *giullarate: Mistero buffo, Fabulazzo osceno (Obscene Fables), Storia della tigre (The Tale of the Tiger)*, and *Johan Padan a la descoverta de le Americhe (Johan Padan—The Discovery of the Americas)*. Sketches from the most successful and well known of these, *Mistero buffo*, have been performed by other artists, such as Robbie Coltrane in Great Britain, Bjorn Granath in Sweden, and various artists in Italy, including Antonio Venturino, who did a version in Sicilian dialect.

Although for contemporary audiences Fo's *giullarata* may seem unique and even unusual, it is based on techniques of popular performers found in many traditions around the world. His first and most lasting experiences were in his childhood, listening to the *fabulatori*, the storytellers of the lake region in Lombardy. In particular, his methods for framing and improvisation are akin to the methods often used by folk and popular players. "Framing" refers to the techniques used for keying in and out of performance and the rapport it establishes with the audience. By using popular methods of framing, Fo strives to destroy the "fourth wall" and create a player-audience rapport that is more akin to street performance. Improvisation concerns the contextualization of narrative formulas, whereby the actual utterances are not memorized verbatim but are "composed" at the moment of performance.[9]

The specific tradition Fo intends to emulate in his *giullarata* is that of the medieval street performer, specifically the tradition of the storyteller-mime, principally pantomime and mime, that may well have had Roman origins. The Roman pantomime consisted of a single silent dancer who played out all the parts in consecutive solo scenes, accompanied by musicians and either a singer or chorus to provide narrative continuity. Lucian reports: "In general, the dancer undertakes to present and enact characters and emotions, introducing now a lover and now an angry person, one afflicted with madness, another with grief" (Beacham 1991:142–43).

In terms of social prestige, mime for the Romans was the lowest form of performance, existing primarily at the street level.

Whatever did not fit the generic categories of tragedy or comedy, Atellane or the Italian togate comedy, was mime: a narrative entertainment in the *media* of speech, song and dance. Like *Commedia dell'arte* these performances were largely improvisational with a plot outline devised by the Archimimus, who would roughly assign dialogue sequences (scenes) for the other players to *ad lib*. There would be traditional scenarios based on confidence tricks, disguise and cheating lovers, in which the leading role might vary between the trickster and his elderly miserly or foolish dupe.[10] (Fantham 1989:154–55)

We may safely assume that as the Roman Empire disintegrated and formal theaters stopped functioning and institutionalized forms of entertainment ceased to exist, many performers continued their art at the street level, joining the ranks of wandering players. In the early Middle Ages, the learned Latin word *histriones*, originally from the Etruscan *ister* ("player"), became a generic term for all roving popular performers and was used "until the ninth century, when the word *jongleur* came into fashion" (Towsen 1976:47). *Jongleur* is a derivative of the Latin *joculator* ("joker," "jester"), as are the Provençal *joglar*, the Spanish *juglar*, the German *Gaukler*, the English *juggler*, and the Italian *giullare*. The *jongleurs*, or *giullari*, were itinerant players, mostly of the lower classes, who worked within the oral tradition. They included a wide variety of performers: musicians, dancers, acrobats, tumblers, jugglers, actors, mountebanks, storytellers, and so forth. Versatility was a common trait of the individual performers as well, and it seems most *giullari* were able to perform in a wide variety of ways (Towsen 1976:48).

Modes of performance bearing resemblance to both Roman pantomime and mime were part of the medieval *giulleria* (*jongleur* tradition), and "Italy seems in particular to have been noted for its mimes and actors" (Beacham 1991:200). Besides playing in streets, piazzas, carnivals, and fairgrounds, the *giullari* would often entertain nobles at banquets and parties. And in Renaissance Italy, they were also being invited to perform for upper-class audiences during the intermezzi of literary plays. We have an account from 1515 of a performance by the celebrated *giullare* Zan Polo. His comic sketch was played during the intermezzo of a staging of Plautus's *Miles Gloriosus* in Venice. Evidence points to a confluence of the performance techniques and versatility of the professional street players and the literary knowledge, particularly of extant Terentian and Plautine texts, of the court dilettantes[11] as the formula for the creation of the *commedia dell'arte*. Like the pantomimists of ancient Rome, Zan Polo played the various roles of the sketch, including a sorcerer and the god of love (Richards and Richards 1990:24).

Pietro Aretino describes a performance, also in Venice, by another
sixteenth-century *giullare* or *buffone*, Cimador. Aretino reports that by imitating "an assortment of voices," the buffoon performed a sketch about a Bergamasque porter cuckolding a senile old husband. Cimador played all the various roles in turn, including the wife and a servant girl (Richards and Richards 1990:24–25). The plot of Cimador's sketch was reminiscent of the Roman mime, as were his characters. They were also the characters that were to become *maschere* (stock characters) of the *commedia dell'arte*: The Bergamasque porter, the old man, and the servant girl are the prototypes of the *commedia*'s Zanni-Arlecchino, Magnifico-Pantalone, and the *servetta*-Colombina, respectively.

As in many traditions of verbal art around the world, Fo tells a story by combining narration, dialogue, and gestural language. Ruth Finnegan's description of African narrative traditions, for example, may be used to describe Fo's solo technique as well:

> Stories are often enacted in the sense that, to a greater or smaller degree, the speech and gestures of their characters are imitated by the narrator, and the action is largely exhibited through dialogue in which the storyteller directly portrays various characters in turn. It is true that such enactment of character is not sustained or complete, that straight narration, as well as dramatic dialogue, is used to communicate the events of the story, and that only one real "actor" could be said to be involved. (1970:501–2)

Although Fo claims to emulate the *jongleurs* of the Middle Ages, and this may very well be, it is difficult to verify, since extant textual descriptions of such performances are extremely rare. However, certain aspects of his *giullarata* do bear a striking resemblance to the type of proto-*commedia*, one-man performance described above. Like Zan Polo and Cimador, the language Fo uses suggests the performance of a proto-*commedia buffone*. And like the *buffone*, he plays all the roles of the various characters in his stories.

The piece in which this technique may be considered a tour de force is *Resurrezione di Lazzaro* (The Resurrection of Lazarus), from *Mistero buffo*. A crowd of people are waiting for Jesus to come to perform a miracle. The Saturnalian inversion lies in presenting the miracle as a magic act with an emphasis on its entertainment value. Money is collected for the show, people are concerned about being able to see, and others profit by selling refreshments and chairs. In the introduction, Fo mentions fifteen to sixteen characters (1977:96), and, in fact, he conveys the sense of an entire crowd, including a gatekeeper, several vendors, and a variety of spectators, all engaged in frenetic interaction with each other.

The Language of the *Giullarata*

Fo's farces are performed in standard Italian, but for his *giullarate*, he developed a special language, which consists of a Lombard-Venetan dialect base and *grammelot*, both of which are pertinent to the proto-*commedia* and *commedia* traditions. The *giullari*, being primarily from the lower classes and working in the oral tradition, would have performed in dialects, that is, codes that were primarily spoken and not written. Dialects and regional variants of Italian then became the speech of the *vecchi* (old men) and *zanni* of the *commedia*.[12] In an idiom that would suggest northern Italian *giullari*, the performance language Fo uses is based primarily on his native Lombard dialect, with some Venetan and (to a lesser extent) some Emilian mixed in. Existing in close geographic proximity and typologically similar, these dialects share many elements, so combining them into a hybrid code is not terribly difficult. The result suggests the generic speech of the *Padana* region, that is, the area of the Po valley (hence the name of the protagonist, Johan Padan.)

The Lombard-Venetan code is pertinent to the proto-*commedia giullarata* and to the *commedia dell'arte* in various ways. First, the tradition of the *commedia* is closely tied with the Veneto region, where much of the proto-*commedia* and early *commedia* activities originated. The *commedia* continued to be popular in Venice up until the work of Carlo Goldoni (1707–93), who wrote many plays entirely or in part in Venetian dialect, arguably the most illustrious of the Venetan dialects (still spoken today by Venetians of all social classes). Second, there is Arlecchino, one of the most important characters of the *commedia dell'arte* and from whom Fo draws much comical inspiration. Arlecchino evolved from Zanni, the stereotyped porter from Bergamo, mentioned above, whose speech, therefore, is based on Bergamasque, a Lombard dialect. Finally, there is the work of the playwright Ruzzante (Angelo Beolco, c. 1495–1542), who wrote in Pavano, a rustic register of Paduan dialect, also of the Venetan family. Ruzzante is important in bringing elements of the popular traditions to literary theater and is one of Fo's greatest influences (see Farrell, in this volume).

Fo intends his solo-performance language to be an intricate and loosely assembled hybrid, thus there are lexical elements of other northern Italian dialects and sometimes from other languages grafted onto the Lombard-Venetan base.[13] This hybrid quality has special sociopolitical connotations, for he asserts that it is the language of a disenfranchised people forced to wander and assimilate elements from host languages and dialects (1986:35).

In his *Manuale minimo*, he discusses the origins of the stock character Zanni. Zanni, Venetan for Gianni (Johnny), was the name given in the sixteenth century to indigent Bergamasque farmers who were forced to abandon their land and seek work in Venice. The Bergamasque men who could find employment worked primarily as porters (Fo 1987:60–62). As was noted above in Aretino's account of Cimador's performance, the Zanni became stereotyped in Venetian proto-*commedia* performances. In the *commedia*, he was stylized as the stock character Zanni, and later, the word *zanni* became a generic term for all of the servant-class characters. Through the enormous influence of the *commedia* in Europe, it became a generic term for *clown* and gave us the English word *zany*. For Fo, Zanni is an allegory of all oppressed and disenfranchised people, and this is evident in another sketch from *Mistero buffo*, *La fame dello zanni* (The zanni's hunger). In this sketch, starvation drives the *zanni* to wild hallucinations of preparing a pantagruelean meal and devouring everything in sight, including himself.

Typically, in his *giullarata* performance, there is also a good dose of modern standard Italian. Since all Italian dialects and the standard language derive from Latin, the similarities create many opportunities for interference. The resulting speech of many Italians is often a tour de force of code-switching and code-mixing, "in which the syntactic constituents of a sentence belong to different linguistic systems" (Berruto 1997:398), and thus more of a dialect-standard hybrid rather than purely one or the other. Like most educated Italians who can speak their local dialects, Fo incorporates a good deal of modern standard Italian, whether he intends to or not.[14]

The other important element in the performance language for Fo's *giullarata* is *grammelot*, which in the recent edition of a major standard dictionary of Italian is defined as the "utterance of sounds that are similar in rhythm and intonation to the discourse of a given language without the pronunciation of actual words and that characterizes the comic or farcical recitation of certain actors" (Zingarelli 1995:797). According to John Rudlin, Fo most likely learned the technique from Jacques

Lecoq, "who certainly got it from Jean Dasté who had used it with the Copiaus (the touring troupe that emerged from Jacques Copeau's Vieux Colombier School), which called it *grummelot*" (1994:59–60). The etymology of the term is uncertain, and there are various theories, such as Gianfranco Folena's assertion that the word may derive from the French *grommeler*, which means to mutter or to speak through one's teeth (1991:121). Fo postulates that the term was coined by Italian *commedia* players in Paris (1987:81), which was the most important center of *commedia* activity (for other theories on the origin of the word, see Pizza 1996:104–10); Pozzo 1998:70–73).

It is very likely that itinerant players, such as the *giullari* and early traveling *commedia* troupes—performing outside the realm of their native speech and thus faced with the situation of not sharing a common language with their audiences—had developed certain performance languages that relied less on precise semantics, serving more to suggest real speech while accompanying histrionics and mime. Whether or not it already existed in some form, *grammelot* became a necessary skill for some of the players of the later *commedia*, as John Rudlin explains:

> The technique was originally developed through necessity by the Italian players at the end of the seventeenth century, when they were banished from the Parisian theatres to the fairground booths. Since spoken dialogue was prohibited except on the legitimate stage, they were obliged to turn to oratorio, placards, scrolls and *grummelots*. (1994:60)

Fo is a master of *grammelot*, and in his *giullarate*, he can perform entire sketches while pretending to speak a foreign tongue. In *Mistero buffo*, there were sketches in *grammelot* that conveyed American English, British English, and French. There are also moments of *grammelot* in his farces. For example, in *Il papa e la strega*, John Paul II sings a childhood song in Polish *grammelot*: "Acuni bonnja inanolijae / A la-stroní-nijamihiae acooniàat!" (1994:253). Fo often uses a form of Italian *grammelot* to signal bureaucratic double talk, radio broadcasts, and so forth.

It should be mentioned that Fo often refers to the performance language of his *giullarate* (discussed above) as *grammelot*. This can serve to create an air of mystique. For example, in the introduction to a performance of *Johan Padan*, he explains to the audience that he will only be using *grammelot*, "which, as you know, is an onomatopoeic language.

I don't say anything, I pretend to say things. Naturally this creates a very subtle mood and sometimes, thanks to *grammelot,* the mood of the discourse is understood more than the words" (1992a). It is an interesting theatrical device, but it is simply not "true," except for those moments of pure *grammelot,* such as signaling Native American speech or the sounds of rain and fireworks (discussed below).

In the same prologue, before explaining that he will be speaking in *grammelot,* Fo claims and then disclaims that the language of the performance will be an incredible hybrid of old Romance dialects and some Arabic, the lingua franca typical of the Mediterranean sailors of Columbus's time. He also explains that the inspiration for this speech was found in the writings of Michele da Cuneo, who had sailed with Columbus. None of this, including Da Cuneo's language, is true; it simply serves to create a linguistic mystique. Michele da Cuneo, born in Savona, wrote in Italian typical of an educated man of the period, that is, in a maritime register and with some regionalisms. Since Fo is notorious for throwing scholars red herrings, it is interesting, yet not surprising, to note that the only extant letter by Da Cuneo (1893) was discovered in 1885 by Olindo Guerrini, a notorious scholarly prankster, which puts its authenticity into question (Bignardelli 1962).

Often in a well-executed *grammelot,* an occasional, identifiable key word will be inserted amidst nonsensical syllables. Following is an example of Native American *grammelot* from the published text of *Johan Padan.* After being shipwrecked somewhere in the Caribbean, Johan and his companions encounter a group of aborigines. They need help from these people but can only hope that they have not yet encountered Europeans, for having suffered at their hands, they may turn out to be less than helpful.

> I take heart and begin yelling words in their language that I learned:
> "Aghiu du, en lì salà, chiomé saridde aabasjia *jaspania* in obrioci *cristeani* emebradì."
> Which means: "Friends, we are shipwrecked *Christians* from a *Spanish* ship that went down."
> They understand me!
> They answer: "Huh? What did you say?"
> "Mujacia cocecajo mobaputio *cristiàn* posietricio *espaniol.*"
> Which means: "Excuse us but we don't know what you mean when you say *Christians* and *Spaniards.*"
> Whew!
>
> (1992b:28; emphasis added)

The insertion of a limited number of key words that are identifiable to the audience conveys a sense of semantic value and thus a sense of real speech to the otherwise nonsensical sounds. In this case, the key words crucial to the protagonists' well-being are *jaspania, espaniol* (Spanish), *cristeani,* and *cristiàn* (Christian). These are the words that would identify Johan and friends to the aborigines, if in fact they had previous close encounters with Europeans. By varying the forms of the identifiable words, he gives the impression that the same words are being used in both nominal and adjectival forms or in different declensions, conveying a sense of morphological complexity.

In his report of Cimador's performance (cited above), Aretino mentions that as part of his act, the *giullare* produced sound effects, such as the old man "farting all the while" and "snoring away in his sleep" and the noise of the porter and the lady "to-ing and fro-ing together" (Richards and Richards 1990:25). In a performance, these sound effects can be interspersed within actual speech or within *grammelot*. An example of the latter occurs in "Il tecnocrate americano" (The American technocrat), in *Mistero buffo*. Fo mimes an American aerospace scientist demonstrating extraordinary and elaborate machinery. Interspersed in the nonsensical discourse in American-English *grammelot* are the pops and pings of the technocrat's space-age devices. There are times when Fo uses extended periods of pure sounds, and these often represent tours de force of this technique. There are several examples of this in *Johan Padan,* such as when Fo aurally depicts raindrops striking the ground or fireworks by imitating the whistling sounds of bombs sailing into the air, followed by multiple explosions.

Many contemporary comic actors use the technique of *grammelot* by imitating the sounds, cadences, and intonations of a given language. But as he does in many other ways, Fo distinguishes himself from most other performers by recovering techniques and methods of older comedic traditions. His *grammelot* is marked by the use of sound effects and by being synchronized to his extraordinary body language.

Fo's Gestural Code

Fo's *giullarata* is essentially an act of storytelling in his performance language, accompanied by gestures, movements, and facial expressions. Such accompaniments are an essential aspect of popular verbal art around the world and was noted by some of the earliest folklorists. We find this expressed in the writings of one of the greatest folklorists of the

nineteenth century, Giuseppe Pitrè, when he discusses verbal art in the
Sicilian tradition of epic storytelling, *lu cuntu*: "Head, arms, legs, everything must take part in the narration, mime being an essential part of
the work of the narrator" (1884:346). In discussing the historical development of the art of gesturing as it developed in theater, Fo distinguishes
between the two great traditions of pantomime and mime. He defines
pantomime as expression purely through gesture; mime, "as defined
since ancient times," entails using every means at the performer's dis-
posal (1987:229).

At the end of the seventeenth century, the same restrictions on spoken dialogue that led the Italian players in France to develop *grammelot*
also resulted in the development of the pantomime show. It was not long
before this mode of performance was brought to Britain by Gallo-Italian
players. An important character for both the French and the British pantomime and harlequinade of the nineteenth century was Pierrot, who is
related to a series of white-smocked, white-faced characters such as
Gian Farina.[15] His immediate antecedent was Pedrolino, originally Gal-
licized by the actor Giuseppe Giratoni in the 1660s (Findlater 1978:154).
In the nineteenth century, the pantomime tradition reached levels of
performance genius in France with the Pierrot, Jean-Gaspard Deburau;
on the London stage, Pierrot was transformed into the Clown of the
English pantomime by Joe Grimaldi. The direct heir of these traditions
is Marcel Marceau, one of the most influential figures in the performing
arts of the twentieth century.[16]

Fo studied with another great artist of the French tradition, Jacques
Lecoq, who, like Marceau, can trace his performance heritage to the
school of Jacques Copeau. Whereas Marceau works primarily in the tradition of the purely silent *pantomime blanche*, Lecoq's technique incorporates sounds and words as well. Lecoq worked with Fo in 1953, super-
vising the rehearsals for the variety review *Il dito nell'occhio* (A *Finger
in the Eye*). He taught Fo the technique of *grammelot* and how to control
his voice in performance. He also taught him how to move onstage by
employing the particular qualities of his face and body for maximum
comic effect.

Fo has developed a sophisticated code to complement his narratives, and it stands out as an essential part of his artistry. His science of
theatrical movements entails creating for a particular character a series
of physical actions, reactions, and fragments of actions, which he exe-
cutes in a variety of sequences during a narrative (Barba and Savarese

1991:175). This method of creating a visual code of gestures and movements for a given character shares a close affinity with performance traditions of other cultures—for example, Kabuki or the various forms of Indian dance theater—that employ stylized movements. Of course, there is the direct influence of the *commedia*, from which Fo incorporated the stylized movements of the various *maschere*.

Like the stylized movements of various other performance traditions of other cultures, Fo's gestural language includes to an extent movements suggestive of animals. In his *Manuale minimo*, he discusses the zoomorphic qualities of the *commedia* masks and gives his theory of their origins and social implications (1987:27–32). This aspect of Fo's gestural art is worth mentioning because his portrayals of animals in the *giullarate* have often represented tours de force. These include the tigress and her cubs in *Storia della tigre* and the many animals depicted in *Johan Padan*, including parrots, donkeys, cows, pigs, monkeys, turkeys, and iguanas and an extensive sequence that involves a mare, a colt, and a stallion.

Besides portraying animals directly, at times movements suggestive of zoomorphism have subtly informed the gestural code of human characters. In a segment from a workshop for young actors (Marks 1984), Fo demonstrates the *maschera* of the Magnifico, whom he interprets as the embodiment of a has-been aristocracy. He explains and demonstrates the character's pomposity and unfounded sense of importance in movements reminiscent of a cockerel: strutting about while turning his head briskly from side to side as if the eyes were placed somewhere at the temples, like those of a bird. The Magnifico's bird qualities are suggested as well by his strident voice and by the feathers and beak of his mask. Watching Fo perform *Mistero buffo*, one can notice how certain elements of the Magnifico's gestural code are incorporated into the character of Pope Boniface VIII. The false sense of dignity inherent in the Magnifico is most appropriate for the depraved and corrupted pope, whose authority has absolutely no spiritual or moral foundation.

Fo's techniques are highly regarded in theater communities. He has conducted many workshops on the subject, even at the international level (e.g., Eugenio Barba's Odin Theatret conferences, which emphasize cross-cultural exchanges). At workshops, he demonstrates techniques, such as that of performing the same sketch with and without a mask—the mask obstructs facial expressivity and forces a wider area of expression with the rest of the body (1987:51–66). As a teacher, he advises his students to avoid conventional and stereotypical gestures, such as resting cheek in hands to convey sleepiness. Theatrical gestures, like theatrical language, should be a product of a creative imagination and should be constantly reinvented, based on reality, not on convention. In order to master the art of gestural language, Fo recommends learning acrobatic skills, how to breathe in time to movements, and the art of signaling the existence of imaginary objects with one's hands. He explains how and why certain gestures should be overstated for optimum effect and admonishes against using too many gestures as a means of flaunting one's technical skills. A performer should be selective in his/ her choice of gestures and masterful in their execution (1987:229–31).

In developing his trademark solo performance, Fo intended to emulate what he believed was the performance art of the storyteller-mimes of the medieval *giulleria*. This tradition, which may have inherited qualities of the Roman mime and pantomime, was an essential ingredient in the formation of the *commedia dell'arte*, and there is evidence that Fo's version shares similarities with the proto-*commedia* art of northern Italian Renaissance *giullari*. He has also assimilated elements directly from the *commedia* and from techniques that were passed down from the *commedia* to other traditions, such as the French pantomime. But ultimately, Fo's *giullarata* is part of a greater tradition of popular storytelling that combines narrative and movement and is based primarily on performance and audience rapport rather than on written text. At the same time, having brought together and incorporated elements from all these traditions, Fo has created something new and unique. And like the Renaissance *giullari* who brought their art from the streets to upper-class theaters, Fo has transposed a piazza performance onto a conventional stage.

All translations are by the author.

Notes

I would like to thank Thomas D. Cravens at the University of Wisconsin-Madison and Hermann W. Haller at Queens College and City University of New York Graduate Center for sharing their expertise in linguistics; my colleagues David Christiansen in Classics and Patrick Lobert in French; and my friend Vittorio Cenini for providing the material on Michele da Cuneo.
    1. The Fescennine verses may be related to a similar type of licentious rural

entertainment, the Greek *phallica*, which was practiced in the southern Italian colonies of Magna Graecia.

2. The *fabula palliata* (plays in Greek dress) were set in Greece as a disclaimer to direct ridicule of Roman society and culture.

3. The discovery of sixteen Plautine plays by Nicholas Trevirius in 1429 represents one of the greatest literary inputs into Renaissance comedy.

4. It appears that the term is first used by Plautus himself, in *Amphitruo*, to describe Jupiter, who transforms his appearance to that of Amphitruo in order to bed his wife.

5. In the seventeenth-century *commedia* scenario, *Arlequin Lingère du Palais*, we find Arlecchino "dressed half like a woman and half like a man" (Beaumont 1967:65). By turning and exposing one side or the other, Arlecchino alternates between a draper and a refreshment vendor, both hawking their wares and vying for the patronage of the unsuspecting Pasquariello.

6. For an in-depth discussion on the self-conscious aspect of the Plautine *servus*, see Slater (1985:4, 9, 56, 58, 104). For a discussion on the aspects of Arlecchino and Pulcinella that were transmitted from primordial carnival rites to the *commedia dell'arte*, see Toschi (1955) and Scuderi (2000).

7. *Servant of Two Masters* was written for one of the greatest interpreters of the role, Antonio Sacchi, who created Truffaldino, a variation of Arlecchino. It was first staged in 1746.

8. Another reason is that in *Servant of Two Masters*, there is no *primo zanni*, who typically functioned as a straight-man clown. Arlecchino carries all of the *zanni* intrigue by himself, in a sense, playing both roles. The same can be said for the *Matto* in *Morte accidentale*.

9. For a discussion of these techniques and the way Fo adapted them from popular traditions, see Scuderi (1996b, 1998).

10. "By its very nature, such activity left little concrete evidence behind, although in the mid-fifteenth century when the *commedia dell'arte* first emerges from the mists (already it seems in a fairly well-developed form) its striking resemblance to earlier popular drama makes it difficult indeed to doubt the survival of an ancient craft" (Beacham 1991:200).

11. *Dilettante* here refers to people of the middle and upper classes at that time who were interested in the performing arts and who wrote and performed plays, mainly for their friends.

12. The *innamorati* spoke in a literary register of Tuscan-based Italian.

13. For example, in order to convey the historic context of *Johan Padan*, he inserts occasional Spanish words. But in an entire performance lasting nearly two and one-half hours (Fo 1992a), there are only a dozen or so such words. These include *sangre* (blood), *Dios* (God), *puede* (s/he can), *trabajar* (work), *hombre* (man), *suerte* (luck), *negro* (black), *amarillo* (yellow), and *fiesta* (celebration). Not only is the use of Spanish lexicon sporadic and limited, but the Italian and/or Lombard equivalents of these words are used as well.

14. Francesco Sabatini (1984) presents some of the various schemata devised by Italian linguists in an attempt to categorize the various levels of language codes that exist within the polarity of standard/dialect. This issue is also discussed in Berruto (1987).

15. *Farina* (flour) refers to the character's white-powdered face.

16. One of Marceau's first performances in the 1940s was in the role of Arlequin in the pantomime "Baptiste," a tribute to Deburau. Marceau was cast by Jean-Louis

Barrault, who had interpreted Deburau-Pierrot in the film *Les Enfants Du Paradis*. In a performance-lecture in 1993 in Columbus, Ohio, Marceau suggested that Grimaldi is considered by many in the tradition—himself included—to have been the greatest mime ever.

References

Arden, Heather. 1980. *Fools' Plays: A Study of Satire in the Sotie*. London: Cambridge UP.

Bakhtin, Mikhail. 1984. *Rabelais and His World*. Tr. Hélène Iswolsky. Bloomington: Indiana UP.

Barba, Eugenio, and Nicola Savarese. 1991. *A Dictionary of Theatre Anthropology: The Secret Art of the Performer*. Tr. Richard Fowler. Ed. Richard Gough. London: Routledge.

Beacham, Richard C. 1991. *The Roman Theatre and Its Audience*. Cambridge: Harvard UP.

Beaumont, Cyril W. 1967. *The History of Harlequin*. New York: Benjamin Blom.

Berruto, Gaetano. 1987. *Sociolinguistica dell'italiano contemporaneo*. Rome: Nuova Italia Scientifica.

———. 1997. "Code-Switching and Code-Mixing." In *The Dialects of Italy*, ed. Martin Maiden and Mair Parry, 394–400. London: Routledge.

Bignardelli, Ignazio O. 1962. "Una delle tante beffe del Guerrini?" *L'universo* 42.1:177–82.

Conte, Gian Biagio. 1994. *Latin Literature: A History*. Tr. Joseph B. Solodow. Baltimore: Johns Hopkins UP.

Da Cuneo, Michele. 1893. "Michele da Cuneo. Lettera" (1495). In *Raccolta di documenti e studi*, 95–107. Rome: Reale Commissione Colombiana.

Fantham, R. Elaine. 1989. "Mime: The Missing Link in Roman Literary History." *Classical World* 82.3:153–63.

Findlater, Richard. 1978. *Joe Grimaldi: His Life and Theatre*. 2d ed. Cambridge: Cambridge UP.

Finnegan, Ruth. 1970. *Oral Tradition in Africa*. Oxford: Clarendon.

Fo, Dario. 1966–98. *Le commedie di Dario Fo*. 13 vols. to date. Turin: Einaudi.

———. 1977. *Mistero buffo*. In Fo 1966–98, Vol. 5, 5–171.

———. 1986. "Arlecchino è il paradosso." *Ulisse 2000* 29 (February/March):35.

———. 1987. *Manuale minimo dell'attore*. Ed. Franca Rame. Turin: Einaudi.

———. 1988. *Morte accidentale di un anarchico*. In Fo 1966–98, Vol. 7, 5–83.

———. 1992a. *Johan Padan a la discoverta de le Americhe*. Milan: C.T.F.R. Videocassette.

———. 1992b. *Johan Padan a la discoverta de le Americhe*. Ed. Franca Rame. Firenze: Giunti Gruppo Editoriale.

———. 1993. Interviews by Antonio Scuderi. Milan, 1–6 October.

———. 1994. *Il Papa e la strega*. In Fo 1966–98, Vol. 10, 215–301.

Folena, Gianfranco. 1991. *Il linguaggio del caos: Studi sul plurilinguismo rinascimentale*. Turin: Boringhieri.

Goldoni, Carlo. 1983. *Il servitore di due padroni*. In *Commedie*, Vol 1. Ed. Guido Davico Bonino, 2–90. 4th ed. 2 vols. Milan: Garzanti.

Jenkins, Ron. 1986. "Clowns, Politics, and Miracles." *American Theatre* 3.3:10–16.

Marks, Dennis. 1984. *The Theatre of Dario Fo*. TV documentary. BBC.

Mitchell, Tony. 1999. *Dario Fo: People's Court Jester*. 3d ed. London: Methuen.

Pitrè, Giuseppe. 1884. "Le tradizioni cavalleresche popolari in Sicilia." *Romania* 13:315–98.

Pizza, Marisa. 1996. *Il gesto, la parola, l'azione: poetica, drammaturgia e storia dei monologhi di Dario Fo*. Rome: Bulzoni Editore.

Pozzo, Alessandra. 1998. *Grr . . . grammelot: parlare senza parole*. Bologna: CLUEB.

Richards, Kenneth, and Laura Richards. 1990. *The Commedia dell'Arte: A Documentary History*. Oxford: Shakespeare Head P.

Rudlin, John. 1994. *Commedia dell'Arte: An Actor's Handbook*. London: Routledge.

Sabatini, Francesco. 1984. "L'italiano dell'uso medio: una realtà tra varietà linguistiche italiane." In *Studies in Italian Applied Linguistics*. Ed. Nicoletta Villa and Marcel Danesi, 139–70. Ottawa: Biblioteca di Quaderni d'italianistica.

Scafoglio, Domenico, and Luigi M. Lombardi Satriani. 1992. *Pulcinella: Il mito e la storia*. Milan: Leonardo Editore.

Scuderi, Antonio. 1996a. "Subverting Religious Authority: Dario Fo and Folk Laughter." *Text and Performance Quarterly* 16.3:216–32.

——. 1996b. "Framing and Improvisation in Dario Fo's *Johan Padan*." *Theatre Annual* 49:76–91.

——. 1998. *Dario Fo and Popular Performance*. Ottawa: Legas.

——. 2000. "Arlecchino Revisited: Tracing the Demon from the Carnival to Kramer and Mr. Bean." *Theatre History Studies* 20:143–55.

Segal, Erich. 1968. *Roman Laughter: The Comedy of Plautus*. Cambridge: Harvard UP.

Slater, Niall W. 1985. *Plautus in Performance: The Theatre of the Mind*. Princeton: Princeton UP.

Toschi, Paolo. 1955. *Le origini del teatro italiano*. Turin: Einaudi.

Towsen, John H. 1976. *Clowns*. New York: Hawthorn Books.

Wing, Joylynn. 1990. "The Performance of Power and the Power of Performance: Rewriting the Police State in Dario Fo's *Accidental Death of an Anarchist*." *Modern Drama* 22:139–49.

Zingarelli, Nicola, ed. 1995. *Vocabolario della lingua italiana*. 12th ed. Bologna: Zanichelli.

CHAPTER 4

Mistero buffo:
Negating Textual Certainty, the Individual, and Time

COSTANTINO MAEDER

istero buffo (Comic mystery), together with *Morte accidentale di un anarchico (Accidental Death of an Anarchist)*, is recognized as one of Dario Fo's masterpieces. This judgment is partial, based on an unstated canon of aesthetics: that a script must be "completed," or at least "organic" and essentially "nontemporal." As such, it fails to render full justice to both Fo's vision and the quality of his other works. These criteria do not take into account his fundamental conception of a theatrical work, which is built on what could be termed simultaneity between performance and context of enunciation: The play should reflect and discuss concrete problems that concern the audience and that are inspired by current events. Fo explains:

> The *hypocrites* for the Greeks was the performer who had the task
> not only of replying to the chorus but also of retelling the stories
> of the myths, translating them into a language and into a dimen-
> sion that was accessible to the "living audience" who came to hear
> them. And it was by no means a question of talking down to or of

flattering these spectators. I would like to emphasize the expression "living audience," in the sense that we are talking about a theater packed with people who reacted, who took part, who applauded but who were also prone to throw insults and to get upset. (1987:173)

It can hardly be, then, a matter of surprise if a large number of Fo's scripts deal with themes that are closely related to the time and socio-cultural context of his own audience. In addition to revealing particular techniques of staging and improvisation—based on a tradition of traveling theater, of cabaret, and of *commedia dell'arte* and, above all, on the dramaturgical genius of Fo—they retain a historical-cultural interest. All these characteristics are evident in, for instance, *La guerra del popolo in Cile* (*The people's war in Chile*), which was put together in a very brief time in the immediate aftermath of Pinochet's coup d'etat.[1]

Nor should there be any surprise if certain scripts show, even in the printed version, traces of improvisation and of the haste with which they were put together. These scripts have not acquired that stylistic and theatrical depth that comes with the process of gradual development, characteristic of "works in progress" such as *Mistero buffo*, the fruit of years of work, reflection, and refinement. The successive changes are also, and principally, due to a process of interaction with audiences and of continual rethinking in the light of a changing political-cultural situation. This fact seems to cause endless surprise to critics who are accustomed to considering theatrical texts as fixed entities and who are incapable of coping with the substantial changes that can be introduced into Fo's works even in the course of the one season.

> We put on *Trumpets and Raspberries* [*Clacson, trombette e pernacchi*] once again the following year and once again it was transformed. At a distance of a year from the last performance, various events of great importance had occurred, and these compelled us to vary the action and the situations. The news bulletins themselves were snapping at our heels, clambering over us and tripping us up, just as we were to do with the critics themselves. (1987:167)

There exist various editions of *Mistero buffo*, plus several video recordings.[2] The differences between the various published editions are of importance precisely because of the glimpse they afford of the development and adaptation of the original *canovaccio*[3] and of the whole

project. Of particular interest are the alterations and the
addition of new episodes, and the fact that in the Einaudi (Fo 1977) edition, there is no bibliography. In the Mazzotta (Fo 1970) and Bertani
(Fo 1974) editions, the bibliography occupies a prominent place and
contributes to the creation of an aura of scientific and historical truth.
The video recording (Fo n.d.) offers the possibility of reconsidering certain aspects of a script that would be otherwise written and fixed for
readers and scholars. It serves to fill in the breaks that are present in
the script but not detectable, because they are not indicated in the published script. I do not, in this context, refer to the happenstance of live
performance or to the serendipity of improvisation and asides, such as
those remarks Fo addresses to spectators entering late and trying to find
a seat, but rather to those "transitions" from one episode to the next dealing with events topical at the time of staging. Being the product of his
ad hoc wit, they cannot be fixed in any published version.

In spite of these free-ranging elements, *Mistero buffo* is a complete
and completed work: The improvisations are inserted into a precise
framework, and their absence in the written text does not create any difficulty for comprehension. The language, in general a kind of Lombard-
Venetan koine, and the economy of the script have now received in
the final elaboration of the text an intrinsic, organic wholeness that allows it both to remain fresh even for future audiences and to satisfy the
most demanding critic while still making it clear to the reader that the
script he has in his hands remains open for further developments and
adaptations.

It is precisely the apparent fixed and organic quality of the written
version, divided as it is into didactic and introductory sections on the
one hand and dramatic sections on the other, that permits us to apply
literary standards to *Mistero buffo*, but it is the same quality that lulls the
reader into a deceptive certainty. The written text, in the Einaudi or
Bertani editions, reveals its own constituent ambiguities only with re-
reading.

The Structure of the Script: Three Variants

Our investigation is based on the analysis of the three successive scripts and the one video recording of *Mistero buffo*. It might be

convenient to outline the content of each edition to make clear the variations:

MISTERO BUFFO

Mazzotta (1970)	Bertani (1974) and Einaudi (1977)
"The Flagellants' Laude"	"Definition of Mystery Play"
"The Drunkard"	"Rosa fresca aulentissima"
"The Raising of Lazarus"	"The Flagellants' Laude"
"Passion"	"The Slaughter of the Innocents"
"Death and the Fool"	"The Morality Play of the Blind Man
"The Morality Play of the Blind	and the Cripple"
Man and the Cripple"	"The Marriage Feast at Cana"
"Mary Hears of the Sentence Imposed	"The Birth of the *Giullare*"
on Her Son"	"The Birth of the Peasant"
"The Crucifixion"	"The Raising of Lazarus"
"Boniface VIII"	"Boniface VIII"
"The Birth of the Peasant"	THE PASSION PLAYS
Glossary	"Death and the Fool"
Bibliographical notes, sources,	"Mary Hears of the Sentence Imposed
performances	on Her Son"
	"The Fool Beneath the Cross, Laying
	a Wager"
	"The Passion: Mary at the Cross"
	Bibliography (Bertani edition only)

The first edition, published by Mazzotta in 1970, presents a series of episodes, in dialect, that are a calque of a medieval Passion play, with comic and tragicomic scenes inspired by the life and Passion of Christ, together with some additional texts of a pseudomedieval character. Two episodes, thematically less in keeping with the spirit of a mystery play, "Boniface VIII" and "Birth of the Peasant," are consigned to the appendix, followed by a bibliography.

It is worth noting, however, that the episodes are not presented in chronological order; the Passion play is presented before "The Morality Play of the Blind Man and the Cripple." One could further note that individual scenes are not introduced by any explanatory material. The Bertani and Einaudi editions are, in practice, identical, but in the Einaudi edition, the bibliography, which had been enlarged in the Bertani edition from that given in the Mazzotta edition, is omitted. In the Bertani and Einaudi editions, there is a greater richness and variety of episodes, as well as various extracts in standard Italian, which I would like for the moment to call "transitions," passages that, not infrequently, have a didactic-explanatory function.

Textual Elements

In spite of the variety of situation, action, and characters, and of its multilayered time structure, *Mistero buffo,* "a *giullarata* in the Padan language," is characterized by a limited number of themes and constituent elements. We will see later how these categories contain in themselves the germ of the destruction of textual certainty.

Historicism

Fo has spoken on various occasions—notably in the discussions that took place after performances of *Mistero buffo,* which were subsequently printed in the Mazzotta edition—of the importance of knowing one's own history in order to "know oneself." Having a sense or a consciousness of ones own origin is of utmost importance.

> It means, in other words, knowing that situations do not change, knowing the history of humankind, because without some knowledge of what we were, we can never arrive at some knowledge of what we want to become. If a person knows nothing of his own origin, of his own world, of his own movements, of what it means to be human, the very meaning of culture is undermined. (1970:46)

And in answer to the observation made by someone in the audience, who preferred the use of modern models instead of the recycling of "archaeological," medieval structures, Fo replied:

> So you are telling me that Gramsci's statement "if you don't know where you come from, you don't know where you can go" is worthless. You are telling me that he has got it all wrong, that he hasn't understood a thing! Excuse me, but if you don't know your own history, if you don't understand what you are talking about, if you avoid the theater, you are going to stay right where you are. It's the people's culture that is up-to-date. When I speak about the peasant, for me it could be the steel worker, the clerk in an office, even the student—they're all exactly the same as a peasant from other times. The peasant who was born from the arse of a donkey is with us still, he is a constant of every moment of time. (1970:47)

It is in this sense that the vast bibliography that Fo appends to the Bertani and Mazzotta editions of *Mistero buffo* is to be understood. Not only do they give the text an atmosphere of academic reliability, but they also underline the presumed continuity of history. It almost seems as though he reveals himself in *Mistero buffo* as a disciple of early Romanticism, collecting medieval texts in order to be able to focus on the roots of his own people, but also to deny, as firmly as Leopardi, ideas of "progress" and "development" (cf. Hirst 1989:14). Here are Fo's own words, recorded verbatim in the heat of debate:

> The Enlightenment idea of society as a continual state of becoming . . . leads us to believe that the medieval period, for example, was one step, then gradually we progressed, one step at a time, and history turned out to be as it is today. But the middle ages are still with us. If, on the other hand, you view our situation, not outside time, but as a constant of all civilization, with all its persecutions, as something that is still alive and present today, you see that nothing has changed, that the boss figure is still what he always was, that he has the same appearance, the same form. (1970:47)

At the same time, Fo has his sights on the behavior of those critics who annexed for the ruling class all works of popular origin. It is not by chance that in the Bertani and Einaudi versions, *Mistero buffo* opens not with an episode dealing with the Passion but with the medieval poem "Rosa fresca aulentissima" (Fresh and fragrant rose), in which, in an exercise of deconstruction, he reexamines, from a "popular" perspective and with the weaponry of corrosive sarcasm, a poem by Cielo (or Ciullo) d'Alcamo. With his comprehensive demythologizing of this work, Fo has prepared the way for a reexamination of Jesus Christ, the central figure of the mystery plays—even if he rarely intervenes—in order to restore to him that "popular" and topical dimension that history and educators, in the course of the centuries, have taken from him. The rehabilitation of the mystery play format is to be seen in this context, the obvious influence of Mayakovsky's *Mystery Bouffe* notwithstanding.

The Cancellation of the Individual

Another indispensable element of this work is the elimination of the individual. Although the play is ideally based upon the work of one actor, the cancellation of individuality is effected. The same actor or actress is required to impersonate various characters simultaneously, in a space given no scenic definition. The script contains no indications concerning the stage, and the actor or actress takes possession of the stage space without individualizing it. Similarly, the techniques of performance and character construction avoid giving a concrete, naturalistic substance to the characters, thus not permitting them to emerge as pseudo-individuals, as they would if, for example, the techniques of the Actor's Studio were applied. The video recordings confirm this fact. Fo or Franca Rame do not make use of costumes or props for their performances. Their gestures and movements do not have the purpose of distinguishing and individualizing particular characters but rather of describing them from above, from a distance. The same gestures, the same acting devices, are often found in different characters, permitting the bringing together of several characters and the demonstration of their extratemporal quality. This approach, unlike that employed in naturalistic theater, in which the aim would be to underline the total uniqueness of each individual character, also highlights the characters' interchangeability.[4]

With the possible exception of Rame, with her passionate and overcharged but somewhat dated interpretation of the Virgin Mary, it is notable that the actor is not permitted to get under the skin of the characters. At most, Rame makes use of a simple prop, for example, a shawl for the part of the Virgin at the foot of the cross. The audience is invited to concentrate on the words and on those tiny gestures that create the illusion of a role switch. The individual is never indicated by specific attributes, such as clothing, objects, or other adjuncts, but becomes an extratemporal "type," an example of human behavior that is not to be located in time. This is even the case when one character dominates a particular scene, as with the "Boniface VIII" episode, because performance techniques, poses, and gestures make Boniface resemble other characters in *Mistero buffo*. Neither form nor appearance change, and the inner beings of the characters remain unaltered as well. At the essence of humanity is an extraordinary reconciliation of contradiction.

The Cancellation of Time

The cancellation of the individual involves perforce the cancellation of historical and linear time, but this does not mean the absence of a precise temporal structure. Even a superficial glance at the succession of episodes in the three versions of the script is sufficient to alert the reader to the fact that the Passion is interrupted by some pieces that destroy logical, temporal succession, even if the entire work ends with the death of Christ. In the Mazzotta version, the first, there is an initial flash forward: "Passion" and the scene with Mary at the foot of the cross are presented before "The Crucifixion," while two episodes ("Boniface VIII" and "The Birth of the Peasant") are given in an appendix, thus removing them from the temporal context of the Passion. In the Bertani and Einaudi editions, on the other hand, there is a bipartition between two separate series of episodes. The first contains scenes that bestride the centuries and that follow one another without any precise temporal order: Besides "The Raising of Lazarus" and "The Marriage Feast at Cana" there are, among other pieces, "The Flagellants' Laude," "Boniface VIII," "The Birth of the *Giullare*," and "The Birth of the Peasant," not to mention the introductory material on the poem "Rosa fresca aulentissima." The second series contains the Passion scripts: "Death and the Fool," "Mary Hears of the Sentence Imposed on Her Son," "The Fool Beneath the Cross," and "The Passion: Mary at the Cross." Unlike the first series, the single episodes follow each other in linear progression without interruptions or transitions.

In both versions, the decisive element is not narrative logic but the creation of what could be called a nontemporal, causal logic that leads to the death of Jesus. Such anachronisms as the "Birth of the *Giullare*," "The Birth of the Peasant," or the "Boniface VIII" episode serve to support the principal thrust of the overall piece, even if they appear at times removed from the immediate context. The destruction of the linear, temporal, or teleological axis induces the spectator/reader to opt for a discursive reading. "The Crucifixion" is inserted in a network of conflicting events that focus on the causes of the death of Christ but that simultaneously give the impression that this event could occur again today and that, in consequence, the systems that create injustice and abuse have remained essentially unchanged throughout the ages.

In addition to these two forms of the destruction of linear, temporal logic, it is worth drawing attention to an additional dramatic-didactic double structure that finds expression in a double plot. On the one hand, there is the main plot, made up of dialect texts, and on the other, there are texts in standard Italian. At first sight, the principal plot may appear dramatic, while the second has a more systematic, cabaret-style charac-

ter that requires an actor-narrator of high skill to recount, explain, prepare the individual episodes, and even make use of slides.

In discussing this structure, Cappa and Nepoti adopt the terminology
of theater and metatheater (1982:75–85). The same structure can be detected in the dramatic text itself. In the Mazzotta version, Fo gives only
the extracts strictly linked to the main plot; in the Bertani and Einaudi
editions, Fo inserts miniplays between the individual episodes, miniplays that are often complete dramatic units in themselves. In the Bertani and Einaudi editions, a logical relationship exists between the two
levels of plot, which is, at least in part, of a genuinely metatheatrical
character, but it can be seen from the video recordings that, onstage, the
preparatory and transitional texts acquire in the transformation of scenes
a genuinely theatrical dimension. In the video recording, as distinct
from the written text, Fo improvises scenes that can be viewed as organic, autonomous dramas in miniature. These new "plays" are drawn
from cues provided by the "here and now" of enunciation-time and deal
with, for instance, the politics of the day or topical aspects of Italian
culture in its widest sense.

Perhaps it would be more accurate to speak of a dual play rather
than of metatheater, inasmuch as both the episodes of the mystery play
and the so-called transitions or introductions to these pieces are often
self-sufficient. The discussion of "Rosa fresca aulentissima" is a wholly
independent piece. The version televised by RAI, the Italian state broadcasting body, confirms the extent to which many of these transitions are
complete and capable of being enjoyed in themselves, even without any
knowledge of the episode they introduce. The apposition of the twin
plot structure serves to indicate possible parallels between today and the
past. This obviously destroys the linear, temporal axis in favor of a concept of time as cyclical if not indeed static, but above all it underlines
the inevitability of certain aspects of the human condition.

The twin plays resemble each other in other ways too: Not only do
the transitions form so many autonomous plays, but the very structure
of the first play is characterized by the autonomy of *jouissance* of each
single episode. The cancellation of the individual, which is made apparent even by the absence of one genuine, overall protagonist, indicates
not only the cancellation of linear time but also the cancellation of the
narrative component. The order of events is not fixed. The text remains
precarious, in the sense that each production, through improvisation
and the temporal freedom afforded, can still reorder the episodes. Not

even the death of Christ has to be situated at the end, as is clear from the Mazzotta edition.

Clashes and Contrasts

The mosaic, multilayered structure, without any seemingly overriding sense of order, cannot fail to generate clashes that a play of a more classical character, especially one guided by Aristotelian principles and by a strong narrative thrust, tends to conceal. These conflicts are not to be viewed as an indication of some supposed structural inconsistency in *Mistero buffo*, or as an indication of some inability on Fo's part to create an organic theatrical work. If anything, they indicate a negative vision of life that, to confound our expectations, seems to pervade his aesthetics (Maeder 1995:217–26).

Fo's historical approach, in spite of the vast bibliography appended to the Mazzotta and Bertani editions, is anything but rigorous. The most superficial checks are sufficient to identify ideological distortions in his texts. Michele L. Straniero and many others have pointed to these problems and to others regarding the accuracy or reliability of Fo's texts, falling thus into a trap cunningly laid by Fo himself.[5] In *Manuale minimo dell'attore* (The actor's mini-manual, published in English as *Tricks of the Trade*), he warns readers from the outset against giving too much importance to his words:

> So, there you are then, it is quite true, I often invent but be careful, let me make it quite clear, the stories that I fabricate will always seem to you completely authentic, almost banal, while those that you would swear were invented, almost impossible, or downright paradoxical will be on the contrary entirely authentic and able to be documented. I am a professional liar. (1987:4)

What matters is the reasoning that permeates his discussion of, for example, "Rosa fresca aulentissima." Fo's principal aim is to show how a line of reasoning based on considerations that may not be altogether correct is nonetheless capable of producing a causal series of coherent events and deductions. It is extremely easy to oppose one official truth with another that is equally persuasive and logical. It is no surprise if reality is, in the last analysis, more complicated than that proposed either by Fo or by historians, whose own assumptions have now entered the realm of academic myth. This is true not only as regards the interpretation of poems like "Rosa fresca aulentissima" but also for the mythical figure of the *giullare,* so dear to Fo but, if recent historical research is to be credited, ever more and more elusive (see Oldoni 1978).

Manipulation

With "Rosa fresca aulentissima," Fo does not wish to present a "new," absolute truth as opposed to an "academic" truth, which was already dated at the time of the first performances of *Mistero buffo.* He deconstructs certain styles of reasoning that were liable to lead to the formation of static, fixed systems. The manipulation concerns the treatment of the scripts themselves.

The historicizing dimension itself, as much as the apparent incongruences, is a sign of this manipulation. The supposed "historicity," if understood as the presentation of a historical truth, is not to be trusted. Preparatory research for *Mistero buffo,* undertaken along Gramscian lines, turns out to be a kind of research into Fo himself and his own artistic credo. The fond notion that artistic creation could be consigned to a culture that contained, and would offer, everything, leaving the artist to do no more than collect and re-present, has been shown to be, obviously, a mirage. Modern Western historiography has taken as its basis a temporal divide between, on the one hand, an unknown, "different" past to be studied and, on the other, a present, that of the historian (see De Certeau 1975). This tendency is unknown to Fo, who prefers to focus on the concrete links with this past.

The treatment of scripts such as "The Birth of the Peasant" can serve as a starting point to allow us to bring together the data so far gathered. The episode of "The Birth of the Peasant" is based on "Nativitas rusticorum et qualiter debent tractari" by Matazone da Caligano. The original is itself caustic and ironic, but Fo has chosen to eliminate many fundamental elements of the "Nativitas," even if this once more contrasts with his declared intentions of wishing to adhere to historical truth and to present the will and social awareness of the people who were given expression in the *giullarate.*

From the outset, a revealing ambiguity exists: A *giullare* presents to an audience of lords and knights a monologue written by Matazone da Caligano, a peasant, while the *giullare* performing the monologue is also a peasant. The social difference among the person performing, the person creating, and those listening is highlighted from the first lines and will be superimposed with increasing force onto the supposed justification that allows the nobles to beat the peasants, those lowly beasts, who have, however, the ability to write and perform.

> Il detto di Matazone da Caligano
>
> A voi, segnor e cavaler,
> sí lo conto volenter
> e a tuta bona zente,
> tuta comunamente.
> Intendí 'sta raxone,
> la qual fe' Matazone
> e' fo da Caligano
> e nacque d'un vilano.
> (1975:35–44)

> [Matazone da Caligano's Ditty]
>
> [To you, lords and knights,
> I will gladly tell
> and to all good people,
> communally united.
> Heed this monologue,
> created by Matazone
> who hails from Caligano
> and of a peasant born.]

Matazone's "Nativitas" is in three parts. In the first, a *giullare* addresses a noble audience, making reference to the tensions that exist among knights, lords, and peasants and justifying all the actions of the former on the grounds that the peasants are unwilling or unable to behave correctly and, in any case, that the nobles make too few demands. In the second part, on the other hand, he narrates the birth of the peasant from an ass's fart, so as to underline the congenital superiority of the noble class, willed by God, who is not expressly named in the script. In the third and final part, he discusses the origin of the aristocracy.

Cesare Molinari (1972) highlights the comic ambiguity of Matazone's "Detto." Even if the peasants are at first sight the objects of the satire, the sarcasm is directed with greater subtlety at the nobility. In his introduction to the "Detto," Fo presents certain facts that are not to be found in the versions of either Contini or Molinari before going on to observe: "There you are: from now on I follow the original script. It is Matazone da Caligano who is speaking" (1977:83).

The differences with Matazone are obvious, even if Fo avoids criticism by drawing attention to the fact that there are alternative versions. He reduces the "Detto" to the second part alone. Both the argument between the peasants and the lords and the section on the birth of the nobles are cut out. Since both of these parts are extremely interesting in themselves, particularly given the ideological framework adopted by Fo, we are left to conjecture at the reasons why this adaptation of the original script was made. Plainly it was no accident.

The Struggle Between Father and Son

The data gathered up to this point are not such as to permit only one reading of the text. *Mistero buffo* is too complex and ambiguous. The entirely obvious ideological component, typical of the 1960s and 1970s, conceals components of greater artistic interest. The political thought, so overwhelming at first sight, can be easily deconstructed. Matazone's "Detto" permits us to proceed with this operation. The decision to highlight the central part of Matazone's poem finds its justification in the perspective of the entire work. In Fo's introduction, but not in the "Detto" itself, the peasant is figuratively paired with Christ. Like Christ, the peasant remains subdued, accepts his fate, and humbly submits to being spat upon without rebelling against his oppressors.

Mistero buffo insistently proposes an evidently Freudian dialectic between father and son. While the angel of the Lord, in "The Birth of the Peasant," underlines the status quo and gives legitimacy to the prevailing situation, and while God the Father creates the peasants, Jesus Christ aligns himself with the latter, as he does also in "The Birth of the Giullare." In this latter piece, the plot tells of how a peasant, attempting to cultivate a piece of land that belongs to no one, is finally punished by the system. Having lost everything—wife, honor, and land—he wishes to kill himself. Jesus passes by, kisses him, and, with this kiss, enables the peasant to become a *giullare*, that is, a person who is endowed with the power of the word and can reveal truth.

Jesus, who will himself be covered with spittle during his Passion, and who will himself endure the injustices of the world, does not, how-ever, intervene; he does not alter the fundamental situation of the op-pressed. The madman and the other figures who attempt to put up some resistance, like the Virgin Mary at the foot of the cross, cannot move Christ or persuade him to struggle against the Father and against oppres-sion. On the contrary, if Christ does enable the peasant in "The Birth of the Giullare" to understand his situation, and if he gives him the capacity to express himself and to make truth known, this ability, this awareness, will remain abstract and without concrete expression, as both history and the present day teach.

Fo states that the peasant, the *giullare*, and the people of the Middle Ages were aware of their own situation or that they were at least in a position to understand that situation (1974:110–15), but his own recon-struction also underlines that this human condition, which made the peasant an outsider, remains exactly as it was. The peasant will not be able to liberate himself, and sooner or later, everything will be bundled up into the culture of the powerful. The peasant must either become a *giullare* whose tongue will be pulled out or else learn to accept his fate. Just as the peasant lost everything, so too the worker will remain a victim of the system.

The multilayered temporal structure itself and the numerous paral-lels all demonstrate this one fact: Attempts to gain control of one's own fate can only end in destruction. The peasants of Vercelli, Fra Dolcino, Jesus, and even the *giullare* are all punished. In this way, the advice to people to learn their own history in order to understand where they are going becomes an expression of extreme cynicism, illustrating the im-possibility of exiting from this vicious circle. At best, it can help the spectator to understand that human life is governed by severe, harsh rules that we are able to understand and even fight but that, as history shows, we cannot change.

Translated from Italian by Joseph Farrell.

Notes

1. Cf. Fo's reflections on the Rame family of actors and their improvisational abili-ties (1987:10–11).

2. Editions of *Mistero buffo* were published in 1970, 1974, and 1977. A videocas-sette performance (n.d.) exists as well.

3. The term *canovaccio* is derived from the *commedia dell'arte* and can be trans-lated as "plot outline."

4. With regard to Fo's theories on "focus" in one-man performance and his views on the relationship between naturalistic and epic popular theater, cf. Fo (1987:142–54) and Binni (1975:238–45).

5. In particular Straniero (1978) is extremely critical of Fo and his work.

References

Binni, Lanfranco. 1975. *Attento te! . . . Il teatro politico di Dario Fo.* Verona: Bertani.

Cappa, Marina, and Roberto Nepoti. 1982. *Dario Fo.* Rome: Gremese.

Da Caligano. 1975. "Detto dei villani." In *Il teatro italiano*, vol. 1, Dalle origini al Quattrocento. Ed. Emilio Faccioli, 35–44. Turin: Einaudi.

De Certeau, Michel. 1975. *L'écriture de l'histoire.* Paris: Gallimard.

Fo, Dario. 1970. *Mistero buffo.* In *Compagni senza censura: il teatro politico di Dario Fo,* Vol 1, 11–38. Milan: Mazzotta.

———. 1974. *Mistero buffo.* Ed. Franca Rame. Verona: Bertani.

———. 1977. *Mistero buffo.* In *Le commedie di Dario Fo,* Vol. 5. Ed. Franca Rame, 5–171. Turin: Einaudi.

———. 1987. *Manuale minimo dell'attore.* Turin: Einaudi.

———. N.d. *Mistero buffo.* Rome: Videoregistrazione RAI. Videocassette.

Hirst, David. 1989. *Dario Fo and Franca Rame.* London: Macmillan.

Maeder, Costantino. 1995. "Zu Dario Fos Aesthetik: das Volk auf der Buehne." In *Wehe, wehe du armes, betrogenes Volk.* Ed. Peter Csóbadi, Gernot Gruber, Jürgen Kühnel, Ulrich Müller, Oswald Panagl, and Franz Viktor Spechtler, 217–26. Anif/Salzburg: Verlag Ursula Muller-Speiser.

Molinari, Cesare. 1972. "Il detto di Matazone di Caligano." *Biblioteca teatrale* 4:1–19.

Oldoni, Massimo. 1978. "Tecniche di scena e comportamenti narrativi nel teatro profano mediolatino." In *Il contributo dei giullari alla drammaturgia italiana delle origini.* Rome: Bulzoni.

Straniero, Michele. 1978. *Giullari and Fo: Mistero bluff?* Rome: Lato Side.

CHAPTER 5

Fo and Ruzzante
Debts and Obligations

JOSEPH FARRELL

ario Fo's most public act of homage to Ruzzante was made in the course of his Nobel Prize lecture in Stockholm, when he identified Ruzzante as the theatrical predecessor with whom he felt the closest affinity.[1] The paean of praise delivered in Sweden came as no surprise to those who knew how frequently Ruzzante's name had been invoked by Fo over the years, always as an exemplar and model representing the type of theater Fo aspired to write, or providing support for opinions held tenaciously by Fo himself. Recognizing that Ruzzante's was not likely to be a name familiar to his largely Swedish audience, Fo expatiated on the qualities that made him, in his view, the "greatest writer of the Italian sixteenth century," explained why he found his influence so powerful, and then, as an encore, performed an extract from one of Ruzzante's plays.

Ruzzante's life is shrouded in the same obscurity as Shakespeare's, to whom Fo has often compared him. His real name was Angelo Beolco, and the probable years of his life were 1495 or 1496 to 1542. He was a native of the Veneto and took the name Ruzzante from the peasant character he invented and played in the plays he himself wrote. Although illegitimate, he received a high standard of education and had the fortune in his adulthood to enjoy the patronage of the aristocrat Alvise Cornaro and his family. His work as steward to Cornaro gave him a knowledge of the realities of peasant life, so the characters in his theater are far removed from the prissy, idealized peasants who people the poetry and drama of Arcadia, a contemporary literary movement. Ruzzante was an actor-author of the same stamp as Fo and wrote the same style of hard-edged comedy. His characters are moved not by Platonic passions but by primary appetites, by hunger, lust, avarice, or greed; his plays are set in lived, not imagined, history; and he portrays the realities of war as experienced by the foot soldiers, not as fantasized by poets.

Fo's veneration for his distinguished predecessor falls not far short of idolatry. The piece chosen for performance before the Swedish Academy was part of a program of selected extracts and monologues by Ruzzante that Fo had performed in the 1993 and 1995 seasons.[2] In the context of Fo's career, this performance was decidedly unexpected, since Fo, the quintessential actor-author, has rarely staged the works of other writers. At the beginning of his career, a play by Feydeau, *Ne te promènes donc pas toute nue* (Don't walk in the nude), was for a time part of the program of four works staged under the overall title *Ladri, manichini e donne nude* (Thieves, mannequins, and naked women) in 1957, but it was removed shortly after the beginning of the run and replaced by *I cadaveri si spediscono, e le donne si spogliano* (Bodies in the post, and women in the nude), a new one-act farce by Fo himself. That switch set the tone for Fo's subsequent career in all its successive phases. Neither in what he later termed his "bourgeois period" in the early 1960s nor in the political period that followed his break with commercial theater in 1968 had Fo either written for other actors or performed the work of other writers.

Previously, not even his admiration for Ruzzante could tempt him to deviate from this practice. As early as 1958, he was invited by Gianfranco De Bosio, then director of the Teatro Stabile of Turin, to play Ruzzante in a production that De Bosio would direct. Fo refused, in part because he was ill at ease with De Bosio's interpretation of the author but also because, as his biographer Chiara Valentini explained, to accept would have meant "giving up his own autonomy in research, renouncing the invention of an absolutely personal style of theatrical writing,

and in some way taking his place among the ranks of the officially sanctioned" (1977:60). Fo intended to follow Ruzzante by following him as
actor-author, rather than by reviving him.

By 1993, Fo felt at liberty to revise this earlier stance. Having established his own reputation and "personal style of theatrical writing," he
was now in a position to pay his own homage to Ruzzante and to give
expression to his own interpretation of him. Fo was in his full maturity
as a writer, so the fear that his own distinctive creativity might be stifled
by overexposure to such a "strong" predecessor as Ruzzante—a fear for
which Harold Bloom coined the term "anxiety of influence"—was now
less acute. Further, a production of Ruzzante would be seen as a coherent part of his overall theatrical activity in the 1990s. During this decade,
Fo had been less prolific in the output of original plays than previously
and had devoted more time to directing. He had not become in any
sense a jobbing director, undertaking work commissioned by theater
managements according to their programming needs, but one whose
choice of play was dictated by fondness and esteem for the work in question and by its conformity to his own wider theatrical-political philosophy. The choice and treatment of the works he has directed can, in turn,
help clarify the nature of the tradition in which he operates and, by extension, his own self-image as playwright.

Fo's stance as a director has invariably been as polemical, revision-
ist, and idiosyncratic as his work as a writer or performer. The resultant
relationship between him as director to text or performance is complex.
His productions are *engagés,* not necessarily in a political sense, and
reflect Fo's standpoint at least as much as they illuminate the work of the
author being staged. Fo possesses every text, reshaping and refocusing it
to a greater extent than any exponent of "director's theater." He has always identified himself as operating within a popular tradition and, in
his directing style, has sought to justify his conviction that many plays
have been more or less systematically misinterpreted by being wrenched
from their true context in that tradition and situated in an inappropriate
line of patrician, high culture. This *parti pris* was behind his production of Molière's *Le Malade Imaginaire* at the Comédie Française in
1992, of Rossini's *Il Barbiere di Siviglia* for Amsterdam Opera in 1993,
and of the same composer's *L'Italiana in Algeri* for the Pesaro Festival
in 1994. With all these productions, Fo planned to explore the impact
of *commedia dell'arte* on European theater. That project could have

been regarded as safely mainstream had he not aimed simultaneously to encourage a revision of accepted notions of *commedia dell'arte*, which he believes has been neutered by many contemporary critics and directors. The surprise, or outrage, that greeted some of his productions was occasioned in part by the clash between critical preconceptions that *commedia dell'arte* required an elegant, elaborately stylized display of delicately devised movement techniques and Fo's belief that it involved the clowning, horseplay, acrobatic tumbles, and vulgarity that are associated in the twentieth century with low farce.

Similar convictions lay behind his production of Ruzzante. In its original conception, the work was to be entitled *I dialoghi di Ruzzante* (Dialogues by Ruzzante), directed by Fo, and performed at the 1993 Spoleto Festival by a fifteen-strong cast drawn from the (private) Fo/Rame troupe and the (public) *Teatro degli Incamminati*. A ministerial communiqué, circulated at a late stage (when rehearsals were well advanced), uncovered, or invented, an obscure law forbidding coproductions between public and private companies. The actors employed by the publicly funded company were required to withdraw, but in the best traditions of traveling theater, the general conviction was that the "show must go on." The work was renamed *Dario Fo incontra Ruzzante* (Dario Fo meets Ruzzante) and given a different cast, including Franca Rame and Fo himself. Fo performed in some individual pieces and provided overall continuity and introductions to some extracts in the style he had employed for *Mistero buffo* (Comic mystery) and *Storia della tigre* (The Tale of the Tiger). A revised version, recast as a one-man work, was taken on tour during the 1994–95 theater season under the slightly altered title *Fo recita Ruzzante* (Fo performs Ruzzante).

Fo recita Ruzzante was essentially an act of devotion, or the acknowledgement of a debt. Fo has, in his own word, "stolen" from various playwrights, but no single writer has so influenced his writing and performing style, or was so important in shaping his vision of the potential of theater, as Ruzzante. He told an interviewer: "An encounter with Ruzzante is an obligation towards the man I have always considered my master, and whose work I have plundered for years. Without him I could not have written *Mistero buffo*" (1995:5).

At an earlier period of his life, he had given Ruzzante credit for helping him to identify the inner essence of popular theater and the most appropriate theatrical approach to the complex tangle of historical and political events from which he was to shape *Morte accidentale di un anarchico (Accidental Death of an Anarchist)*. The motivating vision underlying all that Ruzzante achieved in the theater was not, in Fo's view, the quest for subtle analysis of character, as it would be with such bourgeois writers as Pirandello and Chekhov, but the development of the implications of "situation." The predominance of "situation" over character constituted for Fo the very heart of the style of theater he identified as "popular." Groping for an adequate explanation, his analysis of Ruzzante's connections with the history of his own time led him to suggest that the principal feature of theater of "situation" was "the fact that the contradictions, the mood, the anger, the joy of the characters, their emergence on the stage is determined by facts and clashes that are class conflicts and, therefore, clearly belong to political struggle." This analysis of Ruzzante also enabled him to clarify the kind of theater he and the cooperative La Comune were aiming to stage in the 1970s.

> Our theater, then, unlike that of Pirandello and Chekhov, is not bourgeois theater, a theater of characters who recount their own stories, their own moods, which then become the mechanical basis of conflict. We always aimed to establish a different basis, with "situation." For example, in *Accidental Death of an Anarchist*, the situation is a real event. Where in Ruzzante there is the return (from the war), here there is the madman who finds himself in a police station, putting the police on trial, overturning the basis. The situation is the basis, but it plays on reality. (Fo 1970:8–9)

The combination of the names of Fo and Ruzzante in the very title *Fo recita Ruzzante* signals that the standard relationship between actor and author has been overturned. The two will meet as theater makers of like mind, on an equal footing. Fo gives himself the freedom to interpret, reinvent, reform, and remake Ruzzante. His operation is more akin to the reworking of Velasquez by Picasso, or Poussin by Manet, than to the faithful reproduction attempted by an engraver: There is no attempt at parody or pastiche, and the act of homage implied is genuine, but Ruzzante will be incorporated into a developing tradition rather than left moored in the past. The affinities between the two are so deep that the one may be viewed as the alter ego of the other. Fo is a modern-day Ruzzante, or Ruzzante a Renaissance Fo. Fo believed that Ruzzante's innate stagecraft, his capacity for constructing texts for performance rather than publication, had presented readers, including potential directors, with a challenge beyond their capacities and was one of the reasons why Ruzzante had been so infrequently staged.

Fo was impressed by a judgment delivered by Bertolt Brecht on Shakespeare: Shakespeare's "one, great defect is that he reads so beautifully on the printed page" (Fo 1991:183), whereas the qualities of a real dramatist should become apparent only in performance. In Fo's view, Ruzzante had baffled directors precisely because he could be made to come to life only onstage. Fo held tenaciously to the belief that theater and literature, even dramatic literature, were separate categories, to be judged by different criteria. There were certain major writers, notably Pier Paolo Pasolini, who were incapable of making the switch from page to stage precisely because they had never understood the rhythms, the logic, the exigencies of plot, the scenic qualities, the differentiated pace of action and dialogue that were specific to theater. For Fo, part of Ruzzante's attraction was that his works were innately theatrical, even if this involved the paradoxical consequence that his works could appear uninspired or limp when read:

> What are we to make of the complete works of Ruzzante? Show me the hypocrite who will dare suggest that we have before us a great literary output! For centuries, Ruzzante's scripts lay buried for the reason that they did not conform to literary canons, they could not be integrated; mere dialect works dealing with such themes as hunger, sex, poverty, violence . . . what had they had to do with the sublimity of art? (Fo 1987:283)

The mixture of mastery of form and starkness of content created a brew that Fo found intoxicating. Angelo Beolco, known as Ruzzante, rubbed shoulders with courtiers, bishops, and princes, but in his plays, he focused on the mainsprings of human misery, particularly as it affected the lower orders. His was not an escapist wit, for he turned an unflinching eye on society and did so with satirical laughter. In an 1987 interview on the publication of *Manuale minimo dell'attore* (The actor's mini-manual, published in English as *Tricks of the Trade*), Fo told the critic Rita Cirio that in spite of his refusal of De Bosio's offer years previously, Ruzzante was one of the few authors he would consider performing because he found in Ruzzante that mixture of farce and tragedy that he held as an ideal and that he had himself tried to realize in such works as *Morte accidentale:* "With Ruzzante, I could be both comic and tragic at the same time, and I would enjoy that" (1992:125). In his 1990 interview with Luigi Allegri, he expatiated on the same point. He found his first model in Aristophanes and traces of the same approach in *commedia dell'arte*, notably in the Arlecchino figure, as well as in Molière, but the supreme practitioner was Ruzzante:

> You only have to open the comedy of the Paduan writer to come across a myriad of tragic situations transferred into grotesque mode: the beatings, the insolence, the rapes, the cravings of an unexpressed sexuality, the trade in women as mere instruments of pleasure and relief, women as soft bed-warmers for men with money and power. And then, constantly in Ruzzante, the misery of death and poverty, but with him fluttering around, pulling funny faces and blowing raspberries. (Fo 1990:9)

Fo recita Ruzzante, as a selection presented in a context manipulated by Fo, is founded on an act of criticism, which itself clarifies the nature of criticism in Fo and its overlap with practice. Fo has always written copiously about authors and performers, but his tastes are not catholic. Literary or dramatic criticism for its own sake has no interest and no appeal. His criticism is akin to an exercise in tomb robbing for immediate profit rather than to an archaeological dig for preservation in a museum. A critique is an applied activity, inseparable from his creative needs, reflecting the dilemmas of his own thinking, illuminating or exemplifying the kind of drama he himself wishes to write. It is preliminary to action or is a means of establishing affinities with, or divergences from, the tradition of theater to which he accords validity. The most fundamental errors of valuation of Fo have been committed by those who refuse to recognize the extent to which a consciousness of operating within a tradition is central, not peripheral, to him. The act of criticism represents a corrective or concomitant to the techniques and approaches he employs and the values he aims to express.

Being so closely determined by his own needs and aspirations, his criticism has an unavoidable element of egocentricity. Fo is incapable of appreciating writers whose approach differs widely from his own. There is no point in scanning Fo for a discussion of the subtle dilemmas of Chekhov's frustrated landowners, or for an assessment of the techniques of the dream theater of the later Strindberg. During the Nobel Prize ceremonies, he expressed appreciation of Strindberg as a writer who had also performed his own works and who was held in contempt by the academies of his time; but that was the limit of his admiration. The admiration was accorded, in reality, to an image, however partial, of himself. When Franca Angelini gave her 1976 study of modern theater the title *Il teatro italiano del novecento da Pirandello a Fo* (Twentieth-century Italian theater from Pirandello to Fo), Fo balked at the implied comparison, and not out of modesty. He simply did not recognize any lineage that could open with Pirandello and lead to an actor-author of the popular tradition (Fo 1977:1–2). The two belonged to different political, philosophical, and moral universes. The dilemmas and problems that underlie Pirandello's theater—the dissolution of the personality, the stability of truth, the crisis of values, the feasibility of communication—are of no interest to Fo. On one of the few occasions he mentions Pirandello favorably, it is, significantly, to make his writing habits similar to those of an actor-author:

> This was Pirandello's great discovery—"learning to write on the set." Pirandello did not himself perform, but he lived in symbiosis with the actors. So as to get his plays performed he transformed himself into a *capocomico* (actor-director): The first actress of the company was often his woman. He put everything, even his last penny, into the theater. He was not one of those who drop by with the script under his arm and offer his latest work directly to some impresario. He wrote his plays on the spot, in the green room, writing and rewriting while the rehearsals were underway, right up until the last minute before the opening. (Fo 1987:284)

This portrait of Pirandello is not easily recognizable. In the early part of his career as a playwright, while writing the Sicilian dialect plays for the actor-manager Angelo Musco, Pirandello did incorporate some of Musco's improvised routines into his work. But in later periods, far from living in symbiosis with actors, Pirandello developed a visceral distrust of the acting profession; he could be persuaded to regard actors as perhaps a necessary evil, but he more commonly viewed them as an intrusive force that disturbed communication between author and public. The statement about the first actress is true as regards Marta Abba, but that special case apart, Fo's account differs from the biographical facts. The description of Pirandello undertaking his writing on the set or in the greenroom, in collaboration with actors, reflects Fo's own aims and practices rather than Pirandello's. Unconsciously, Fo makes Pirandello conform to the model of the playwright best known to him. It is hard to avoid the conclusion that much of his criticism is more a vicarious description of his own beliefs than those of the person he is overtly discussing, but it is equally misleading to be unaware that attempts to "correct" Fo's views of other writers are mere pedantry, of little value in discussing Fo's own work. Any misunderstandings or distorted assessments of others are, according to Harold Bloom's ideological framework, "necessary and inventive," since his criticism is a prop to creativity in his own world, not an insight into an alternative world.

Fo's performance techniques and style as a writer are based on instinct guided and honed by learning. If theater, unlike literature, deals of its essence with the ephemeral, then tradition, with its continuing dialectic between past and present, represents the attempted suppression of ephemerality. The dispute over the existence or nonexistence, the value, and the ideal content of one all-inclusive, great Western tradition has been raised by Harold Bloom, who has made himself, in the face of those who seek to redefine that tradition, the most resolute defender of an established Western canon (1994:22). However, as Bloom himself has argued, every tradition is founded on a "principle of selectivity," and no tradition or canon is created by some pseudonatural process; it is akin to a series of rock carvings uncovered in a cave, not to a row of stalactite formations located in the same place. Further, as Bloom recognizes to his chagrin, a tradition can never be viewed as immutable. Bloom acutely identifies Antonio Gramsci as inspiration and patron saint of those he terms the "anticanonizers" and draws attention to Gramsci's distaste for the "esprit de corps [among] various categories of traditional intellectual" (1994:22), which they express as loyalty to the category itself and as self-deception regarding their capacity for autonomous action. Fo does not have the overarching ambition Bloom attributed to the "anticanonizers"—of dismissing or dismantling the literary and culture achievement of the great Western writers—but he must be numbered among them. Fo is indeed an admirer of Gramsci (see Binni 1975:241–43), who provides him with the ideological tools for his analysis of the concept of culture and with the philosophical underpinning both for his

identification of the class interests of "traditional intellectuals" and for
the establishment of an alternative, popular canon that would give status
and dignity to those excluded from the established pantheons.

Following Gramsci, Fo believed that while the canon feted those
who had been servants of the status quo, genuinely subversive writers
had either suffered neglect or been neutered by academic mystification.
As he announced during an interview on French television:

> The task of theater has been to serve and reinforce power struc-
> tures. For those who are opposed to established power, it is a mat-
> ter of fighting, of winning spaces, of letting people see an alterna-
> tive system, a different culture, another vision of the world. That's
> why many actors and performers in the middle ages ended up be-
> ing burned at the stake. (Fo 1992:349)

Fo's anticanon is deliberately, militantly, stridently heretical and
dissident, including of those who had offered an alternative vision and
had been excluded by the keepers of the flame. His preference was for
the "lesser trodden paths," not the great highways of the Western theatrical tradition. Nonetheless, there would be many unexpected absences
and presences. Not every *giullare* or Arlecchino would merit a place, for
some performed in the courts of bishops or dukes and so were numbered among those who served "power structures." Molière, the supreme writer of comedy and imp of the subversive, would have a place
of honor. Shakespeare would be there, because it would be an act of
impiety to keep him out, but he would not be numbered among the
inner elite. There would be reservations over Goldoni, whose domesti-
cated Arlecchino does not attain the favored status of the earlier, earthy
Arlecchino of *commedia dell'arte*. Fo had a high measure of esteem
for such theatrical forms as vaudeville, *pochade*, bedroom farce, and
boulevardier theater of nineteenth-century France, even if, in the case
of the latter, it was limited to an admiration for the mastery of comic
technique displayed by Feydeau, Labiche, and their contemporaries. He
had the highest esteem for the abilities of clowns and circus performers.
He also respected Neapolitan theater, particularly the performance
skills of Peppino De Filippo and Totò, as well as the complete theatrical
expertise of Eduardo De Filippo. However, the supreme figure in this
tradition, or antitradition, is undoubtedly Ruzzante.

In Ruzzante, Fo saw an image of himself as he would have himself viewed. Ruzzante was the last representative of the medieval *giullare* and the precursor of the Arlecchino. Like Fo, Ruzzante was an actor-author; like Fo, his preferred genre was a kind of bitter farce whose poignant, or bawdy and broad, humor concealed an undercurrent of tragic emotion; like Fo, he dealt not with fantasy but with history; like Fo, he created characters who came from the people, and who spoke in popular dialects. There are other points of resemblance. With Ruzzante, the writer Beolco created a proto-Arlecchino figure, whose plucky, inventive ingenuity was his only defense against the assaults of entrenched power. Beolco devised the kind of theater Fo aspired to create, one which had the range, depth, and strength to depict primitive instincts and dark forces — death, fear, violence, brutality, hunger, sexual desire — and one in which the attitudes displayed toward power structures were always adversarial, and voiced in tones of satirical derision.

Fo also attributed to Ruzzante the actor the invention of a version of what became known as "epic" or "third person" performance style. In his monologues, Fo used the freedom afforded by popular theater — to move into and out of part, to adopt or abandon the fiction as required —

Sketch for *Hallequin, Harlekin, Arlecchino* by Dario Fo. (Courtesy C.T.F.R.).

and believed that Ruzzante too had availed himself of this privilege. Fo explains:

> Ruzzante too made use of direct address to the audience. But not in a trivial way, from some aesthetic desire for upheaval. No, it was because he needed to have the audience take part in the what was going on on-stage, but with an awareness that it was a constant fiction. (Binni 1975:151)

Fo detected in Ruzzante a disturbing, threatening imagination, which exposed the dark underside of a Venetian Renaissance normally viewed only in the splendid colors made familiar by the canvases of Carpaccio, Titian, Bellini, or Veronese. The character Ruzzante became the voice of the Veneto peasant uprooted by the War of the League of Cambrai in *Parlamento de Ruzzante che iera vegnú de campo* (Story of Ruzzante returning from the wars, published in English as *The Veteran*); of the poor man who finds himself deserted by his wife in favor of a wealthy man whom she does not love but who can put food in her stomach in *La bilora (The Weasel)*; but also, in *La moscheta (Posh Talk)*, of the unscrupulous, scoundrelly, but likable booby who loses wife and home to a fellow countryman whose only assets are superior physical and financial power. The character Ruzzante moves in a pitiless, loveless world devised by Ruzzante the writer, a world where the superego has lost its grip and the id is out of control, where the human, rational values dictated by ethics, affections, solidarity, and compassion have been replaced by the all-consuming drive to satisfy the primary, animal needs for shelter, sex, and nourishment.[3]

It may be this Ruzzante is as much a creation of Fo's as was the Edgar Allan Poe admired with such fervor by Baudelaire and Paul Valéry. There are discrepancies between Fo's Ruzzante and the Ruzzante championed by other critics, most notably Ludovico Zorzi, the critic-dramaturg who, as Fo readily conceded, was largely responsible for the reintroduction of Ruzzante to the Italian theatergoing public. In Zorzi's view, in only one of Ruzzante's works, *La Betia*, was there any trace of any "vein of popular theater" (Zorzi 1990:35). Mario Baratto (1990:72–75) too entertained doubts on this score. Zorzi emphasized the aristocratic connections and university education afforded Ruzzante, seeing his predilection for farce not as a symptom of his cultivation of any popular tradition but as the choice of a genre favored by the educated milieus in which he moved and dictated by his "goliardic associations (in which a taste for farce and masques had been prevalent for some time)" (Zorzi 1990:42). His knowledge of peasant conditions Zorzi saw as springing from his leisure time spent in rural, aristocratic circles (1990:15–16). Zorzi distances himself from those who would see Ruzzante as endowed with some "populist sentiment," something that as an "intelligent bourgeois but complete child of his time he could not have, and certainly did not have" (1990:26), although he does qualify this view by his apparently grudging agreement that Ruzzante was an acute observer of the mores of his age, endowed with a deep understanding of his own society. There was a certain fluidity to Zorzi's views, since he stated elsewhere that if "Ruzzante is not of the people," he nevertheless "pursued the creation of a repertoire of largely popular drama" (1990:48).

When Fo and Zorzi met in 1979 at a conference on questions relating to language and theater, it was Fo who underlined these differing interpretations of Ruzzante. Benedetto Croce had dismissed *La bilora* as a kind of "North Italian *Cavalleria rusticana*" (Fo 1992:84–91), and where Zorzi had been guarded in his disagreement with Croce, Fo was sarcastic and dismissive, seeing that misinterpretation as motivated by ideological prejudice and emblematic of a systematic blunting of the cutting edge of Ruzzante's work. Croce, in failing both to give due weight to the interplay of complex historical and political forces that Ruzzante's work expressed and to detect the "tragic-satirical discourse" with which Ruzzante's vision was imbued (Fo 1992:86), had been guilty not of defective critical insight but of that act of class-based, cultural expropriation that Fo particularly abominated. For Fo, Ruzzante was the spokesperson of the dispossessed peasant class, which had taken refuge in Venice from the ravages of war, and the visionary who understood the nature of the commercial economics of nascent capitalism and its resultant ethic in which money alone constituted the basis of all value. When Bilora asks payment in exchange for his wife, Fo interprets this act not as the behavior of a pimp but as a faltering gesture of compliance with the new mercantilist ethic, in which price determined value. Fo provides his own "paraphrase" and comment of the words he attributes to Ruzzante's Bilora:

> "Am I a cuckold? No, I am no longer a cuckold if I sell my woman, because money cleanses; it is a filter which washes away every

stain." Money is health, it is the antidote to every indecency, it is honest and clean. If you pay me, I am no longer dishonored, and my wife is no longer a whore but an object supplied at market value. (Fo 1992:88)

Bilora, however, remains a peasant with other values and cannot make himself totally accept the new economics and the new culture. He is driven to return to the rich merchant who had taken his wife, but the killing that ensues is almost an accident, a matter of uncalculated chance. The problem for a more literal-minded critic is that there are no lines that correspond even approximately to those that Fo puts in the mouth of Bilora. His reading can be viewed, gently, as a creative misinterpretation, diverging somewhat from the historical Ruzzante but in keeping with Fo's Ruzzante.

Fo's Ruzzante is a writer with a critical view of the historical developments of his own time. If he was a "bourgeois" by birth and educational background, his illegitimate birth had given him an instinctive sympathy with the underdog and the exploited peasant. His illegitimacy was crucial to Fo's characterization of him and provided Fo with an answer to a dilemma posed by Baratto and Zorzi (one that, *mutatis mutandis*, many critics have raised in connection with Fo himself): Since Ruzzante had received a court education, had been brought up in the company of the bluest of blue blood, and was the companion of cardinals and nobles, how could he pose as the spokesperson for ordinary people, and how could he justify his claim to be producing popular theater?

Beolco is a bastard, a bastard who has studied, who was witty, who had an enormous sense of the theater, but he was relegated to the lower end of the table. He found himself on the same level as the farm manager or the head waiter, perhaps even lower. He identified himself with the condition of the people with whom he had to share a daily struggle for survival. Ruzzante was a bastard like every servant, however much he may have been held in high esteem by the prince. Here we find the reason for his rage against every form of hypocrisy, every false manner invented to sustain the hegemony of one particular class. . . . I believe that Beolco chose the part of the hard-done-by peasant character not only because that role suggested to him various comic situations. I am convinced that Ruzzante stood shoulder to shoulder with the peasant, adopting his dress and language because he shared his culture, that is, the poetic style of anger and resentment. (Fo 1992:88–89)

The vocabulary and tone of this piece are intriguing and revealing. The reference to Ruzzante's "anger" recalls Fo's description of his own theater as a blend of "anger with laughter," but there is a much deeper level of identification suggested by the passage as a whole. The slightest acquaintance with Fo's own political and theatrical beliefs is sufficient to make it clear that this supposed biographical sketch of Ruzzante by Fo is in reality a self-portrait. Fo allied himself with a culture, a political ideology, a philosophy by choice not by spontaneous osmosis. His socialism, his identification with a proletariat cause, like his championing of popular culture, and his dedication to a vein of what he called people's theater were rational, were all willed decisions, not consequences of birth, self-interest, or class determinism. He is a classic meritocrat who, like Ruzzante, could have selected different companions and a different life philosophy but who forged his own beliefs out of ethical and aesthetic conviction.

There is little common ground between the image of Ruzzante presented by Zorzi and that presented by Fo. Both insisted that Ruzzante be seen in the context of his own age, but for Zorzi, that implied a recognition of the shaping power of the prevailing cultural and literary conventions and stereotypes; for Fo, it involved taking into account Ruzzante's adversarial reaction to the political-economic substructure he saw developing around him. Zorzi agreed that Ruzzante's opus was incomprehensible if the anti-Arcadia polemic intrinsic to it was ignored, but he held that the focus on the countryside and on the peasant was dictated by the cultural trends prevalent in his lifetime. Ruzzante's peasant may have been neither the *rusticus fatuus* nor the idealized shepherd, but he emerged from a contemporary (upper-class, or court) cultivation of pseudopastoral culture in which such figures were fashionable. For Fo, the concentration on the peasant was an ideological choice, motivated by a fellow feeling for the unprivileged. Zorzi stresses that Ruzzante lived a privileged life as the court poet of his noble patron, Alvise Cornaro; Fo, while wholly aware of the friendship with Cornaro, depicts Ruzzante as a free spirit. In his introduction to Ruzzante's *First Oration* in *Fo recita Ruzzante*, Fo writes that "Ruzzante is a man of his time," before adding the gloss that he was "perhaps the only great free author of his own century. The others, however illustrious they may have been, like Ariosto, Bembo, Aretino, Bibbiena are and remain authors of the court . . . of the regime" (1993a).[4] Fo's Ruzzante was a militantly committed playwright who adopted the politics of the peasant class and whose poetics were a consequence of that stance. Zorzi's Ruzzante was a writer who had no sense of the popular theater and wrote and performed farce because the goliardic spirit was in vogue among the cultured elite of the time.

Zorzi and Fo came closer in their shared awareness of the difficulties involved in bringing Ruzzante to a modern stage. In the above mentioned 1979 conference, Fo identified these problems:

> Personally I have tried to perform Ruzzante, with, I have to say, a fear that was near to panic; I have even tried to play about with him. I have tried to rewrite some of the dialogues and have them sewn onto me. It just didn't work, a disaster. But then I spoke to others who have attempted the same operation—directors like De Bosio, actors like Franco Parenti, and they had all experienced the same debacle. Ruzzante is untouchable. (1992:89)

Plainly, he later changed his mind. The pioneering and generally admired productions of Ruzzante in postwar Italy were those undertaken by the actor/director Gianfranco De Bosio in collaboration with Ludovico Zorzi. Fo was outspoken in his criticisms of these ventures.[5] Zorzi, in his essay "Storia di una scoperta" (History of a discovery; 1990:93–110), recounts their quest, starting with the 1950 production of *La moscheta* in its original text, for the most appropriate means of staging Ruzzante for a modern audience. It is interesting to note that in the later (1966–67) production of *I dialoghi di Ruzzante*, Zorzi and De Bosio decided to use as framework-situation a supposed performance by Beolco in the court of Cardinal Marco Cornaro, cousin of Alvise, and to use the *Oration* to the Cardinal as a prologue. Fo was to use the same structure in *Dario Fo incontra Ruzzante*, but he had no admiration for either the underlying vision behind the earlier production or De Bosio's performance. To an interviewer who asked him in 1973 whether there were any examples of popular theater in contemporary Italy, he produced De Bosio as an example of dangers to be avoided: "De Bosio has created a Ruzzante who looks like Goldoni, all little flutters and winks"

(Fo 1992:36). The Zorzi/De Bosio production had, in his view, eliminated all the radical strength from Ruzzante and had made insufficient
effort to reproduce the historical context. In consequence, the production was an exercise in the same kind of mystification and falsification
he believed Strehler had operated on Brecht. He was scarcely any more
sympathetic to the production of *Parlamento de Ruzzante* by Cesco
Baseggio, mounted in the open air in a Venetian *campo*. In any early
version of the prologue to *Fo recita Ruzzante*, he attacks Baseggio for
having failed to grapple with the power of the original: "It's disastrous to
banalize him or make him gratuitously crude (see the operation of
Baseggio with the transposition into the style of farce, almost cabaret)"
(Fo 1993a). In the final, performed version, the reference to Baseggio
was eliminated, but the warning against banalizing Ruzzante remained.

In his own presentation of Ruzzante, the fundamental problem for
Fo continued to be that of finding a means of making the language com-
prehensible and vivid while maintaining something of its authenticity.
Where De Bosio had tried to maintain the original text, leaving the audience to deduce the sense from the actions and gestures of the actors,
Cesco Baseggio had used, at least in part, translations into modern
Italian. On this point, Fo's approach was closer to Baseggio's (D'Amico
1993:9). Fo had no interest in textual purity for its own sake, but he was
convinced there were two contrasting dangers to be avoided. If commu-
nicability by undue reliance on translation ran the risk of destroying the
texture of the language, presenting the unvarnished original risked ob-
scuring Ruzzante's theatricality. The audience could not, however, be
simply left to grasp the sense by instinct. In the Spoleto program, he
wrote that while some things could be left to intuition, "with intuition
you lose all immediacy and people don't laugh, they feel left out, they
don't experience the life of the text and character, as happened when
Ruzzante himself was performing" (Fo 1993a). Fo set himself the task of
reinventing Ruzzante's work, of imbuing it with fresh spirit and making
such transformations as were necessary to show its original qualities.
Once again Fo finds justification for his operation in his identification
with Ruzzante, the kindred spirit. In the Spoleto 1993 program, he
writes:

> The problem with Ruzzante—I become more and more aware
> every day in rehearsals—is that everyone had forgotten that he was

an actor-author, and so nobody has paid heed when he said, please remake this fashion afresh for me. . . . I'm giving you this piece of cloth, but don't even try to dress in the same fashion, because it will be simply ridiculous. (Fo 1993a)

So it's essential to cut Ruzzante's cloth anew, to make it easy for the actors, to give him topical, present-day value. In expressing these sentiments, Ruzzante was, Fo adds, "truly a revolutionary, as well as the greatest Renaissance actor-author in all Europe" (1993a). Having established this basic kinship between actor-authors, Fo felt entitled to offer an adaptation that would preserve the fundamental spirit, rather than a philologically accurate reproduction.

If Fo's adaptations of Ruzzante must illustrate the anger, they must also produce in a modern audience "enjoyment and hilarity." In the "prologue," he agreed that Ruzzante's was "a dead language," even in the countryside around Padua where Ruzzante had lived, but he refused to simply modernize archaic terms. His solution, as he stated in his "anteprologue" to *Fo recita Ruzzante*, was to clarify meaning by the repetition and duplication of synonyms and by inserting some familiar modern words in the middle of lists of dialect terms. This device allowed him to ensure accessibility and comprehensibility while respecting the rhythms, the assonances, the onomatopoeia, and the cadences of Ruzzante's language. In performance, particularly when employing the monologue structure, Fo has access to a range of other techniques. He can unite the rational, communicative aspect of language with the *grammelot*, and with an expressive, nonverbal vocabulary of gesture and sound that he had been developing in all his monologues since *Mistero buffo*. An appearance as the modern *giullare* in works taken from Ruzzante enables him to repeat his conviction that Ruzzante had been his forerunner in that tradition too.[6]

The same suggestion is implied by the choice of extract. In the context created by Fo, the *Oration* to Cardinal Marco Cornaro—mildly erotic in content, with a vein of anticlericalism allied to caricatured social comment—is made to seem part of the same genre of satirical-political routine as many improvised prologues by Fo himself. Other extracts include a letter from Ruzzante to an actor who performed in some of his plays, but in Fo's view, the letter was a pretext for a pseudo-philosophical consideration of life and death. It opens with a whimsical account of the expulsion of Adam and Eve from Eden, and in tone and manner, it resembles several of Fo's early monologues such as "Caino e Abele" (Cain and Abel) or "Davide e Golia" (David and Goliath), from the 1952 radio series, *Poer nano*. Fo also includes the fantastic anecdote recounted by the fisherman Bertevèlo from *La piovana (The Girl from Piove)*, transforming it from an element intrinsic to the play to an exercise in *fabulatore* storytelling of the sort that, as he has often said, and repeated in his Nobel lecture, he heard in his boyhood and were influential in his development as a writer.

In the extract from *La piovana*, which serves as an introduction to the show, Fo enlists Ruzzante's help to resolve the dilemma of the level of respect due to works from other ages. This problem was relevant to his thinking on Ruzzante but had troubled him previously. He had been commissioned in 1980 by the Berliner Ensemble to prepare a new version of Brecht and Weill's *Threepenny Opera*, but when the company saw the final work, they rejected it as too radical a departure from the original. Fo's version was later staged in Turin as a supposed rewriting of John Gay's *The Beggar's Opera*, but the experience led him to rethink the appropriate style of staging classics. Conveniently, Brecht had advised adapters not to be overawed by celebrated texts and not to submit to the "terrorism of the classics" (Fo 1982:5). The same phrase recurs in Fo's opening words on the *Oration*. In his search for a justification for intervention into established texts, he found even deeper support in Ruzzante himself. *Vaccària* (Cow-comedy) was based on Plautus's *Asinaria*, and to defend his right to adapt the plot, Ruzzante had Plautus himself appear to recite a prologue, in which he asserted:

> I wrote this play but if I were alive in these times, I would not make my plays in any way different from the one you are now watching. I also beg you not to make any judgment or comparison between this (production) and the written version of my plays. I swear they were performed differently from the way they are printed, because many things may be good on the pen, but turn out badly on the stage. (Fo 1993a)

In his prologue to *La piovana*, Ruzzante goes further in his defense of the practice of rewriting, comparing it at one point to a seamstress refashioning old styles, but also anticipating Gramsci (and Fo) in his convictions on the role of tradition:

I am here to advise you that this story was born a short time ago. It's also true that you are about to hear a play cut and fashioned from old wood. But it is not new or old that counts. We were all born of that old tree. And how could we know, after all, where we want to arrive if we do not know from where we come? (Fo 1993a)

These words are uncannily reminiscent of words that Fo normally attributes to Gramsci and that he quoted many times in the course of the debates that followed the political plays he performed while touring around his "alternative circuit" in the post-1968 years. He reproached those members of his audience who asked him to do only contemporary pieces and who could not understand his fondness for the medieval material of *Mistero buffo*. "Could Gramsci have been mistaken when he wrote that you can only know where you are headed if you have an understanding of where you have come from," he told one such heckler (Fo 1970:47). Fo had a very clear knowledge of the past from which he came, and of the part Ruzzante had played in that past, even if Ruzzante is to some extent remade in Fo's own image and likeness.

All translations are by the author.

Notes

1. Modern scholars almost invariably prefer the form *Ruzante* rather than *Ruzzante*, since it corresponds to the Venetian-Paduan usage. While Fo has himself occasionally adopted that form, he appears to prefer the Tuscanized *Ruzzante* and has used that spelling in the title of the show under discussion. The latter form has, for consistency's sake, been adopted throughout, even in quotes from authors, such as Ludovico Zorzi, who used the alternative spelling. For biographical and critical material on Ruzzante, see Carroll (1990) and Andrews (1993).

2. For a discussion of the differences in the content of the two shows, see Pizza (1996:319–61).

3. Cf. Ludovico Zorzi (1967). Ronnie Ferguson has translated *La moscheta* as *Posh Talk* (Beolco 1991) and *La bilora* as *The Weasel* (Beolco 1995).

4. *Fo recita Ruzzante* (Fo 1993a) has not been published, but copies of the script were distributed at venues where the production was mounted, and I was able to consult the manuscript of the performance copy in the archives of La Comune, in Milan. The work has been issued by La Comune Theater Company on two audiocassettes, and on videocassette.

5. For a discussion of productions of Ruzzante, see Calendoli (1983:111–24).

6. It is significant that when an interviewer asked him how many "Ruzzantes" he had known in his own experience, Fo referred to his grandfather, a market gardener who was known as Bristin, "a nickname stolen from the seed of the pepper plant," and who did short performances as a means of attracting a crowd to purchase his produce (1993b:25).

References

Andrews, Richards. 1993. *Scripts and Scenarios*. Cambridge: Cambridge UP.

Angelini, Franca. 1976. *Il teatro del Novecento da Pirandello a Fo*. Bari: Laterza.

Baratto, Mario. 1990. *Da Ruzante a Pirandello*. Naples: Liguori.

Beolco, Angelo. 1991. *Posh Talk*. Tr. Ronnie Ferguson. In *Three Renaissance Comedies*. Ed. Christopher Cairns. Lewiston: Edwin Mellen Press.

———. 1995. *The Weasel*. Tr. Ronnie Ferguson. New York: Peter Lang.

Binni, Lanfranco. 1975. *Attento te! . . . il teatro politico di Dario Fo*. Verona: Bertani.

Bloom, Harold. 1994. *The Western Canon*. London: Macmillan.

Calendoli, Giovanni, ed. 1983. *Ruzante sulle scene italiane del secondo dopoguerra*. Padua: Università di Padova.

Carroll, Linda. 1990. *Angelo Beolco (Ruzante)*. Boston: Twayne.

D'Amico, Masolino. 1993. "Fo Recita Ruzzante." Review (Milan). *La Stampa* (10 July).

Fo, Dario. 1970. *Il teatro politico di Dario Fo: Compagni senza censura*. Vol 1. Milan: Mazzotta.

———. 1977. *Dario Fo parla di Dario Fo*. Interview by Erminia Artese. Cosenza: Lerici.

———. 1982. *L'Opera dello sghignazzo*. Milan: La Comune.

———. 1987. *Manuale minimo dell'attore*. Ed. Franca Rame. Turin: Einaudi.

———. 1990. *Dialogo provocatorio sul comico, il tragico, la follia e la ragione*. Interview by Luigi Allegri. Rome: Laterza.

———. 1991. *The Tricks of the Trade*. (*Manuale minimo dell'attore*). Tr. Joseph Farrell. Ed. Stuart Hood. New York: Routledge.

———. 1992. *Fabulazzo*. Ed. Lorenzo Ruggiero and Walter Valeri. Milan: Kaos.

———. 1993a. *Fo recita Ruzzante*. Unpublished. Milan: La Comune.

———. 1993b. Interview (Milan). *Corriere della Sera* (2 July).

———. 1995. "Dario Fo recita Ruzzante." Interview (Milan). *Giornale dello spettacolo* (March/April).

Pizza, Marisa. 1996. *Il gesto, la parola, l'azione: poetica, drammaturgia e storia dei monologhi di Dario Fo*. Rome: Bulzoni Editore.

Valentini, Chiara. 1977. *La storia di Dario Fo*. Milan: Feltrinelli.

Zorzi, Ludovico, ed. 1967. *Ruzante: Teatro*. Turin: Einaudi.

———. 1990. *L'attore, la commedia, il drammaturgo*. Turin: Einaudi.

CHAPTER 6

"The Moon Is a Light Bulb" and Other Stories
Fo, the Songwriter

TONY MITCHELL

Although there is a considerable body of critical writing about Dario Fo's dramaturgy, performance, political and theoretical approaches to theater, and even his work as a visual artist, there has been little or no attempt to isolate Fo's extensive oeuvre of songs, written both for his plays and as individual compositions. What follows is a consideration of the songs that Fo wrote in the early stages of his career, often in collaboration with the Milanese *cantautore* (singer-songwriter) Enzo Jannacci, who has performed many of them in his own repertoire.[1] These songs were usually set to music by Fiorenzo Carpi, a composer who died in 1997, after a long career. From the early 1950s onward, Carpi had done extensive work with Milan's Piccolo Teatro, including writing the music for Giorgio Strehler's celebrated production of Goldoni's *Arlecchino servitore di due padroni* (Harlequin, servant of two masters). He also composed the soundtracks for films by directors such as Luigi Comencini and, more recently, the Nuovo cinema italiano

of Comencini's daughter, Cristina, and other directors, such as Carlo
Mazzacurati. In addition, Carpi worked for the Italian state broadcast-
ing body, RAI, and scored more popular films, such as *Le avventure di
Pinocchio* and the "Christmas film" *Buon natale . . . buon anno* (Merry
Christmas . . . Happy New Year). But according to Sergio Bassetti, Carpi
"never achieved—nor probably sought—any great public popularity":

> The three words "culture," "elegance," and "discretion" could be
> used to summarize Carpi's social and musical personality . . . and
> he has found his appropriate expressive idiom in functional music,
> whether it be for film or theater. (1991:41)

Carpi's work with Fo was often self-effacingly functional in its versatility and ranged from military-style marches to rock and roll, slow
ballads, and jazz-style syncopated comedy songs. The first period of the
Fo-Carpi collaboration began in 1953 with "La luna è una lampadina"
(The moon is a light bulb) and continued until the last play of Fo's
"bourgeois period" in 1967, *La signora è da buttare (Toss the Lady Out)*.
By this time, Fo had discovered "Bella Ciao" and the more politically
oriented work songs, as well as peasant and partisan "roots" music of the
traditional folk group Il nuovo canzoniere italiano. He collaborated with
members of this group on *Ci ragiono e canto* (I think things out and sing
about them) in 1966. In his subsequent, more directly militant plays with
his Nuova Scena company between 1968 and 1973, performed outside conventional theater circuits, the music was provided by Paolo
Ciarchi. The Sicilian *cantastorie* (story-singer), Cicciu Busacca, was
first recruited as a member of Fo and Franca Rame's later company, La
Comune, in 1973 for *Ci ragiono e canto 3* and *La guerra del popolo in
Cile* (The people's war in Chile).

With Nuova Scena and La Comune, Fo was exploring more "authentic" forms of *musica popolare* (people's music), which expressed
aspects of the class struggle. This is perhaps best exemplified by one of
Ciarchi's compositions, "La grande quercia" (The great oak), from the
1971 play *Morte e resurrezione di un pupazzo* (Death and resurrection
of a puppet). In his introduction to his 1976 collection of Fo's songs and
ballads, Lanfranco Binni singles out "La grande quercia," which refers
to the "great oak" of capitalism and imperialism being felled by an army
of worker ants, as a marker of Fo's militancy. In this work, Binni writes:

The musical direction has become unified with the words of the song, drawing on a long tradition, and carrying it a long way, into the hearts of the struggling people, and living in their conception of the world and in the conscience of the people's culture and its enormous creative force. It is no longer Dario Fo solo, with his instinctive attraction to the "low life" that causes him to laugh at the misery of bourgeois culture. It is a Dario Fo who identifies deeply with the force of political consciousness, the process of revolutionary transformation through which the people are constructing their own unity. . . . [He has shifted] from an individual dimension to a choral, collective dimension, from an instinctively anti-bourgeois conception of the world to the understanding that in every society that is divided into classes there can be only two points of view: the bourgeois view and the proletarian view. (Fo 1976:27)

Viewed in retrospect, Binni's rather simplistic, quasi-religious, doctrinaire Marxist rhetoric signals "La grande quercia" as something of a low point in Fo's song writing. A collective ideological solemnity and solidarity of choral posturing has taken over from the individuality, wit, complexity, and distinctive satirical charm of his earlier song writing. Fo's shift from comic, satirical and individualistic songs to collective political songs also marks a shift from *musica leggera* (literally: light, or pop, music) to *musica popolare* (people's music). Carpi's return as a musical collaborator on Fo's 1976 play *La marijuana della mamma è la più bella* (Mother's marijuana is the best) and on subsequent plays such as the 1981 *Clacson, trombette e pernacchi (Trumpets and Raspberries)* marks a welcome return to the more idiosyncratic, abrasively comic and satirical levity of Fo's pre-Nuova Scena period, even if Carpi only provides largely incidental music in these later plays. Fo's 1997 play for the Taormina festival, *Il diavolo con le zinne* (The devil with boobs), with Rame and Giorgio Albertazzi, includes a song written in homage to Carpi. This play was in production in Milan when Fo was awarded the Nobel Prize.

Another musical low point occurred with *L'opera dello sghignazzo (The Opera of the Sneering Laugh)*, Fo's chaotic, misconceived 1981 rock opera version of Brecht's *Threepenny Opera*. Written with the assistance of his son Jacopo, Fo substituted Brecht and Weill's songs with twenty-four mostly banal songs "freely inspired by rock songs by Allen

Ginsberg, Patti Smith, Donovan, Zappa, Janis Joplin, Jimi Hendrix, David Bowie, Nina Hagen, and other notable rock musicians" (Fo 1981:9). These songs, as well as incorporating assorted rock, rhythm and blues, and reggae riffs, showed that Fo's song writing powers had diminished considerably by the 1980s. One only has to compare Brecht and Weill's powerful "Pirate Jenny" with Fo's banal substitute, "Guarda un astronave blu metallo" (Look at the blue metallic spaceship), to illustrate the depths of self-conscious pastiche to which Fo had sunk. Carpi, who did the musical arrangements for the songs in *L'opera,* was clearly not given enough room to produce anything musically distinctive. Fo's musical activities then turned to directing opera, which had begun with his rewritten version of Stravinsky's *Soldier's Tale* for La Scala's "decentered activities program" in 1978. However, Fo and Carpi's songs of the 1950s and early 1960s have been unjustly neglected, and it is to these I wish to turn in an attempt to bring to light some of their distinctive features.

Fo and the *Canzone d'Autore*

In his 1981 essay "The system of *canzone* in Italy today," musicologist Franco Fabbri defines seven types of *canzone* (song) in contemporary Italy: "the traditional song, the pop song, the 'sophisticated song,' the *canzone d'autore* (author's song), the political song, the rock song, and the children's song" (1981:123). Fabbri's categories allow for considerable overlapping, and a cursory glance at Fo's early output of songs could provide examples of the use of elements of almost all of these genres at various times. It could be argued that in most of Fo's songs of the 1950s and 1960s, there is a hybridity in which the *canzone d'autore* predominated. In terms of lyrics, which will be the principal focus of this study, given Fo's involvement largely as a lyricist, Fabbri states that the *canzone d'autore* contains

> the highest level of complexity, with regard to richness of vocabulary, rhetoric and syntax. Both in the music and in the lyrics the different levels of complexity are expressed in the syntax, understood in the wider sense of relationship between parts. . . . The tendency of the *canzone d'autore* towards individual characterization can be seen above all in its lyrical vocabulary, which is

richer and more open to literary suggestion [than other genres]. (1981:124, 127)

Fabbri estimates that the *canzoni d'autore*, and the *cantautori* (singer-songwriters) who wrote and performed them, first appeared in Italy at the end of the 1950s, and its precursors were Domenico Modugno, Renato Carosone, and Fred Buscaglione. All three attempted to rise above the prevailing banality and standardization that characterized Italian popular songs of the time by introducing satire and parody, as well as incorporating elements of contemporary American popular song. They were followed by the more innovative and down-to-earth songs of Umberto Bindi, Gino Paoli, and Luigi Tenco (all from Genoa) and by the Milanese singers Enzo Jannacci and Giorgio Gaber, who both collaborated with Fo, and who both came from a background of theater and cabaret. One characteristic of the new urbanity of the *canzone d'autore* Fabbri outlines was its retention of aspects of older forms of Italian song, such as the dialect song, the traditional song, and the nightclub song; elements of all are present in Fo's early songs. There were also intellectual aspirations, literary influences, overtones of French existentialism, and jazz and rock and roll influences. As Fabbri states:

> The *canzone d'autore* (perhaps this is an aspect of its "sincerity") appears to have a social image that corresponds to its actual area of consumption: that is, lower-middle and middle-class intellectuals, students, the Italy of mass scholarization, the university open to everyone, intellectual unemployment. (1981:132)

The *autori* were in some cases literary figures who wrote song lyrics in the 1950s and 1960s. Fabbri cites Italo Calvino's work with the group Cantocronache, but Pier Paolo Pasolini, Alberto Arbasino, Franco Fortini, Ennio Flaiano, and Alberto Moravia also wrote song lyrics, most notably for the Rome-based actress Laura Betti's 1960 cabaret show, *Giro a vuoto* (Running on empty). Fo also wrote songs for Betti in the 1960 episodic film about the Fascist era, *Cronache di '22* (Reports of 1922). Indeed, despite the ideological differences dividing Fo and Pasolini over theater—Fo rejected Pasolini's profoundly "literary" theater, and Pasolini once described Fo as a "plague on the Italian theater"

(Pasolini 1973)—there are considerable affinities between their song writing activities.[2] Both also worked at different times with the Roman political songwriter Giovanna Marini. Fo's Milanese *canzoni della mala* (songs of the criminal underworld), some of which were recorded by Ornella Vanoni in the late 1950s, bear striking similarities to some of Pasolini's bleak Roman dialect song portraits of Roman prostitutes, unemployed layabouts, and disaffected youth. Both were probably influenced by Brecht and Weill's *Threepenny Opera*, although the predominantly up-tempo comedy arrangements of Fo's songs contrast with the prevailingly black, brooding melancholy of Pasolini's. The Pasolini song that comes closest to the skewed wit and whimsy of Fo's early songs is the 1966 *Uccellacci uccellini (Hawks and Sparrows)*, set to music by Ennio Morricone. This consists of Domenico Modugno singing the opening credits of Pasolini's film of the same name, which starred the great comic actor Totò ("the absurd Totò, the human Totò, the crazy Totò, the sweet Totò," as the song puts it), who, of course, was an enormous influence on Fo. The involvement of literary figures in song writing was later to fuel debates about whether *cantautori* had the right to be referred to as "poets" (see Fiori 1996). But Fabbri characterizes Fo and Jannacci as "decidedly the least literary, most comedy-directed" of these early *cantautori* (1981:141).

Fabbri points out a distinctive aspect of the *canzone d'autore* that relates to Fo's early songs: the tendency of the singer to create a personality that could be identified with the protagonist of the songs. For this personality to dominate,

> things that might be considered mistakes of intonation or bad pronunciation in other genres are accepted as characteristics of individual personality, which is of primary importance in this genre.
> . . . The tendency of the *canzone d'autore* towards individual characterization can be seen above all in its lyrical vocabulary, which is richer and more open to literary suggestion. (1981:126–27)

Another distinctive aspect is the strong emphasis on lyrics rather than music, which Fabbri attributes to a predominantly student audience primarily concerned with "social and political topics" (1981:139). But this political focus, deriving from "a speaking subject who dominates the situation," was markedly different from the political song, in which "the speaking subject assumed itself to be collective" (1981:141).

One distinctive feature of Fo's work with Jannacci, which was show-
cased in 1967 in a Jannacci concert entitled *22 Songs*, directed by Fo,
was his use of Milanese dialect. He also displayed a tendency to create
comic, proletarian protagonists who are either petty criminals or down
on their luck. Lorenzo Coveri has noted that the "dialect inserts" in both
Jannacci's and Giorgio Gaber's songs in the 1960s "reflect a clearly-
defined sociolinguistic realty of dropouts [in English in the original] in
the outer suburbs of Milan" (1996:23).

107
■
"The
Moon Is a
Light Bulb"
and Other
Stories

"La luna è una lampadina"

"La luna è una lampadina" is generally acknowledged as the first
important song Fo and Carpi wrote, and it remains one of their most
characteristic. Binni locates it in 1953 (Fo 1976:25), although one recorded version by Fo (1977) is dated 1962.[3] Jannacci has recorded two
radically different versions of it, the second in 1980. The song takes an
archetypal situation of thwarted love and turns it on its head: The protagonist is standing under a balcony, and his beloved Lina is above him,
carrying on with Nino the barber, who has "heaps of money." Instead of
complaining of a broken heart, he complains that his feet are already
sore from walking up and down the pavement and that the last trams
home have already left and he will have to walk home. In the final verse,
he compares himself to a stray cat he once saw "crying like a madman."

Fo's recorded version of the song, in an arrangement by Gigi Cichellero and his orchestra, has a decidedly rock and roll intonation, almost reminiscent of Bobby Solo, the Italian Elvis. It is set to tinkling
piano, walking bass, snare drums, jazz-styled electric guitar, and saxo-
phone. In the dialect reprises, Fo indulges in some raunchy scat singing that verges on *grammelot*, the invented onomatopoeic language he
was to use in his later solo performance pieces. (Probably Fo's earliest use of full-blown *grammelot* occurs in the song "Pianto dei piantatori di piante" [The plant-planters' lament], recorded in 1962, with a
musical setting by Cichellero that is almost identical to "La luna è una
lampadina.") The jagged, syncopated rhythms of Fo's version of "La
luna è una lampadina" suggest excursions into the "sophisticated song"
genre, but there are obvious overlaps with the dialect song and the rock
and roll song, and its spoken sections could almost be regarded as op-
eratic *recitativo*, or even an early form of rap.[4] The most notable feature
of "La luna è una lampadina" is its double articulation: Each verse is

first spoken in standard Italian prose and then sung in rhyming Milanese dialect. Jannacci's 1980 version is a decidedly cool, laid-back, jazz crooner's rendition with muted trumpet and bursts of swinglike brass, trilling piano, and guitar chops, and he actually incorporates the English word *translation* to signal his switch from Italian to dialect in the first verse.

In an analysis of Jannacci's earlier, more up-tempo version of the song, in which the singer assumes a high-pitched, petulant, childlike voice, backed by piano, frantic guitar, and drums, Carlo Testa refers to a bilingual "schizophrenic storyteller" (1996). This concept resonates for anyone familiar with Fo's monologues in *Mistero buffo* (Comic mystery), such as the "Wedding Feast of Cana," in which an angel and a drunken guest do battle to tell the story. The "schizophrenic" aspect of the dual narration is perhaps most evident in the second verse of "La luna è una lampadina," in which the prose lyric states "Il 31, inteso come tram, è già passato; di 28 non ce n' è più'" (The 31, referring to a tram, has already gone; there are no more 28s either) (1996:30).[5] This rather pompous, pedantic footnote provided by the narrator suggests someone unfamiliar with public transport; but as Testa points out, the dialect version refers to "the only thirty-one or twenty-eight that can be pertinent on a moonlit night in a working-class neighborhood. Dialect does not offer the context; it is the context." He adds the historical footnote that "in the Fifties and Sixties, both the 31 and 28 lines operated away from the flashy city center and through working class neighborhoods" (1996:31). Hence, definite class distinctions are being made between the standard Italian and the dialect versions of the lyric. While this is not to present a simplistically binary scheme, like Binni's insistence on a bourgeois and a proletarian view, it is to emphasize a working-class perspective. This mocks the standard narrative of courtly love and insists on a more down-to-earth, dialogic, even carnivalesque, perspective that domesticates the moon as an engine of romance and substitutes sore feet for a broken heart.

Mikhail Bakhtin's notions of dialogism, carnival, the world upside down, grotesque realism, and bringing down to earth (mocking the head and heart by reference to the genitals and excretion) have been applied to Fo's one-man shows, for example, *Mistero buffo* and *Fabulazzo osceno* (*Obscene Fables*; see Scuderi 1998). They could equally be applied to "La luna è una lampadina" and other songs, such as "Il mondo alla rovescia" (The world upside down). This latter song was included in the

1960 play *Aveva due pistole con gli occhi bianchi e neri (He Had Two Pistols with White and Black Eyes)*, a mistaken identity farce about the criminal underworld, heavily influenced by Brecht's *Threepenny Opera*. It derives from popular carnivalesque traditions of topsy-turvy bestiaries, set to a catchy Carpi melody and adding a few religious and political reversals:

> Horses fly through the sky
> Fishes swim through flowering trees
> A flower sucks butterflies
> And settles on a hornet's back
> You see a thief hearing a priest's confession
> And a little orphan giving a home to nuns
> Government ministers join a political rally
> And cops beat them up with their truncheons.[6]

(1976:42)

The hymnlike group chorus on the final line consolidates the song's satirical inversion. This befits a play in which a priest with amnesia is mistaken for his double, a gangster, but who turns out not to be what he appears, after organizing a thieves' strike in which they demand a percentage of the profits made by those who benefit from their thefts, for example, insurance companies, crime reporters, and dog trainers.

Testa argues that the protagonists of Jannacci's songs of the 1950s and 1960s are usually grotesque in the Bakhtinian sense rather than absurd in the existentialist sense. They are also often juxtaposed with the natural, inanimate, and animal spheres:

> By choosing to be the storyteller of the Milanese poor folk of the '50s and '60s, the early Jannacci arguably even chooses to be, in a sense, "rear guard": he opts to lend a voice to the Otherness of those who cannot yet be concerned with the void that modern Reason has discovered at the center of the cosmos, because they are still too concerned with the void inside their stomachs.
> (1996:33)

If this suggests affinities with the *grammelot* of the starving Zanni of *Mistero buffo*, who imagines he has gorged himself on a sumptuous meal and then eats a fly, or with the other peasant figures in Fo's monologues, then the affinities are apt. Another of Fo's songs written collaboratively for Jannacci's 1967 show, *22 Songs*, that has strong affinities with

Mistero buffo and, in particular, Fo's celebrated carnivalesque, dialogic monologue, "Resurrezione di Lazzaro" ("The Resurrection of Lazarus"), is "Prete Liprando e il giudizio di Dio" (Liprando the priest and the judgment of God). Set to a mock-liturgical, dirgelike organ and drum roll, the song is almost totally lyric-driven, and it is sung by Jannacci in an almost Gregorian chant mode. A spoken introduction, which the authors have "tried to set to music with a certain degree of commitment," states that the story derives from an account by Landolfo, a twelfth-century Milanese historian. They dedicate it to all those who bear witness to important historical events even if they don't realize it. Liprando accuses the Archbishop Teosolano of Sant'Ambrogio of being a thief, a miser, and the emperor's lackey and calls for him to be brought to justice. The archbishop calls down the judgment of God on the priest and demands that he walk over red-hot charcoal from a fire made from forty faggots and that if he emerges unscathed, the Archbishop will leave Milan on foot. People come from outside the city to witness the spectacle, but the pope forbids it. Liprando insists nonetheless, and the spectators provide him with the requisite forty faggots. In the course of the fire-walking spectacle, three women faint and one gives birth, and Liprando "is all in a sweat but isn't burnt" and succeeds in ridding Milan of the corrupt archbishop (1976:143–44).

The song is presented as a dialogue in direct speech between Liprando and the emperor, with a chorus singing the narrative links, the crowd's comments, the pope's edict, the judgment of God, and, finally, a litany of praise to Liprando. The narrator's voice gradually emerges as that of a spectator from Como who is unable to see much of the event through the crowd. This narrative structure, as well as the subject matter of public religious spectacle, anticipates the more complex, multiviewpoint narration of "The Resurrection of Lazarus." There, Fo portrays an entire crowd, switching from one character to another, and ending with a spectator whose pocket has been picked. Liprando, and the narrator, represent the underdog, or "little man," who succeeds in overcoming a corrupt and unjust authority figure similar to the figure of Pope Boniface VIII in *Mistero buffo*, which also uses elements of liturgical music.

Another carnivalesque Fo-Jannacci song that Testa analyses is "Ho visto un re" (I saw a king), first aired in *Ci ragiono e canto 2* in 1969, and performed by the folk group Duo di Piadena as well as by Jannacci. "Ho visto un re" represents a transitional phase between Fo the individualist *cantautore* and Fo the folklorist and political *giullare* (jester). Like "La

111

■

"The
Moon Is a
Light Bulb"
and Other
Stories

luna è una lampadina," it is split dialogically. Here there is a call and response structure in standard Italian and dialect as the narrator tells a group of initially uncomprehending peasants a kind of parable about confiscation of property that illustrates the power of social hierarchies in a dog-eat-dog world. Testa suggests the narrator is "a modern equivalent of the poor folk's Gramscian 'organic intellectual,'" and the song, "La nascita del villano" ("The Birth of the Villeyn"), appears to be an early version of one of the monologues included in *Mistero buffo* (1996:20). Following the accumulative, repetitive structure of many traditional Italian folk songs and children's songs, the narrator tells of a king who is crying atop his horse because he has had one of his thirty-two castles taken away by the emperor. He is followed by a bishop who is crying and biting his sacristan's hand because he has had one of his thirty-two abbeys taken away by the cardinal, and by a rich man who is crying into his goblet of wine because he has had three of his thirty-two houses and one apartment taken away from him by the king, the bishop, the emperor, and the cardinal. He then describes the plight of a peasant (which he has to translate from the dialect *vilan* to the Italian *contadino* before his peasant audience understands what he means). The peasant has had his son taken into military service, and his chicken, his turkey, his wife, his farm, and his pig taken away from him by the king, the rich man, the bishop, the emperor, and even the cardinal. After a pause, the narrator then starts laughing, to illustrate that the peasant did not cry, as the peasant's lot must be a happy one, because the king, the cardinal, and capital in general would be upset to see him cry. The song ends with a rousing chorus, a "frenzied Rossinian crescendo" (Testa 1996:23), in which narrator and peasant chorus are united in expressing their *allegria*. Indeed, the entire tone of the song is *molto allegro*, with a bouncy piano accompaniment, and Jannacci adds a nonsensical rhythmical refrain—"ah be' sì be'" (oh well, yes well)—which adds an air of silliness to the proceedings.[7] Textual variants on the list of possessions confiscated from the peasant include a violin, a chess set, a transistor radio, and some records by Little Tony (later updated to Miguel Bosé), which gives what is essentially a medieval parable a more modern cast (Testa 1996:22).[8] But unlike the more brutal and bitter version of the story of the peasant in *Mistero buffo*, the song "Ho visto un re" maintains an air of mocking irony within a context of *musica leggera* (pop music) rather than being a full-blown *giullarata*. Storyteller and chorus may be united at the end, as in the political songs Fo was writing at the time, but there

that sooner or later justice will prevail over injustice. The sneering laugh [*sghignazzo*] of a "sucker" today will become the guffaw of a winner tomorrow. It is a language that is immediate, alive, never abstract or literary, and that is brought to life through the external projection of communication with others, which gets under our skin and pins the audience to their seats. As such it operates in a dimension that is not static but mobile and vivid. Fiorenzo Carpi's music . . . expresses completely this affirmative atmosphere of movement, with its fast rhythms and its satirical counterpoints. (Fo 1976:26–27)

One of Fo's songs that deals with the "industrial outskirts" of Milan but perhaps does not entirely express this sense of optimism in justice prevailing is "La brutta città che è la mia" (This ugly city of mine). Fo wrote and first performed this song (with music by Carpi) for the television program *Canzonissima* in 1962. Loosely based on Jacques Brel's 1962 "Le plat pays" (The flat country), the refrain of which it borrows, it is a melancholy but satirical lament. Fo's recorded version has a plangent flute and piano accompaniment, with orchestral augmentation in the choruses that reprise the title. A world of pipes and pylons and "walls disguised as houses" is described, with only one tree, on which "all the dogs queue up to pee." The land is flat, the wind is "afraid to dirty itself with snow," the Duomo of Milan is "a marble quarry dressed as a bride," and the Naviglio (one of the canals that run through Milan) is a stagnant pond in which the fish suffocate. Nonetheless, going into the piazza on Sundays to meet up with girls creates wind and movement, and the song ends with the image of doves flying over the holy ground of "this ugly city of mine" (1976:51–52). It is an evocative but sad, if slightly tongue-in-cheek, song and was recorded by the popular singer Milly. It anticipates a later tradition of Italian *canzoni d'autore* about cities, such as Lucio Dalla's "Milano" ("where you speak to someone in German and they reply in Sicilian dialect"), Antonello Venditti's sentimental paeons "Roma Capoccia" (Rome's the boss) and "Torino," and Paolo Conte's "Genova per noi" (Genoa for us). The first verse of Fo's song is quoted, without comment, as an example of songs that portray Milan in Gianni Borgna's 1992 history of Italian song, *Storia della canzone italiana*.

Another song featured in *Canzonissima* (and later performed and recorded by Jannacci) is "Il foruncolo" (The pimple), a parody of the *canzonetta* (trivial love song), which prevailed in the Italian pop music industry of the early 1960s. The protagonist has discovered a pimple on his ear while he is shaving. As his girlfriend cannot bear pimples, or cysts, or blackheads, or any other form of acne, he knows this is the end of their relationship. The song fades out on a debate with himself as to whether it is a pimple or a blackhead (1976:51–52). Fo performs the song with a mock *gravitas* that underscores the triteness of the teenage romance content of what must be his silliest song. Jannacci milks this gap between content and presentation even further, assuming a grief-stricken, cracked voice, backed by a cheesy organ and slow, loping bass and drums that mock 1950s sentimental ballads (1976:50).

Other mock love songs by Fo recorded by Jannacci include "Veronica," about a woman who loved symphonic music, which she played on the accordion, who wanted to be a nun but swore at priests and who "didn't risk platonic love." She was remembered by the narrator as a "canonic first love." This lighthearted, slightly nonsensical song, with its silly refrain, "m'beh ooh," seemed mainly an opportunity to rhyme Veronica with *fisarmonica* (accordion), *monaca* (nun), *platonica*, and *canonica*. "Sopra i vetri" (On the window panes) announces itself as a "serious love song of heartbreak and pain" and describes the forlorn, empty room of a man whose lover has left him. To a slow, mock-mournful beat, the protagonist describes the dirty windows, which seem to be covered in raindrops even when it isn't raining, and the eyes of his ex-beloved, which look like the flies in his room, and he hasn't any DDT. He goes on to list the things she's left—cigarette butts, canaries, a gun in the kitchen, mattresses, a knife—and some of the things she's taken, which include the silver. He ends by deciding to report her to the police. The existential angst signaled by the cigarette butts, gun, and knife, which evoke a 1950s French film noir scenario, is mocked by the details of the flies and the DDT.

Fo proved he was capable of writing "straight" sentimental love ballads with "Stringimi forte i polsi" (Hold my wrists tightly together), a song from his 1959 play *Gli arcangeli non giocano a flipper (Archangels Don't Play Pinball)*. A fairly trite love ballad sung by the play's "street kid" protagonist Il Lungo (Stretch, played by Fo) to the "Albanian" prostitute (played by Rame), it evolves from the mock wedding Il Lungo's mates set up for him, in which the couple have their wrists bound together. The song later became the theme tune to *Canzonissima*. In Fo's detached, bemused, but resonant rendition, with music by Carpi, the bluesy setting, with "boppy," rhythmic piano and "whiplash" scratch guitar effects, gives the song an urbane quality that rescues it from sentimentality. Even the flute solo between verses manages to avoid too much emotion. A later version recorded by prominent Italian pop singer Mina is less successful, milking emotion from the rather corny lyrics:

> Hold my wrists tightly together
> Tightly in your hands
> And even though my eyes are closed
> I'll see you with my heart.

> (1976:41)

The celebrated Italian jazz trumpeter Enrico Rava rather surprisingly included his jazzed-up, Latinized version of this song, with vocals by Barbara Casini, on his 1997 album *Italian Ballads*, recorded in New York. This placed Fo's humble song in the canonical company of Nino Rota's "Gelsomina" theme from Fellini's *La Strada* and "Un bel Dì"; Rota's theme from Fellini's *Juliet of the Spirits*; the aria "Vedremo" from Puccini's *Madama Butterfly*; the Neapolitan favorite "Return to Sorrento"; and Riz Ortolani's "More," the theme from the 1960s scandal film *Mondo Cane*.

"Non fare tilt" (Don't go into tilt), the opening song from *Gli arcangeli*, is also worth noting for its pop art style portrayal of Il Lungo and his gang as a group of petty criminals playing the city like a pinball machine. Late 1950s U.S. rock and roll influences are apparent, with jazzy brass and flute arrangements and a rhythmic jive-dance beat. Fo and Jannacci also collaborated on "La forza dell'amore" (The power of love), a Milanese version of "La Bamba," transposing names of streets and piazzas in Milan and absurd lyrics such as "un uomo incinto" (a pregnant man) for the nonsense Spanish lyrics of Ritchie Valens's Mexican American rock and roll adaptation of a traditional Mexican song. Another song from *Gli arcangeli*, which also has the distinction of being the first of Fo's plays to identify its protagonist with the *giullari*, "Fratelli d'ufficio" (Brothers of the office), is a satire on bureaucracy that parodies the Italian national anthem "Fratelli d'Italia."

Two songs have survived from Fo's early revue shows in 1953 and 1954 with Franco Parenti and Giustino Durano, both in versions by Jannacci. "Il primo furto non si scorda mai" (You never forget your first robbery), which featured in Fo's first revue, *Il dito nell'occhio* (A *Finger in the Eye*), is a jaunty, frantic cabaret-style song with a mock-flamenco opening and chickenlike vocalizations. It deals with a chicken thief who steals a turkey that turns out to be an eagle. The thief ends up in prison for insults to the Fascist regime (the eagle was a Fascist symbol). "Il taxi nero" (The black taxi) (1976:35–36) came from *I sani da legare* (A madhouse for the sane), a series of sketches satirizing everyday life in a big city. This was described by Nobel Prize-winning poet Salvatore Quasimodo as "a form of popular theater . . . recalling the late French decadent poets" (1954). "Il taxi nero" is basically an absurdist comic sketch in song form with a contemporary Milanese version of Cain and Abel. Abel is a taxi driver, Cain steals his tires, and Abel dies after one of his stolen tires explodes. Jannacci's recorded version (1990) is set to a tango beat by Carpi and even incorporates an accompaniment on spoons.

"Il taxi nero" anticipates the *povero cristo* (poor bastard) theme Binni identifies in Fo's early songs. This is also featured in another dialect song written by Fo in 1954 and performed by Jannacci, "T'ho cumprà i calzett de seda con la riga nera" (I bought you some silk stockings with black seams).[11] This song draws on wartime imagery to portray a pimp who buys his prostitute-girlfriend some silk stockings, and who is proud when she walks with him along the street "like a panther." But passersby call him a *pistola* (pimp), and he describes himself as a *povero cristo*, nailed to a cross, sitting in a cafe spending money as he watches his girlfriend ply her trade and try to make money in the piazza. The song ends with a defiant challenge to those who call him a "pimp," asserting that people who work all day long and support a wife are pimps too. But there is no self-pity in the jaunty, bouncy arrangement of the song, which resembles "La luna è una lampadina." Jannacci even breaks into a whistle before making the Christ analogy.

This song's controversial subject matter and its reference to Christ make it particularly bold for its time. The protagonist's apparent lack of remorse is conveyed with a sense of sympathy, as is his denigration of the institutions of work and marriage: This "poor bastard" is certainly no underdog. Indeed, he is much more assertive than other protagonists of Fo's "canzoni della mala" (songs of the criminal underworld). In "Hanno Ammazzato il Mario in Bicicletta" (They killed Mario on his bicycle; 1976:139–40), for example, the victim of a gang shooting is described as cycling to visit his girlfriend Lina when he is shot at from a tram. He is "hit right in the brain, pedals a few more times, then collapses like a calf after they give it its last blow." The song, which was recorded by Ornella Vanoni in 1959, goes on to present a brief biography of Mario, a petty thief who operated from a stolen bicycle, and who was responsible for killing a police superintendent with a bomb. But the graphic description of Mario's death, repeated in the final verse of the song, leaves a residue of sympathy for him despite his actions.

In "La sirena" (The siren; 1976:138), also recorded by Vanoni, there is similar sympathy for the victim of a police ambush. A woman describes sirens as the police race to the Corso Sempione in pursuit of her husband Nino "il Barbisa" (Nino with the Moustache), a criminal who has killed the chief of police, robbed trains, and sold stolen goods. The police have found him because his wife discovered him with a prostitute and threw him out of the house. When she arrives at the scene, she finds the police have shot and killed Nino, so she goes up to him, washes the blood off him, closes his eyes, and crosses his arms. Nino thus becomes a popular hero of proletarian urban legend.

A more comic variation on a criminal narrative occurs in "L'Armando" (1976:142), recorded by Jannacci as a jaunty, anachronistically cheerful ballad, with a final scat chorus. The protagonist is being interrogated by the police as a suspect for the murder of Armando, who has fallen to his death from a bridge. The suspect claims he has an alibi (in a restaurant in Jannacci's version, but just "went out" in Fo's original version). He goes on to say that he and Armando were like twins, even sharing the same woman, but that Armando used to hit him in the eyes with a hammer so that he would look less handsome and push him off a bridge into a dried-up river to amuse his friends. He admits that the knife found on the body was his and reiterates his alibi before letting slip that he pushed Armando out of the car (1976:138).

Affinities between Fo's early songs and his plays are inevitable. Many of the songs seem like miniplays that share a consistently abrasive, grotesque, and carnivalesque sense of comedy and a sympathy with the underdog, and poke fun at the police bourgeois respectability and authority in all its forms. They are also free of Marxist dogma, yet even the songs that lean most closely towards *musica leggera* (pop music) contain, in their performance by Fo or Jannacci, a sense of satiric and ironic theatricality that gives them an affiliation with cabaret and revue. But Fo has insisted that the tradition within which he worked in the early to mid-1950s was that of *avanspettacolo* (curtain-raiser), the musical variety shows performed between film screenings in the 1930s and 1940s, a tradition from which the great Roman film actress Anna Magnani also emerged. Fo has described this tradition as "flung out" (to the audience), involving considerable physical expression and "a popular element that consisted of the storyteller's visual narration" (1978:36). This element of physical narration is also present in most of the songs, and it involves a considerable degree of acting out. Nonetheless, Carpi's musical settings give them a self-contained sonic idiosyncrasy that helps them to stand alone as musical texts, rather than theatrical adjuncts to the plays. As Testa has pointed out, the *canzone* "lends itself considerably less than theater to being rendered in another language" (1996:19), which means that Fo's songs and Jannacci's recordings have received little attention outside Italy. Unfortunately, they have also been unjustifiably ignored in Italy, but it is hoped that in the rush to revive Fo's oeuvre in the wake of his 1997 Nobel Prize, the songs will not be neglected yet again. Fo and Jannacci's collaboration on a new song, "C'è la luna in mezzo al mare" (The moon in the middle of the sea), for Jannacci's 1998 album suggests a revival, as does Jannacci's weekly 1997 television program on Rai Uno and his appearance at the popular Sanremo song festival in 1998.

All translations are by the author.

Notes

I would like to thank Franco Minganti of the University of Bologna for his helpful comments and Antonio Scuderi and Joe Farrell for their editorial suggestions.

1. There is no mention of Fo, for example, in two of the standard texts on Italian song writing of the 1950s: *Cantocronache: Un' avventura politico-musicale degli anni cinquanta* and *Le canzoni della cattiva coscienza*. The only collection of texts of Fo's songs is in Fo 1976, edited by Lanfranco Binni (an updated reissue of a 1974 Bertani edition). It includes the lyrics of 103 of Fo's songs, most of them from his plays, but not "La luna è una lampadina." Binni includes the music of seven songs that were also composed by Fo (the final two of which are dealt with here): "La pojana," "Ancora una volta," "La rivoluzione la vincerò," "Canzone del cavallo bendato," "C'è chi dice che è un delitto di stato" (all written for plays between 1971 and 1973), as well as "La sirena" and "Hanno ammazzato il Mario in bicicletta." Fo and Jannacci are credited as cowriters on "L'Armando," "Veronica" (with Ciotti), "Sei minuti all'alba," "Il primo furto non si scorda mai," "Prete Liprando," and "T'ho cumprà i calzett de seda." The three editions of *Ci ragiono e canto* have also been published. Jannacci has recorded at least eighteen of Fo's songs (see Discography). Gianni Borgna's *Storia della canzone italiana* (1992) includes a few cryptic, passing references to Fo, citing *Ci ragiono e canto* (264; as an example of Il Nuovo Canzoniere's work rather than Fo's), Milly's version of "La brutta città" (269, 282), Vanoni's version of "Hanno ammazzato il Mario" (271), the singer Nada's role as Polly in *L'opera* (343), and Fo's collaboration with Jannacci (287), about whom he offers some analysis (285–88). His brief accounts of Jannacci's versions of "La luna è una lampadina" and "Vengo anch'io" (286) and citations of "Taxi nero," "Veronica," "L'Armando," and "Ho visto un re" do not even acknowledge Fo's authorship. Paolo Jacha's *La canzone d'autore italiana 1958–1997* (1998) includes Jannacci but not Fo among the

109 *autori* he considers, categorizing Jannacci's repertoire as comprising elements of rock, folk, jazz, funk/soul, and melodic tradition, but not pop. He gives him a five-star rating for "elements of innovation" (223). He also briefly discusses Fo's collaboration with Jannacci (74) and stylistic influence on both Jannacci and Giorgio Gaber (82).

2. Pasolini's (1995) songs are collected in versions by Laura Betti, Anna Nogara, Domenico Modugno, Daniela Davoli, Sergio Endrigo, Chetro and Co., Alice, Avion Travel, Giovanna Marini, and Fabrizio de André.

3. Binni, infuriatingly, does not cite dates for the early recordings by Fo and Jannacci.

4. See Mitchell (1995) for an analysis of Italian rap music and its relation to *recitativo*.

5. Testa follows the text of the lyrics in Jannacci's *Canzoni* (1980a).

6. There seems to be no recording of this song. I discovered it by chance on a tape of the music from *Aveva due pistole* in the Milan archives of La Comune in 1985.

7. In an interview with Antonio Scuderi (Fo 1993), Fo explained that this "ah be' sì be'" chorus was based on a type of Tuscan popular song, similar to the *canto sardo* (Sardinian song), in which a background drone of male voices rhythmically sings either onomatopoeic animal sounds or "bah bim bam bu." It should be pointed out that variations of "bim bam bu bah" are to be found in Italian children's songs and games as well.

8. The Miguel Bosé reference occurs in a rerecording of the song by Jannacci (1980b).

9. Fo's text of the song is in *Dario Fo: Ballate e canzoni* (1976:145–46); Jannacci's version is on the rerecorded album (1980b).

10. The lyrics in *Dario Fo: Ballate e canzoni* (1976) are in dialect (140–41) and Italian (158–59). Jannacci's *I successi di Enzo Jannacci* (1990) includes his recording of the song.

11. The lyrics in *Dario Fo: Ballate e canzoni* (1976) are in dialect (137–38) and Italian (157–58).

References

Bassetti, Sergio. 1991. "Alla voce giungla: Musica cinematografica italiana anni '90." *Segnocinema* (May–June).

Borgna, Gianni. 1992. *Storia della canzone italiana*. Milan: Mondadori.

Coveri, Lorenzo. 1996. "Lingua e dialetto nella canzone popolare italiana recente." In Dalmonte 1996.

Dalmonte, Rossana, ed. 1996. *Analisi e canzone*. Trento: Università degli Studi di Trento.

Fabbri, Franco. 1989. "The system of canzone in Italy Today." In *World Music and Social Change*, ed. Simon Frith. Manchester: Manchester UP.

Fiori, Umberto. 1996. "'In un supremo anelito.' L'idea di poesia nella canzone italiana." In Dalmonte 1996.

Fo, Dario. 1976. *Dario Fo: Ballate e canzoni*. Ed. Lanfranco Binni. Rome: Newton Compton.

———. 1977. *Ma che aspettate a batterci le mani*. Dischi Ricordi (Serie orizzonte). Recording.

———. 1978. "Dario Fo Explains." Interview by Luigi Ballerini and Giuseppe Risso. *The Drama Review* 22.1(March):34–48.

———. 1981. *L'opera dello sghignazzo*. Milan: La Comune.

121

■

"The
Moon Is a
Light Bulb"
and Other
Stories

———. 1993. Interviews by Antonio Scuderi (Milan). 9–20 October. Tape recording.
———. N.d. Le canzoni, vol. 1. La Comune. Recording.
Jacha, Paolo. 1998. La canzone d'autore italiana, 1958–1997. Milan: Feltrinelli.
Jannacci, Enzo. 1980a. Canzoni. Ed. Gianfranco Manfredi. Rome: Lato Side.
———. 1980b. Nuove registrazioni 1980. Dischi Ricordi. Recording.
———. 1990. I successi di Enzo Jannacci. International Joker Production. Recording.
Mitchell, Tony. 1986. Dario Fo: People's Court Jester. London: Methuen.
———. 1995. "Questions of Style: Notes on Italian Hip Hop." Popular Music 14(3).
Pasolini, Pier Paolo. 1973. Interview. Panorama (22 November).
———. 1995. Luna di giorno: Le canzoni di Pier Paolo Pasolini. BMG/Ricordi. Recording.
Quasimodo, Salvatore. 1954. Review. Tempo (1 July).
Rava, Enrico. 1997. Italian Ballads. Music Masters. Recording.
Scuderi, Antonio. 1998. Dario Fo and Popular Performance. Ottawa: Legas.
Testa, Carlo. 1996. "The Dialectics of Dialect: Enzo Jannacci and Existentialism." Ca-
nadian Journal of Italian Studies 19(29, 52).

Discography

Fo, Dario. 1977. Ma che aspettate a batterci le mani includes Fo's 1962 versions of "La
luna è una lampadina," "Il foruncolo," "Pianto dei piantatori di piante," and "La
brutta città."
———. N.d. Le canzoni, vol. 1, includes "Non fare tilt," "Fratelli d'ufficio," and "Stringimi forte i polsi."
Jannacci, Enzo. 1980. Nuove registrazioni 1980 includes "Vengo anch'io, tu no," "L'Armando, La luna è una lampadina," and "Ho visto un re."
———. 1990. I successi di Enzo Jannacci includes "L'Armando," "La luna è una lampadina," "Veronica," "Un taxi nero," "Sei minuti all'alba," "Il primo furto non si
scorda mai," "La forza dell'amore," "Prete Liprando e il giudizio di Dio," "T'ho
compraa i calzett de seda," "Un foruncolo," and "Sopra i vetri."
Rava, Enrico. 1997. Italian Ballads includes "Stringimi forte."

CHAPTER 7

Dario Fo's "Bourgeois Period"
Carnival and Criticism

BENT HOLM

S ince the late 1960s, when Dario Fo decided to transform himself from the *giullare della borghesia* (the jester of the bourgeoisie) into the *giullare del popolo* (the people's jester), there has been a tendency to consider all his previous activities as a kind of prehistory. In consequence, the 1957–67 period has come to be conventionally described as Fo's "bourgeois period," but this is an inadequate judgment, made with the benefit of hindsight.

The New Left of those years set itself the ambitious task of creating the world anew. According to this vision, anything previously existing was consigned to an uncertain sphere as a preliminary stage for what was to be. The problem with this approach, and with evaluations made on the basis of it, is that historical context and viewpoint are ignored or downplayed. In any consideration of Fo's "bourgeois period," the role of censorship as imposed by the Christian Democratic regime tends to be disregarded, as is the awkward fact that basic attitudes displayed by Fo, and the thematics of the plays written in this period, are far from bourgeois.

Even if Fo himself declared in 1968 that he had previously been the

"Alka-Seltzer," the *digestif,* of the bourgeoisie, there is every reason to take the historical-political context into account in any (long overdue) reconsideration of the 1960s as an autonomous period. This decade was the era of the Cold War in Europe and of Christian Democratic rule in Italy. The myth of the "bourgeois" Fo comes down to the fact that Fo in those years worked inside the conventional theatrical framework, the only one in existence at the time. Nobody would dream of calling Brecht a bourgeois playwright because his "epic" plays, such as *Life of*

Sketch for *Gli arcangeli non giocano a flipper* (*Archangels Don't Play Pinball*) by Dario Fo. (Courtesy C.T.F.R.).

Galileo or *Mother Courage,* as distinct from the ideologically more correct *Lehrstücke* (didactic plays), were written for traditional theaters. It
took the 1968 movement to create an "alternative" structure.

The 1960s was the period when Fo matured as a playwright, moving
from reviews, one-act farces, and film scripts to full-length plays. These
plays were produced by the Compagnia di prosa Fo-Rame, founded by
Fo and Franca Rame in 1959. In 1966, he directed *Ci ragiono e canto* (I
think things out and sing about them), based on research into the popular music tradition. This show represented a break with conventional
theatrical concepts of staging techniques and use of space (and pointed
to such later works as the 1969 one-man show *Mistero buffo* [Comic
mystery]). In 1967, the explicit political satire of *La signora è da buttare*
(Toss the Lady Out) made a move from conventional structures inevitable. That break occurred in 1968, with *Grande pantomima con bandiere e pupazzi piccoli e medi* (Grand pantomime with flags and small
and medium-sized puppets), a satirical panorama of postwar Italian history presented in "alternative" venues—the *case del popolo,*[1] or facto-
ries. The post-1968 company, Nuova Scena, was established as a private
club, which meant, at least in theory, that censorship could not be imposed and that the police could be denied entrance from the performing
spaces. The company's style of expression changed: It played to an audience that was already politically engaged, but the move in subject matter from *La signora* to *Grande pantomima* was, in fact, very small.

There was a definite pattern to the 1957–67 period, with one premiere per year at the Odeon in Milan. The exceptions were *La signora,*
which had its debut at the Manzoni, Milan, *Ci ragiono e canto,* which
premiered in Turin, and the adaptation of a Georges Michel play, given
the title *La passeggiata della domenica* (The Sunday stroll), which was
given its first production at the Teatro Durini, Milan. Normally, the productions contained music, song, and choreographed movement.

First Comedies

Fo presented his first full-length comedy, *Gli arcangeli non giocano
a flipper (Archangels Don't Play Pinball),* in 1959. The work has an
episodic and associative structure, in part a reflection of Fo's recent cinema experiences, and in part due to the fact that the work is an account
of a dream by the main character following a blow to the head. The

protagonist is a kind of *giullare* (jester) in a gang of semicriminal youths, who make him believe he is to marry a beautiful woman, who turns out to be a prostitute. After a series of chase scenes, executed in a style that had echoes of burlesque or harlequinade, and episodes that subject bureaucracy and authority to satire, he wakes up in time for his wedding. The satiric content and direct language of the play were viewed with suspicion by the authorities. From a theatrical point of view, the work represented a renewal of the comedy genre, mixing song, choreography, stylization, gags, and satire with the undemanding tradition of theater-as-entertainment.

The following year, 1960, Fo staged *Aveva due pistole con gli occhi bianchi e neri (He Had Two Pistols with White and Black Eyes)*, which has, even by Fo's standards, a highly complex plot. The play is set in the post–World War I period and opens in a hospital. The main character is a patient suffering from amnesia, later revealed to be a priest. The complication is that he has a double, a ruthless gangster, the two being played by the same actor. The priest is taken "home" by the gangster's lover, who believes the patient to be her partner, but this leads to complications when the real gangster comes on the scene. The priest is held prisoner by the gangster to provide an alibi for his criminal activities. In the course of a shoot-out with the police, one of the two is killed, and for some time, the audience is convinced that the gangster had killed the priest. In a further twist, the criminals declare a strike against society, which, unable to function in the absence of crime, is driven to negotiate. It transpires that it was the gangster who had been killed by the priest and the priest who had conducted the war on society.

The play on identity is of almost Pirandellian sophistication, although more of a logical and less of a metaphysical order. The main character is akin to Brecht's Macheath from *Threepenny Opera*, and as in Brecht, the official and criminal worlds are linked. In Fo's comedy, the priest-gangster double suggests connivance between the ultraconservative ("black") forces and the political-Catholic ("white") rulers. The introductory stage directions describe the hospital as resembling a monastery; it is peopled by doctors, one of whom is a military man, and by nurses who wear "on top of their white outfit . . . cloaks also in white, with a red cross sewn onto the dress at the height of the left shoulder, in the style of the Knights of Malta" (Fo 1966a:97) (The ecclesiastical outfit is said to be the dress of the future.) The dramatic universe, an implied portrait of contemporary Italy, suggests an insane society run by quasi-Fascist, Christian (Democratic) characters. It is interesting to note that the gangster-priest goes through a "death" experience, after which, when he declares his subversive project, all the bandits wear "carnival noses." Besides being an ecclesiastical-political figure, he is a kind of madman or anarchist operating in the upside-down dimension of comedy.

In the 1961 play *Chi ruba un piede è fortunato in amore* (Whoever steals a foot is lucky in love), the satire is veiled but undeniable. Of all Fo's comedies, this comes closest to conventional theater. There are no songs, the environment is upper bourgeois, and the plot slightly piquant, but the underlying concern with "social" themes is unmistakable. Class differences make any union between the two principal characters, a taxi driver named Apollo and an upper-class lady named Daphne, impossible. The ancient myth is reenacted, with the ingenuous taxi driver, Apollo, making off at the end with the plant, which he believes to be his transformed Daphne. There may be an echo of the don Calogero of Eduardo de Filippo's *Grand Magic*, in which the husband believes he has a box containing the wife, who has "disappeared," but the use of the myth as the basis of the comedy is another reminder of the formative influence on Fo of the storytellers *(fabulatori)* of Lake Maggiore. However, in spite of the light comedy tone, the work satirizes corruption scandals, and the blood transfusion sketch, depicting the donation of blood from the lower to the upper class, continues the ironic glance at class differentiation. The taxi driver, being a blood donor, happens to know his blood type. The society lady, Daphne, who is going to receive his blood, reacts uncertainly: "A blood donor? You? Congratulations. That's very nice, highly altruistic." The taxi driver replies:

> I did not do it out of altruism. I was in Switzerland, and I was out of work . . . and since they paid something like three thousand lire a liter, I put my name down. But then I discovered I was losing out. With three thousand lire, I couldn't even make up a quarter of the blood I was donating. So I threw in the towel and came back to Italy. (Fo 1966a:239)

The allegory is clear, without being overdemonstrative. The seemingly realistic situation is combined skillfully with such archaic and anarchic images of "a world upside down" as the supposed pregnancy of the male, achieved by having the taxi driver attached to a blood transfusion machine so as to share the symptoms of his beloved Daphne. In the end, it is revealed to be a trick of his to enable him to stay close to her.

Isabella, tre caravelle e un cacciaballe

Sources and Plot

In 1963, Fo staged *Isabella, tre caravelle e un cacciaballe* (*Isabella, Three Sailing Ships, and a Con Man*), a grand, satirical portrait of Christopher Columbus, the "con man" of the title. Apart from sketches of world history, performed back in 1953 in *Il dito nell'occhio* (*A Finger in the Eye*), *Isabella* was Fo's first historical play. The style was noticeably different from that of the preceding comedies. The work contains a number of songs, partly integrated into the dramatic situations, partly a comment on them. The choice of topic, with its satirical treatment of a national hero, was in itself controversial, and the reaction from the Right was largely hostile.

The opening scene features an actor condemned to death because of his irreverent choice of repertoire. There are initiatives underway to have the death penalty commuted, and before being executed, he is allowed to present, on the scaffold, the play of Columbus. The play within a play follows Columbus's complex maneuvers to obtain finance for his expedition. The rulers are depicted as grotesque and childish, even if Isabella emerges as an intelligent person in a complex situation. Columbus, who is far from honest, steals and lies to attain his goal. The trial of Columbus on his return involves a number of flashbacks, each presented in a different key, depending on the perspective of the various agents involved. In the end, no mercy is accorded to the poor actor. Columbus realizes that an alliance with the rulers is impossible, and he himself is offered as a sacrificial lamb. The actor lays his head on the block. The execution is carried out by means of an old theatrical device. The stage directions read:

> The executioner raises the axe. All kneel. Darkness. In the darkness, the shouts of the crowd are heard. The lights go up: the severed head of the condemned man appears on the block. The condemned man, minus his head, is standing next to the block and

lays a hand on his own severed head. It is a trick, and can be seen to be such. (Fo 1966b:86)

In dramatic terms, *Gli arcangeli* is a dream, told in a cinematic style, involving a return to the point of departure; as such, it obeys its own "logic." The following comedies, even if grotesque and paradoxical, respect a kind of rational structure, although *La signora* draws in style and structure on the revue and the circus. The real innovation with *Isabella* is the structural experiment, the attempt to give voice to varying points of view, all reminiscent of such works as Brecht's *The Measures Taken*. Similarly, Fo features a range of testimonies in the various flashbacks, with the result that they lose the value of objective truth otherwise associated with that technique, especially when employed in cinema. The basic fiction is that of the condemned actor, and inside that fiction, the play within a play unfolds. The play within a play is watched by an "audience" who experiences on the scaffold-stage events from thirty years previous, the whole combined with yet another level, that is, the reality known to the contemporary, 1963, audience, which includes the prevailing political reality of the Francoist regime in Spain. This almost Pirandellian toying with illusions is, to an extent, repeated later, in 1983, with *Coppia aperta, quasi spalancata (Open Couple)*. It exemplifies Fo's delight in the demolition of the "fourth wall," always central to bourgeois theater. Fo's technique, unlike that of Pirandello, is not aimed at the negation of objective reality but is a method of inducing in the audience a level of analytic awareness, and it is thus closer to Brechtian concepts. The final and basic layer of illusion is the implicit reference to Italian reality in general and specifically to Fo's own situation. We will return to this point.

The distortion of a myth points back to Fo's earliest period. Fo has spoken many times of his debt to the *fabulatori*, the storytellers he had known in his childhood, describing their repertoire as surreal, grotesque, and disrespectful. His breakthrough as writer and performer came with *Poer nano* (Poor sod), a series of monologues created for Italian radio. Conceived in the manner of the *fabulatori*, these works took as their subject, and treated subversively, such figures as Hamlet, Samson and Delilah, and Romulus and Remus, not to mention Columbus himself. Similarly, mythological references, to Apollo and Daphne in *Chi ruba un piede* or to Aeneas in *Settimo: ruba un po' meno (Seventh Commandment:*

Steal a Bit Less), underlie some of Fo's plays, but this is myth twisted in irreverent ways. Perhaps the Rigoletto story in the *Poer nano* series, with its account of the *giullare* sacrificed, may be viewed as a foretaste of the Columbus comedy (Pizza 1996:154n).

In the *Poer nano* version of the Columbus story (Pizza 1996:150n), the hero is described as a little boy who has a passion for eggs, and who wants to go to America. He fails to raise money for his project in Italy and, therefore, goes to see Ferdinand and Isabella in Spain. The queen is depicted as beautiful and arrogant, the king as foolish and oppressed, and Columbus as imprudent, characteristics they were to have in the play. The characterizations in the monologue can be viewed as a sketch for the same parts in *Isabella*. In the story, Columbus, like a traveling salesman, sells his project to the queen, emphasizing that he needs only "twelve caravels." His famous egg experiment ends up in confusion, with the queen's dress stained. "Take your caravels and never let me see you again! Get out!" she screams.[2]

Political Context

One of the favorite devices of the *fabulatore* was to tell one story through another, or to devise a complex system of allusions and suggestions and leave the audience to create its own tale. The choice of subject for *Isabella* was controversial in itself, given the status of Christopher Columbus in Italy as quasi-national myth, and given Fo's notorious lack of reverence, but the political context, the background to the creation of the text, was just as important. The portrait of a dark, Catholic Spain in the fifteenth and sixteenth centuries is evidently a transferred portrait of twentieth-century Italy, subject to restrictions and censorship. The church and clergymen are, in Fo's comedies, synonymous with the regime, as instanced by the introductory stage directions, quoted above, for *Aveva due pistole*, which give a portrait of the country as a psychiatric hospital in the hands of some military-ecclesiastical clique.

The early 1960s in Italy was the period of the *apertura a sinistra* (opening to the left). In 1960, the dominant Christian Democratic Party, then led by Fernando Tambroni, had turned to the neo-Fascist MSI for support in creating a government coalition, but the move led to widespread revolts in several Italian cities, especially Genoa, and the initiative was dropped. Instead, Amintore Fanfani invited the Socialist Party to abandon its alliance with the Communist Party and enter government.

Discussions dragged on, and it was only in 1963 that the *apertura a sinistra* was completed, with the formation of a Center-Left government. The Christian Democratic Party remained the strongest party, but pressures for social reforms were difficult to ignore. The hopes placed in the Center-Left alliance were enormous and, perhaps, exaggerated. This was the period of growing prosperity later tagged the "economic miracle," and general democratic reform of the state was expected. The possibility of creating a Scandinavian-type welfare state was floated, and reforms in the judicial, health, fiscal, and many other fields were planned. In a broader context, the whole operation was seen by some as an attempt to recreate the national unity the Resistance movement had aimed at creating.

There were, on the other hand, fears expressed in some sections of the Left over the use to which the newly acquired power of the Socialists would be put and concern that the Socialists would be dragged into the existing system of state influence and patronage. In the event, the Socialist Party acquired political responsibility, but the optimistic expectations were disappointed, and few concrete results were achieved. The Socialist Party went down to a heavy defeat in the 1968 elections.

The Christian Democratic Party was made up of a number of factions, whose shifting internal strength determined the direction of Italian politics as a whole. The party's left wing conceived the notion of *apertura*, but it was the right wing that brought it into being. It would be absurd to claim a perfect analogy between *Isabella* and the prevailing political conditions, but it is the case that Fo's depiction of the centers of power in the comedy is two sided. Queen Isabella takes a relatively more enlightened and positive position in relation to Columbus's request for support, while Ferdinand is shown as reactionary to the point of paranoia.

In the cultural area, *apertura* brought about, in 1962, abolition of preventive censorship, although cultural freedom could be restricted by other means. One of the most significant theater productions after the abolition of censorship was Giorgio Strehler's staging at the Piccolo theater in Milan of Brecht's *Life of Galileo*. The critical image of the church given in *Galileo* meant that it had not been possible to present that work before. It is natural to relate *Isabella* to *Galileo*. Thematically, there are interesting relations between the two dramas, presented a few hundred yards from each other in two theaters in Milan. *Galileo* deals with the relationship of the intellectual, or of the scientist, to power and rulers, a theme that had gained new urgency with the new Center-Left alliance.

Personal Background and *Canzonissima*

As a consequence of the climate created by the *apertura*, Fo had been invited to present a popular TV entertainment program, *Canzonissima*. Fo saw the invitation as an opportunity to use the institution as a platform for communicating his own views. At the outset, an agreement had been struck that there should be no censorship, so Fo and Rame began performing the kind of satirical sketches that had been agreed upon. The network's directors began to grow uneasy, and the crunch came over a sketch concerning building workers' safety at a time when a strike was in progress in that sector. The cancellation of that sketch caused Fo and Rame to walk off the set a few minutes before the program was scheduled for transmission. The move made headlines all over Italy.

In some interesting notes written in 1962 on the basis of the *Canzonissima* experience, Fo reflected on his own relationship with people in authority. He saw the possible advantages in his alliance with the broadcasting institution, but also the risks.

I said to myself, ah-ha! here we go, be careful. Instead I fell for it . . . RAI [the Italian state broadcasting body] . . . put me into the position where I had to ask—do I go or do I stay? At one point, I thought—that's it, I'm off. Then I thought—no, if I do that I'm playing into their hands, I'm giving in. (Fo 1992:23)

Later, Fo emphasized there were connections between the thinking behind *Isabella* and the situation created by the Center-Left alliance, especially with regard to the role of intellectuals. As he told Chiara Valentini:

When I wrote *Isabella, Three Sailing Ships, and a Con Man*, there were many things I wanted to say. I wanted to attack those intellectuals involved with the Center-Left and the Socialist party who had discovered power and its attractions, and who threw themselves at it like mice onto cheese. I wanted to expose a character . . . who's out to . . . toy with the king, to act smart with people in power and who, unfailingly, ends up trapped and reduced to the status of the *povero cristo* [poor soul]. (Valentini 1977:85)

This is in line with what he wrote in 1977:

> Everything hinges on the intellectual coming to a state of aware-ness in his relationship with classes and their struggles, on the at-titude of the intellectual towards power. It also involves the duty of radical choice and the denunciation of the intellectual who al-ways manages to adapt and who tries to find his own space when-ever people in power issue the summons. (Fo 1977:11)

These were the terms he used in his (very) explicit political period, but there may be a degree of oversimplification involved, a tendency to focus on one aspect of a complex dramatic and thematic structure. No doubt the comedy is a generalized portrait of the relationship of politi-cally progressive forces—especially of the intellectuals among them—to power, but it is also based on very personal experiences with the establishment. It debates the classic dilemma over staying "outside"—outside influence and power—in order to remain free from the risk of being compromised or, alternatively, of attempting to obtain influence and so running the risk of selling one's soul. The final tableau, which has the executed actor standing beside the block on which Fo's own head is resting, represents a coherent conclusion, underlined by the paradoxical words of the closing song, which state that the opportunist is not as smart as the honest man. The honest man makes common cause with the *poveri cristi* and constitutes a greater threat to the rulers. The man who enters the power structure and makes tactical alliances—as Fo's Columbus did with the Spanish court and Fo himself did with state-run television—will inevitably end up neutralized or devoured.

Fo operated as an independent artist in theater, not as part of an official system, even if postwar Italy had set up *teatri stabili* (public thea-ters). Giorgio Strehler had been a key player in that process, but Fo has often been critical toward Strehler's strategy (Fo 1992:42). The *Canzon-issima* episode implied integration in a system but ended in a confusion over who was using whom. It did, on the other hand, give Fo the advan-tage of contact with a mass audience, and this in the longer term eased the way for the growth of his independent theater. However, although

Isabella addresses these issues, the play moves on more than one level and contains more than mere political allegory.

Carnivalism

The basic situation of the comedy is carnivalesque. The set includes, among other things, an *albero della cuccagna* (greasy pole) and a scaffold. The stage directions make reference both to James Ensor and to Goya, both of whom have painted carnival scenes. Ensor painted an *Entry of Christ into Brussels*, which evidently was a source of inspiration for Fo.

Carnival derives from a pre-Christian rite of passage in the annual cycle of nature that was, up until recently, celebrated in many parts of Europe. It often included a purging of the community's misdeeds and negative behavior through a symbolic trial and execution. This was followed by a celebration of "rebirth" into a new period. The rite was centered on the person of Carnival, an ambiguous figure who represented the king of misrule, served as scapegoat, and thus embodied a liberation from the past and the hope for a better future. As a whole, Carnival implied the anarchic reign of the "fool," who criticized and created chaos in the normal order, and who would then be put on trial for a number of crimes. He was permitted to proclaim his last will and testament—a satirical unmasking and criticism of the community—and was then symbolically executed. The character in question was sometimes represented by a puppet but, more often than not, was enacted by a member of the community. With the execution of the Carnival figure, the period of festive anarchy was replaced by a return to "normality" and to the repressive order, which became "Lent" in the Christian context.

In his function as scapegoat, the Carnival figure incarnated all that is negative from the standpoint of official society. Much of the same may be said about the *giullare*-Columbus. The actor in Fo's comedy is a controversial figure facing execution. The play on the scaffold, including the trial of the protagonist, may be seen as a "last will." It is, like the popular "Carnival testament" itself, a satirical portrayal-revelation of society and of the crimes of rulers. The crimes of which the protagonist are accused are exaggerated ad absurdum. He is made the scapegoat for all manner of misdeeds. In the end, he is eliminated.

In *Isabella*, a number of scapegoats are indicated—the heretic *giullare*, Christopher Columbus, Carnival, and Christ—and in a sense, they merge. At the end, Columbus, who now embraces the *giullare*-Carnival, is reduced to the status of *povero cristo*, on the same level as other *poveri cristi* mentioned in the final song. The *Canzone del Dàlli, Dàlli, Dàlli, Dàlli, Dàlli,* the song in the closing section of act 1, also talks about *poveri cristi*. The Conservatives, which here means the mob and/or the pillars of society (an evident reference to the Christian Democratic Party), sing that their symbol of power, the cross, is a reminder that "it will be the end of every *povero cristo*," as it is for Columbus and the *giullare*. In the second act, Columbus is supplied with an alter ego in the shape of the mad and obscene Giovanna. Madness in this sense has overtones of the magical and the demonic, a combination that recalls Christ and the madman in *Mistero buffo*. The execution is ritualistic. Fo's image of Columbus as the intellectual opportunist is modified considerably by the ritual implications of the act.

A number of grotesque bodily elements and deformations—the pregnant queen used as a globe, the martial use of chamber pots as helmets—might point to Mikhail Bakhtin, although his work was not published in Western Europe until 1968. (In *Mistero buffo*, there appears to be evidence of Bakhtin's influence.) Laughter, profanation, the grotesque body, the dialectics of birth and death or death and resurrection, the relationship to the underworld, and the use of obscenity are all traits typical of popular culture—and also of Fo's own dramatic universe. Research into carnival had already been carried out by Paolo Toschi in his fundamental study of the origins of Italian theater (1955). Fo brought carnivalism into his comedies at an early stage. In that perspective, *Isabella* could be read as a fully developed Carnival rite, but it is appropriate to add that Fo's style and structure are based on intuition as well as on research. Fo's universe and perception of the world are as they are thanks to his own background and instincts. His outlook could be described, for those with similar tastes, as Rabelaisian. He once told me that from the beginning, he simply wrote as he wished, instinctively, and only later on, having studied writers like Toschi, did he begin to do so consciously,

A stock structure in many of Fo's texts is the situation in which the main character finds himself/herself under pressure and receives assistance from a phantasm-figure, who functions as a kind of emanation or double. The main character undergoes a kind of symbolic death-rebirth and undertakes a mental transformation. This kind of "helper" figure is common in, among other things, popular fairy tales. In Fo, he may be a ghost, a mad person, or the like. In *Settimo*, it is the *feretrofobo* (coffin-maniac); in "La nascita del giullare" ("The Birth of the Jongleur"), it is Jesus; in *Storia della tigre (The Tale of the Tiger)*, it is the tiger; and in *Abbiamo tutte le stessa storia (Same Old Story)*, it is the naughty puppet. On a symbolic level, that figure is integral to the character, as expressed in the final monologue of *Isabella*: "I nostri . . . siamo noi" (We are our own helpers). The relationship between the more fatalistic Columbus and rebellious Giovanna the Madwoman has similar connotations, as has that of Jesus and the madman in *Mistero buffo*. One could also point to the madwoman as a double of the Madonna in *Mistero buffo* or to the madman in *Morte accidentale di un anarchico (Accidental Death of an Anarchist)*, who is in a way a representative of the sacrificed anarchist. The madman introduces an upside-down justice, a doomsday, and ends up being blown to pieces (in one version of the farce); he thus, in himself, bears traits of a carnival figure.

These two structures, carnival and fairy tale, never appear in their "pure" form in Fo's work; they are often either interwoven together or make a fragmentary appearance. The "mythical" structure of such works as *Isabella* merges, in a complementary symbiosis, with the political allegory, producing a theatrical discourse that is simultaneously clear and ambiguous.

Comparison with *Life of Galileo*: Conclusion

As already stated, *Isabella* was performed at the same time as the Piccolo Teatro's production of the *Life of Galileo*. There are connections. The thematic overlap has already been discussed, and one could point to a generally pragmatic attitude, including a certain relaxed relationship to truth, in both Columbus and Galileo. There are also a number of more external similarities. In *Galileo*, the washstand used as the sun in an astronomic demonstration, the apple made to represent the earth, and the protagonist's act of deception with the eyeglass that he pretends to have invented are all devices that have their counterparts in, for instance, Columbus's more grotesque use of an apple, candle, and female bosom to demonstrate the structure of the universe to the Spanish court, and his trick with Toscanelli's stolen map. There are other moments of greater or lesser importance: In *Galileo*, one of the town councilors focuses on food with the "new" eyeglass and becomes immediately hungry, just as Columbus's demonstration of the "pear-shaped" earth provokes general appetite among his audience and leads to an offer of sandwiches. The cross-examination of Galileo recalls the long interviews of Columbus, although these, as usual in Fo, are transformed into the grotesque.

The parallel in subject matter, the relationship of the intellectual to power, is of primary importance. Fo himself made the comment on the comparison of his character with Galileo: "We are dealing with two opposing characters. My 'con man' is a child of his age, a man of incredible courage who employs his own weapons against the powerful in order to survive. He is not someone who dreams of scientific conquests, but a sailor from Genoa who thinks about finding the shortest route to the Indies for concrete reasons" (Nepoti and Cappa 1997:56). In an interview in connection with the premiere, he stated that

> someone who had lived as a saint, or as an adventurer, would not have stolen Toscanelli's map from the King of Portugal's archives, would not have told a series of lies to Isabella and would not have compromised a stack of courtiers. And so he would never have managed to get himself the three caravels, to become Christopher Columbus and discover America. (Valentini 1977:86)

In the light of later character judgments, quoted above, portraying Columbus in purely negative terms, this positive judgment and Fo's emphasis on Columbus's courage are worthy of comment. It can be taken as an indication of a certain relativity in the character of Columbus and perhaps of some flexibility in the author's statements.

Brecht is paradoxical, his hero is an antihero. Fo's Columbus is not only a visionary, intelligent, and creative character—as such a "hero"—but also in many ways a negative figure, or at least one who is in the wrong. The final picture, already mentioned, of Fo's own head on the block brings together the different aspects—political, personal, historical, and ritualistic. Thus, in the ending, we see, among other things, a pragmatic character, who mixes with the powerful and is executed. He is in some ways similar to Brecht's *schlau* (crafty, clever) type who, in consequence of his antiheroism, secures the survival and spread of truth, except that as a consequence of his collaboration with the mighty, Columbus is destroyed. Galileo is seen in a paradoxical light, not in a satirical light, as is Columbus. To a certain extent, the two plays seem to reach opposite conclusions from similar premises. Fo's message is clear, expressed in the final song. Columbus-*giullare* learns his lesson too late, which is why he has to perish. On the other hand, or on another level, Columbus is evidently not an unambiguously negative figure, as it is he who undermines the unjust ruling order. Perhaps he represents an infantile stratum in humanity, that of the fool and the child. His ruin is not, in that perspective, satisfactory. In other words, these two levels contradict but do not exclude each other; they may even be viewed as complementary. The contradictions generate a series of doubts and uncertainties in the spectator. Is, for example, the character naïve or cynical? There is no final answer, and analysis is left to the cocreative efforts of the audience.

Deeper paradoxes are created by contradictions between the political and the mythological levels, even if these levels interact harmoniously onstage. The audience is required to complete the picture, a process that corresponds with Fo's conception of epic theater. The open structure is dialogical, with space for improvisation and interpretation.

Later Plays

With the 1964 play *Settimo*, Fo returned to the vein of satirical comedy, portraying a contemporary Italy submerged in corruption and scandal. The early scenes are set in a churchyard that is the workplace of a naïve, female grave digger, Enea (Aeneas), who forms an alliance with a supposedly dead businessman. The plot, an account of a coming to consciousness, follows Enea through a multiplicity of intrigues that see her take on a role as a prostitute and later dress as a nun in a convent that is also a psychiatric hospital. The choice of ecclesiastical psychiatric hospital as an image of Italian society is reminiscent of the opening of *Aveva due pistole*. This image of regimentation is made even more forceful by the prospect facing the patients of a form of brainwashing, or brain drilling, by trephine to reduce them to a state of compliance, as happens to the "coffin-maniac" at the end, after he has told the truth about the scandals wracking the country.

The only exception is Enea, a madwoman of a type often used by Fo as a symbol of the people. The very name, Enea (which had been mistaken for a feminine name by her father, since it ends with the letter *a*), is an instance of the overturning or downgrading of myth, the same model used in *Poer nano*. The reference is plainly to Virgil's hero, whose escape at the fall of Troy led to the foundation of Rome and, by extension, of Italy. But the association of that name, which seems to give

Enea a role as founder of a future order, with a mad alcoholic female grave digger is arresting. The structure of carnivalesque ritual underlies, once more, the farcical plot. The businessman, Arnaldo Nascimbene, who assists Enea in her development, is an ambiguous character. He is neutralized, leaving her to continue the liberation mission. Dramatically, his pacification is only vaguely motivated, but ritually, it is absolutely coherent: He is made a sacrificial victim. As was the case with the gangster-priest of *Aveva due pistole*, or indeed with Columbus, one cannot assign *tout court* tags of "good" or "bad" to the role. A study of earlier versions of the text only adds to the impression of the futility of any attempt at ethical categorization.

The words of the title of this comedy, "ruba un po' meno" (steal a bit less), entered general usage in Italy, so much so that Fo ironically claimed author's rights over Tangentopoli, the series of political-financial scandals uncovered by the Milan magistrates in the mid-1990s. Previously, in an 1977 interview on the occasion of the televised version of the comedy, Fo pointed to its prophetic quality: "The aeroplane fraud, which is one of the gags in this play, became reality with the Lockheed affair" (Fo 1992:250). In fact, there is no mention of aircraft in the original version; Fo is an ingenious *fabulatore*.

With the 1965 *La colpa è sempre del diavolo* (Always blame the devil), Fo is more explicitly political. In this play, a farce set in the Middle Ages concerning a dukedom's relation to a mighty imperial protector, Fo chooses a subject and structure from history. The duke is threatened at home by the *communitards*, a movement of peasants dedicated to an ideal of poverty. The references to Italy's domestic and international position throughout could scarcely be more clear, although there is the addition of a number of near-surreal, complex intrigues featuring, among other things, a supposed witch as well as the duke and a devil. It ends with an ironically depicted massacre on the *communitards* and the triumph of the rulers. The final scene shows the imperial troops invading the stage, but as mechanical puppets.

In 1966, Fo made a first step out of conventional theater structures when he directed *Ci ragiono e canto*, premiered at Teatro Carignano, Turin. This production was mounted in collaboration with the group of researchers and artists known as *Il nuovo canzoniere italiano*. The group's performance work was based on research into the tradition of popular song and music, which, on this occasion, they invited Fo to transform into stage rhythms. The formula employed is the one Fo used in many of his productions, from his early one-act farces based on the

Rame family repertory to his version of Ruzzante in 1995. He transforms and recreates traditional material into an unmistakably Fo work, sometimes presenting this operation as one that liberates the real, deeper content.

With *La signora*, which premiered in 1967 at the Manzoni Theater in Milan, Fo moved toward the abolition of plot in any conventional sense in favor of a fool-play of an Aristophanic inventiveness and crudity. Subtitled a comedy *per soli clowns* (for clowns alone), the work takes place in a circus framework, and for the performance, Fo invited clowns from two well-known circus families, the Vitali and the Colombaioni, to participate. The play was a step in the direction of choral structure and represents a deepening of Fo's wish to present history from the point of view of madmen, fools, or clowns. The plot concerns the succession of two "ladies," both played by Rame, in the management of a circus. The Old Lady dies and is followed by the Young Lady (John F. Kennedy), who is killed and succeeded by an ambiguous "lady," played by a male actor. There is no need to belabor the allusions to American history, or the wider portrait contained in the play of Western culture in the 1960s. A riot of music and choreographed movement, *La signora* is a culmination of Fo's work in nonrealistic, total theater. It avoids overt statement or mechanical imitation of external reality and chooses to work with suggestions and allusions, inviting the audience to create its own images. There are, in the vision of history as seen from below, links to Fo's early work, notably *Poer nano* and *Il dito nell'occhio*, while in a wider perspective, this style of satirical theater harks back to Meyerhold and Piscator. Meaning is established by the invitation to the audience to look beyond the circus spectacle, a technique that was to become increasingly characteristic of Fo's theater, with *Mistero buffo* as the supreme exemplar. Images were produced by means of allusion, allegory, or analogy, or all three simultaneously. At one level, *La signora* contains an elimination theme, which has deep roots in popular ritual. The old hag is dressed like the *Befana*, the "witch" of the Italian feast of the Epiphany. The plot includes parodic doctor scenes and mock wills and testaments, all ending with the clowns' expulsion of the "lady," a man in woman's dress. These details are implicitly related to carnivalistic structures and produce patterns of meaning on different levels. They also smash conventional expectations of "political" theater.

After this production, Fo abandoned conventional structures altogether and declared himself the "people's jester." However, it has to be underlined that throughout the so-called "bourgeois period," Fo was on one hand subject to certain restrictions and on the other prepared to systematically violate these restrictions. The political climate and context itself underwent profound changes during these years, and Fo's point of departure with *Il dito nell'occhio* had been anything but bourgeois.

It is of undeniable importance to focus on the political ideas in Fo's theater, but even when these seem clearly and strongly stated, there are other textual levels—fairy tale, myth, and magic—that should not be ignored. There is, in Bakhtin's terminology, a level of dialogism present that causes the total picture to fluctuate and the various levels to interact, producing striking ambiguities. Little has been written on the metaphoric dimension of Fo's work. He is conventionally viewed as a producer of light comedy, or as an exponent of political theater, or as some problematic combination of the two. There is, however, a further dimension and a flow of images that are both of a more universal value than the political parable. It is probably the presence of these other elements that explains why the plays can be moved from their original context, and why some of them will surely remain, in the longer perspective, classics.

The 1979 play *Storia della tigre*, for instance, follows a scheme that is not unusual in Fo, that of the protagonist's transition to another state of consciousness via a kind of death and rebirth, already touched upon in connection with the popular structures in *Isabella*. The *Storia della tigre* is a tale with a Chinese subject, telling of a soldier shot in the leg and who, although at the point of death, forces his way through a storm to a cave, only to discover that the inhabitants are a mother tiger and her cub. An odd ménage à trois is established: The soldier sucks the tiger's bursting breasts, and the tiger cub licks the soldier's gangrene wound, while he is forced to fry meat for them. He makes his escape by river back to the human world, where he is received as a walking dead or a ghost. The tigers follow him and are pressed into service to help the village people against the enemy. When the number of tigers is shown to be inadequate, they assist in the creation of "imitation tigers."

A deeper examination of the operation of the images reveals that the protagonist experiences "death" and initiates his transformation by passing through water into a cave. Initially, the cave, filled with bones, has connotations of death, but its sexual overtones—the tiger that licks him, the focus on the cub's testicles, and the narrator's own erotic dream—become stronger. Further, a fire is lit in the cave, and the tigers eat "his"

flesh, creating a complex of images of intercourse and reciprocal com-
munion. The creatures "absorb" each other. Residence in a cave-uterus
leads to a new birth through water, but at a later stage, he is seen as a
ghost, a member of the "living dead," someone possessing a magical
power he can share among others by use of carnival masks (powerful
references to the "other" dimension). Fo's poster drawing for this monologue shows the narrator, complete with the tiger mask, in exactly the
same position as the *giullare* in the sketch of himself, which Fo uses as
the symbol of his theater. The narrator has undergone a metamorphosis
to become half man, half tiger, man with tiger in himself, exercising a
superhuman power.

Later, in the 1974 "La nascita del giullare," the poor peasant on the
point of suicide receives a ritual, initiatory kiss from Jesus, which transforms him into the *giullare,* the artist who is in contact with deeper,
perhaps mystical, forces, and who is able to give expression to pain and
outrage. These patterns, portraying transformation caused by mystical
contact with a subhuman or superhuman dimension, can be found in
different periods of Fo's development. They can be traced back through
Fo's production to the monologues and farces that were his earliest
scripts. The presence of these deep structures mean that his theater has
the capacity to transcend categories of "bourgeois" or "political."

All translations are by Joseph Farrell.

Notes

1. The *case del popolo* were the local meeting and activity centers run by the
Italian Communist Party.

2. Much in the same vein as the legend of George Washington and the cherry
tree, there is a European legend about Columbus at the Spanish court. When certain
dinner guests tried to discredit the validity of his historic voyage, he challenged them to
stand an egg on its end. When none could, he demonstrated how it is done by first tap-
ping the end flat, thus making this point: "Of course it is easy, once someone shows you
how it is done" (editor's note).

References

Fo, Dario. 1966–98. *Le commedie di Dario Fo.* 13 vols. to date. Turin: Einaudi.

———. 1966a. *Aveva due pistole con gli occhi bianchi e neri.* In Fo 1966–98, Vol. 1,
93–179.

———. 1966b. *Isabella, tre caravelle e un cacciaballe.* In Fo 1966– 98, Vol. 2, 2–86.

———. 1977. *Il teatro politico di Dario Fo: La censura fallita.* Ed. G. A. Cibotto. Milan:
Mazzotta.

———. 1992. *Fabulazzo*. Ed. Lorenzo Ruggiero and Walter Valeri. Milan: Kaos.

Nepoti, Roberto, and Marina Cappa. 1997. *Dario Fo*. 2nd ed. Rome: Gremese.

Pizza, Marisa. 1996. *Il gesto, la parola, l'azione: poetica, drammaturgia e storia dei mono-loghi di Dario Fo*. Rome: Bulzoni Editore.

Toschi, Paolo. 1955. *Le origini del teatro italiano*. Turin: Einaudi.

Valentini, Chiara. 1977. *La Storia di Dario Fo*. Milan: Feltrinelli.

CHAPTER 8

Morte accidentale in English

JENNIFER LORCH

"N owhere is the impossibility of translation so evident as in the theater" (Fitzpatrick and Sawszak 1995:15). Not only does the rendering of a theatrical text into a target language and culture carry with it the problems generally associated with translation—freedom versus faithfulness, the relation of language to culture, the integration of metaphor and subtext—it also has to take into account the added factor of a physical recreation, a performance.[1] There is a place for drama translation: Plays are read as well as performed, and a translator is able to provide a text that is linguistically closer to the original than a version for the theater and can thus refer the reader back to the source text within its own culture. A theater text, however, presupposes performance. In translating fiction or poetry, notions of faithfulness are usually a priority, whereas in the theater, "performability" often takes precedence to enable the text to "work" on the stage. Theatrical texts require theatrical versions, and translators, those invisible and modest handmaids, cannot provide the goods (see Venuti 1995). So the provision of the theatrical text in English is often a double process: the literal translation of the words and sense followed by the theatrical rendering of this intermediary translation. And more often than not this second process renders its maker ostensible rather than invisible; s/he becomes cocreator rather than modest handmaid. This is clearly the case with *Morte acci-dentale di un anarchico (Accidental Death of an Anarchist)*.

Further considerations arise from the various kinds of theater texts. Here I am not referring to genre, such as tragedy, comedy, or farce (though these too provide their own set of problems), but to the status of the text. What place does the text have in the structure of theatrical performance? At one end of the scale, there is text as "original," as "holy writ," dominating all other elements, actors, director, and designer, whose function it is to understand and interpret the text. Pirandello was the arch exponent of this view, even regretting that there had to be "translation" of his creations onto the stage, let alone translation into another language and culture. "Unfortunately there always has to be a third, unavoidable element that intrudes between the dramatic author and his creation in the material being of the performance: the actor" (1993:27). Beckett and Pinter, though working happily with ac-tors, claimed possession of their texts, as various incidents concern-ing the presentation of their plays have indicated (see Billington 1994; Billington 1996:237–40; Lane 1973).[2] At the other end of the scale, the text is so ephemeral that it is remade at each performance, in the manner of a *commedia dell'arte* scenario. Put differently, in a language that befits a society concerned with ownership: To whom does the text belong? The answer to this question will influence translation strategies.

Compared to the aforementioned literary playwrights, Dario Fo is relaxed about his relationship with his text but not so relaxed as to have no attachment to his work. He follows the vicissitudes of his "throwaway theater" with a keen interest. In the continuing debate of "whose text is it?" Fo has sided strongly with the actors, suggesting that they learn "to invent roles for themselves . . . to learn to be authors. . . . *All* actors should do this" (D'Aponte 1989:537). Pirandello had been attracted to improvisation; he considered it as potentially "pure" theater because it provided an unmediated theatrical text closest to his ideal of theater as "being," rather than text that is "translated" onto the stage, but reluc-tantly rejected improvisation because it was "trivial" and could not be "that ideal simplification and concentration of the superior work of art" (1993:34). Fo's approach to theater is dominated by different concerns; for him, the choice of improvisational theater is political rather than aes-thetic "because improvisational theater is never finished, never a closed case, always open-ended . . . [it] is open on an intellectual level." Im-provisational theater is not just a question of a technique of theater making; it is a "theater of ideas" (D'Aponte 1989:537). And it is of the nature of ideas that they are always developing. Fo continually alters his scripts to take into account new historical or political events, suggestions not only from the actors but also from audiences (Cowan 1979:11).

Morte Accidentale in Translation

These notions concerning improvisation are particularly relevant to versions of *Morte accidentale*, which shares with other Fo texts of the 1970s a unique political immediacy and specificity. There are texts that are so topical, so enmeshed in their immediate cultural and political context, that a "faithful" translation is only of use as an explanation of their source culture. *Morte accidentale* is one of these. Anger at the unjust death of Pinelli and the equally unjust imprisonment of Valpreda and the *frisson* evoked by the closeness between the theatrical script and the real-life performance in the courtroom where the Calabresi/Bandelli libel case was being staged cannot be repeated (see Cederna 1971:55–85; Lorch 1997:29). The same holds true for the effect of the presence of Fo in the key role of the 1970 Madman; his presence within the character endorsed the ideas the Madman expressed, and the character protected Fo from having the ideas ascribed to him (see Fo 1973:190; Lorch 1997:26). Performances of a later period have to seek other ways of making the play cohere, and one of the solutions adopted by all versions is an improvisational response to the present political moment. This may be the reason why there are already six English versions of the play, as many, that is, as there are of the 1921 modernist classic *Six Characters in Search of an Author*.

Of the six English versions, four have been used in performance: those by Gavin Richards (adapted from a translation by Gillian Hanna), Richard Nelson (based on Suzanne Cowan's), Tim Supple and Alan Cumming, and Robin Archer's adaptation of this last for the Australian stage. The remaining two, by Suzanne Cowan and Ed Emery, have not, as far as I know, been presented on the stage. This does not imply that the language they have used in their versions is unstageworthy, for both in their different idioms provide colloquial, speakable scripts. It does mean, however, that their versions can be, and are, closer to the Italian versions than those that have been performed and that therefore they are of use to those wanting closer access to the source text.

Richards, Cowan, and Nelson base their versions on the 1973 Italian text; Supple and Cumming (and, of course, Archer) and Ed Emery base theirs on the 1974 Italian text. The 1973 and 1974 texts vary in two main ways. The 1973 text of the play emphasized the framing device, claiming to be transferring an event that happened in 1921 in New York to Milan to make the incident more credible to an Italian audience. This cheeky device was all but dropped in the 1974 version. The two texts also had different endings. In the 1973 text, Bertozzo succeeds in unmasking the Matto, handcuffing his colleagues and the journalist to the coat stand. But the Matto reveals that the bomb in his bag is no facsimile, unarms Bertozzo, and handcuffs him to the coat stand with the others. He tells them he will creep away, having set the lever on the bomb, and if they so much as move, it will explode in such a way as to leave not a trace of them. The lights go out, and there is a prolonged scream, followed by an explosion. When the lights come on again, the Madman has disappeared. The journalist manages to slip off her handcuffs and reports from the window that there is a crowd of people around a man down below; the assumption is that the Madman has fallen from the window. But the actor who played that part appears at the door, this time differently dressed and with a bristly black beard and a great stomach. The policemen rush toward him, dragging the coat stand with them, grabbing at his beard, only to find that the beard is real and that they are attacking the judge, Antonio Garassinti, who has come to conduct the enquiry.

The circular structure of this version, with its sense of unresolved spiraling, a fitting analogue to the experience of those involved in attempting to find out what had actually happened in the fourth floor room of the Milan police station, is cut in the 1974 version. The play ends with the Matto having taken the bomb from his bag, picking up the keys to the handcuffs and the pistol dropped at his command by Bertozzo, and declaiming the same words that occurred earlier in the previous version:

> Who cares a damn? What matters is that the scandal explodes! *Nolimus aut velimus.* So that the Italian people, like the American and English, can become social democratic and modern and can finally say, "We're in the shit right up to our necks, true enough, and that's the reason why we can walk with our heads held high."
> (1974)

This ending releases the play from the agitprop immediacy of the Pinelli and Valpreda affairs and emphasizes the socialist critique of capitalism, indicated in earlier parts of the play and clarified in the final pages with the references to American and English culture. The last image of the play is not of a bearded, paunchy judge settling down to another investigation but of the Madman disguised as a bishop holding a pistol to the policemen.

As Suzanne Cowan has observed, Fo's language in *Morte acciden-tale* "comes very close to the everyday spoken vernacular employed by a people throughout northern Italy, but with a particular inflection and cadence characteristic of the region around Milan" (1979:11). In this play, Fo does not use dialect expressions, but his language is colored by expressive idioms, popular slang, and frequent puns. It is a fast moving, energetic dramatic prose that gains its effect less by vulgarisms than by being strongly verbal and by the frequent use of consonantal clusters beginning with the sibilant *s*, for instance, *sferrare* (to land a blow), *sfot-tuto* (fucked about), *sfruttare* (to exploit), *sghignazzo* (scornful laugh-ter), *stracciare* (to tear up), *stronzata* (bullshit), and *strumento* (instru-ment). As can be seen by the individual translations of these words, only some convey a similar energy in English, and this difference gives some indication of the problems facing a translator. Unlike Stuart Hood, who, in his translations of Fo, has provided "a plain language text" with the suggestion that "actors and directors should find their own solutions" (1989:344), thus endorsing Fo's own approach to actors as creators, all the versions of *Morte accidentale* attempt to provide a colloquially in-flected script. As Cowan and Emery are providing versions that priori-tize meaning over "performability," they are able to use footnotes when a pun or reference resists translation.[3] Others must either omit or at-tempt to find an English or American equivalence.

Something of the process of translating the play can be deduced from the note that prefaces Richard Nelson's adaptation:

The version printed in this volume was first created by Richard Nelson in 1983 for a production at Arena Stage. His adaptation was based on Suzanne Cowan's literal translation, published in *Theater Magazine* in 1979. For the Arena Stage production and the sub-sequent Broadway production, both directed by Douglas Wager, Nelson revised the dialogue for the American stage, and added some references to current politics. Dario Fo approved his adaptation. Subsequently, Fo asked for further changes in the text, which were made by Ron Jenkins and Joel Schechter, in collaboration with Fo and Franca Rame. His changes included some new political references, and dialogue closer in meaning to that of the original Italian text. These changes were made with the consent of Richard Nelson, who remains credited as the American adaptor of the play. Future productions of the text may require further alteration of political references, unless our President is elected for a life term, and outlives the century. (1987:6)

As is to be expected, the texts differ from one another because they come from different linguistic cultures. For instance, the Italian phrase *'sto disgraziato* (1973; 1974) is rendered as "the shit" (Richards), "that sonofabitch" (Cowan and Nelson), "bastard" (Cumming and Supple), and "the bastard" (Emery); *mondo bastardo* (1973; 1974), omitted in Richards, is rendered as "Lousy goddam world!" (Cowan and Nelson), "It's a sick world" (Cumming and Supple), and "what a bastard world!" (Emery). Other choices have less to do with linguistic culture and more with interpretation. There are three words used to translate the name given to the main character, Il Matto: "Maniac" (Richards and Emery), "Madman" (Cumming and Supple), and "Fool" (Cowan and Nelson). These translations influence how the character is viewed: "Fool" carries associations of innocence and jesting, as well as of stupidity, and links with Fo's *giullare* figure; "maniac" provides undertones of obsession; and "madman" provides undertones of insanity. This last is probably the closest to Fo's term, *matto*, which is also used to denote someone who is clinically insane, which the character claims for himself. Richards's choice of Maniac is, however, defensible as a description of the character he has created whom the journalist recognizes as Paulo Davidovitch Gandolpho at the end of the play (see below). Another clear choice on the part of the adapters is the song the Madman forces the police officers to sing at the end of act 1, scene 1: In the Italian texts, this is the anarchist song; Nelson and Cumming and Supple opt for the *Internationale*.[4] Given the fact that Fo was involved in both the Nelson and Cumming and Supple versions, it would seem that this is a choice that he made, or a least approved, perhaps because the *Internationale* carries more resonance in English-speaking countries than the anarchist song and contributes to the socialist theme. Other changes relate to the different theater cultures (Fitzpatrick and Sawszak 1995:27). As mentioned earlier, Fo

created the role for himself. Certain long speeches not only carry important meaning, they are also vehicles for Fo's particular form of entertainment. An obvious example is the one in which he assumes the role of a judge and tries out his various "walks" and speech characteristics. This is maintained as a set piece by Richards, but it is shortened, and stage directions are included. Other monologues, however, are altered to create a more dialogic structure, as has been noted by Fitzpatrick and Sawszak (1995:25–28), thereby taking the focus off the Maniac and allowing for more ensemble acting than in the original. In the "shoe scene," the Maniac disappears from the dialogue altogether, and the police admit to having pushed the anarchist out of the window by their own buffoonery (see Fitzpatrick and Sawszak 1995:27).

The Play in Performance

Translated plays that are staged enter the target culture and begin to assume a life of their own within it. Some also maintain a relationship with their culture of origin. In all cases, the knowledge that the writer came or comes from another culture has some bearing on how the plays are viewed by their target culture spectators, though it is difficult to pinpoint just what the difference is. Chekhov, for instance, has been appropriated by the English, who tend to see his plays through the "filter of the English class system" (Bassnett 1998:91). Most spectators, however, know that Chekhov was Russian — the "strangeness" of the names of the characters alerts them into an awareness of "otherness" — and this knowledge governs some of their responses.

Accidental Death of an Anarchist has kept its distinction as an Italian play while developing a separate life in its English target culture. Its first production stands at a crucial point in the development of British alternative theater.[5] The Belt and Braces Roadshow Company staged it as a touring production, with its opening night at the Barn Theater at Dartington College of Arts, Totnes, Devon, on Friday, 9 February 1979. Dartington College, which offers degree programs in music, theater, and the performing arts, was known at the time for its innovative visiting theater program. The next visitor to the Barn Theater was Caryl Churchill's *Cloud Nine*. After touring, *Accidental Death* transferred to the Half Moon Theater in the East End of London in October of the same year. This theater, a converted synagogue on Alie Street, was one of a number of small London theaters (including the Bush, the Soho Poly, and the King's Head) that arrived "on the tide of late and post sixties idealism that related high artistic standards to a determined political conviction" (Burrows 1981:70).

The Belt and Braces Roadshow Company, one of a number of politically committed alternative theater groups of the 1970s, was created in 1973 by Gavin Richards, when Ken Campbell asked him to take over the Ken Campbell Roadshow (see Craig 1980; Itzin 1980a, 1980b; Mac-Lennan 1990). Previously, Richards had worked at the Liverpool Everyman Theater, when John McGrath of 7.84 was writing for it.[6] Griffiths was an early member of 7.84 and acted in and directed the controversial *Ballygombeen Bequest* (by John Arden and Margeretta D'Arcy) in 1972. After that production and two years on the road, some members of 7.84 left, and it was at this point that Gavin Richards joined the Roadshow. By 1979, and with some seven productions and a European tour behind them, the company was well equipped to undertake a presentation of *Accidental Death*. They had developed a policy: "to strive to present an entertainment that is articulate and socialist" (Itzin 1980a:200); and they had worked out a performance style. Like Fo himself, they were influenced, as were a number of the alternative theater groups of the time, by Brecht. *The Mother* was a popular influence after the impressive performance of it at the Half Moon Theater in 1973.

Gavin Richards based his version of *Morte accidentale* on the 1973 Italian text, provided in a literal translation by Gillian Hanna. Setting the play in Milan provides a frame in this English version. He altered the last part of the play, however, producing alternative endings that polarized the political argument. The Madman (in this version referred to throughout as the Maniac) removes his disguise and is recognized by the journalist as Paulo Davidovitch Gandolpho. He gives the journalist a choice:

> Here. Have you the stomach for this? There's the keys to the handcuffs. I'm off. You can't chuck the bomb out of the window, it's a public street. So . . . Release them, write your story, but the evidence will die with me and this bunch will undoubtedly be acquitted. Don't release them and you become my accomplice—you join the ranks of the extremists. It's all yours. (Richards 1989:73; ellipses in the original)

The Maniac speaks to the audience as it waits to see what the journalist, Miss Feletti, decides to do. She turns and bolts for the door. There is an explosion in which the policemen perish. The Maniac then offers his second ending, to "satisfy the drama critics." This time Miss Feletti unlocks the handcuffs, but the policemen, realizing that she knows everything, tie her to the window frame and run for it. The play, constructed as confrontation from the Left, ends with the Maniac's challenge to the audience, which polarizes the choices open to the spectators: "Oh *Dio!* Whichever way it goes, you see, you've got to decide. Goodnight" (Richards 1989:73).

In the Italian play, Fo achieved effect through reference to one topical incident that provided the political focus. Gavin Richards's version keeps the title and the incident but attempts to compensate for lack of immediacy by introducing a range of political references. There is a wider range of allusion in the 1979–80 version than in any other. They include President Carter, the Thorpe conspiracy, Blair Peach, Watergate, David Frost, Anthony Blunt, Guy Burgess, Pinochet, Chile, Allende, Paris in 1968, Kent State University, and even a feminist reference to Fo's nearly all male cast. There was a British focus, however. A stage direction reads: "detailed examples of political murder and state repression in Britain." The large and informative theater program provided further information on "suicides" in British prisons, with a particular focus on Ireland, an article on Blair Peach's death, and graphic pictures of police brutality. In fact, about half the program is about miscarriage of justice in Britain, the other half being dedicated to an explanation of the Italian situation, that is, the Valpreda and Pinelli affair and the "strategy of tension." The import of both the production and the program was the possibility of a similar incident in Britain. "The story of *Accidental Death of an Anarchist* may be more akin to 'The British Way of Life' than many people would like to admit" (Belt and Braces 1979:5).

The Italian production of the play also had a specific focus because the central character was a vehicle for Fo's particular comic talents. Clearly no other actor, whether Italian or English, can repeat the experience of Fo's acting of the role. In Alfred Molina, who first took this role, however, there were certain positive analogies that contributed to the favorable reception of the production. His theatrical experience was wide: as a comic in variety theater and as an actor with the Royal Shakespeare Company, the Royal Court Theater, and the community theater in Deptford (the Albany Empire). He had also recently gained wider recognition and popularity through his role in the comic television show *The Losers*, on ATV. Both right- and left-wing critics acclaimed Molina's performance as The Maniac. For Sheridan Morley (1979), he was "a consistent and utter joy and the best knockabout farceur to have arrived in our midst in a very long time." John Barber (1979) commented on his "delightful energy" and Michael Billington (1979) on his "wonderful performance," characterizing him as "the dynamo that gives this production its *commedia dell'arte* fizz" and likening him to "Tommy Cooper on speed." Molina's success in this part served him well; he received the Most Promising New Actor Award for his performance and went on to be a successful actor on both stage and screen.

This first English production of *Accidental Death* was also well received as a farce. Sheridan Morley (1979) entitled his review "Full Marx" and asked readers to "imagine the Marx Brothers running a documentary enquiry into the death of Blair Peach," to understand what the play was like. Michael Billington (1979) suggested "Brothers Marx, Karl and Groucho have been working in unison." However, although all reviewers provided an explanation of the Italian source, they were more interested in the play as a farce than as a political catalyst. John Barber of the *Daily Telegraph* (1979) could not be expected to sympathize with the message of the play ("The wild Left-wing ravings . . . make little impact"), but he did enjoy his evening out. He refers to Fo's "beautifully constructed farce" and "a performance of delightful energy." From this first production, the Italian play became part of British and world culture. Both Sheridan Morley and Michael Billington had mentioned Tommy Cooper, and Morley refers to *The Government Inspector*.

Richards's production of *Accidental Death* was timely. Farce, so often denigrated as a "low" form of theater, was coming into its on. Orton's *Loot* and *What the Butler Saw*, and other new farces, showed that farce could be a successful political weapon. It was recognized that farce was not only Brian Rix and vaudeville. Its combination of logic, situation, and humor rendered it an ideal means of conveying thought in the theater, with the result that Gavin Richards's version of the Italian farce not only became assimilated into British culture but also was an influence on that culture (Hastings 1979:12).

The influence of *Accidental Death* was not exhausted, however, with its role in alternative left-wing theater. It also became involved in the economic decline of British entertainment. The situation is not without irony. In 1968, Fo had left the commercial circuit in Italy because, as he put it, he no longer wished to be jester to the bourgeoisie. It was that decision—and the even more radical one, two years later, when he felt no longer able to use the playing places of the Italian Communist Party because his thinking had moved to the left of official party thinking—that contributed to the theatrical context of *Accidental Death*. Its limited set and its third act as a debate with the audience stem from the alternative theatrical environment that Fo was creating at the time.

In 1980, this situation was reversed. *Accidental Death* came to the London West End. The increase in VAT (value-added tax), the recession, inflation, and the accompanying decrease in tourists were making life difficult for commercial theater. Ready-made shows that had proved to be popular were welcome in the West End. *Accidental Death* transferred to the Wyndham's Theater in March of 1980, with Gavin Richards now in the lead role (Radin 1980). It attracted a greater range of reviewers and included those who were willing to put up with the politics of the last part of the play as "the price of the immense pleasure given by the previous two hours" (Young 1980). Some reviewers, such as James Fenton (1981) and Michael Billington (1980), sensed (or knew) that the play had been better elsewhere. The cultural references increased, giving the play an even greater foothold in British and world culture. These now included Zuckermayer's *Captain of Koepernick* (Wardle 1980), variety theater, and the Crazy Gang (Young 1980). But perhaps the most notable result of the transfer (along with other plays such as *Clouds, Bodies,* and *Gloo Joo*) was the gradual loss of subsidies from the Arts Council. The success of the English version of Fo's radical play, which in Italy was an example of counterinformation and counterculture, contributed to the economic crisis of alternative theater in Britain. The final words of Sheridan Morley's 1979 review herald the dark future:

> True, the threatened Arts Council cutbacks (by no means yet confirmed) are appalling, but it ill behooves a company having achieved such an anarchically good box-office success to turn round and demand public money for it. Belt and Braces does after all indicate some form of self-support.

If in 1980 Fo's political farce had been incorporated by the impecunious West End, in 1991 it moved even further into the bastions of established culture. It was staged by the National Theater, no less, even if in its minor theater, the Cottlesloe. The Royal National Theater Education Department mounted the new production as one of their mobile tours. Previous tours had included Molière's *Tartuffe*, Wesker's *Roots*, Hare's *Fansen*, and Brecht's *The Mother*. Tim Supple and Alan Cummings created the new version using a more literal translation from the Italian. In interviews, they reiterated the differences between their version and that of Gavin Richards, but it is not clear whether they were aware that the literal version they were working from was a translation of the 1974 rather than the 1973 Italian text.

The script was the result of a collaboration between director Tim Supple and Scots actor Alan Cumming in the leading role, because as Supple explained, "Whoever was playing the madman would have to inject a lot of his own thoughts and language, because it is such a personal kind of characterization" (Burnett 1990). Preparations included a visit from Fo, who gave Alan Cumming "a few gags"; help from Lord Denning, who gave them "some extra material"; and attendance at some rehearsals from Paul Hill from the Guildford Four. ("He came in and told us all these dreadful things that had happened to him and we were in hysterics because it was so funny. We realized that was what the play was all about, that mixture of farce and tragedy" [Burnett 1990].) Supple and Cumming were determined not to commit what they saw as the mistakes of the Belt and Braces production. They "had increased the comedy and generalized the political comment. It became a debate within the left. But the play is a provocation *from* the left. It's not an abstract debate" (Bardsley 1991). In contrast to Gavin Richards, Supple and Cumming attempted a cultural transfer, by dressing and playing the text as though set in England. In addition, while in 1979–80 the police had been presented as a savagely comic troupe, each policeman was now differentiated into a credible person. Tim Potter's Inspector Bertozzo, Trevor Cooper as the Superintendent bulging uncomfortably from his ill-cut suit, Lorcan Cranitich as the thuggish Inspector Pisani, and Mark Benton as the plump eager-to-please Constable were all distinguishable characters (Hutcheon 1991).

This version of the play did not figure so prominently in the history of British drama as did the Belt and Braces production. Despite good publicity before and during the tour, reception was mixed. Two reviews

while on tour sum this up. At the Alhambra Studio in Bradford, it was
attended by the committed Left: "For one evening at least it was possible
to believe that the Tory decade has never happened. The Bradford Left
had emerged from the ghetto to celebrate its favorite play" (Smith 1990).
At the Gardner Center, in Brighton, Martin Holye for the *Times* found
the experience "oddly unfunny" (Hoyle 1990). Michael Billington, who
had so enjoyed and appreciated the Half Moon version of the play, concluded that what he saw at the Cottlesloe was "Fo shrewdly updated but
without his carnivalesque danger" (1991). By now, English writing about
Fo carried an air of authority; the reviewers "knew" how Fo should
be played. For them, the 1979–80 version had taken on an air of authenticity. Clare Bayley, writing in *What's On*, speaks with assurance:

> Fo's polemical diatribes, which sometimes grate, have been cur-
> tailed thus retaining their political punch, while the pantomime
> style farce is kept tightly under wraps, except for one brief loss of
> control in the second half. Fo is an Italian who was writing during
> those heady days of the 70's and it is hardly surprising if some of
> the exuberance is hard for a 90's British audience, but Supple has
> managed to achieve a necessary sophistication without losing the
> vitality and anarchic humor that characterizes Fo. (1991)

Here again there is some irony, for it is well known that Fo was critical of the Gavin Richards production, which Bayley is claiming as pure
Fo. In the author's note to the printed text, he commented on the omis-
sions that he considered "may have produced some erosion at a satirical
level, that is to say, in the relationship of the tragic to the grotesque,
which was the foundation of the original work, in favor of solutions
that are exclusively comic" (Richards 1989). David Hirst compared the
Richards text with the 1973 Italian version and showed conclusively that
the tight control and discipline exercised by Fo through his long education in comic techniques was not matched by Richards. Some gags were
exaggerated, made more visual than in the Italian version, and the language was made "ruder" (e.g., "a fucking good laugh" and "in his grave
right now pissing himself"); some of the political meaning was reduced
by cuts (Hirst 1989:73–81).

In fact, the whole Richards version is characterized by a lack of faith
in Fo's words, which are either rammed home by vulgarisms or substituted by visual gags. An example is the disguise assumed by the Maniac

when the woman journalist arrives. In Fo's 1973 version, the Matto, already in the role of Marco Maria Malipiero, the investigating judge from the court of appeal, hastily disguises himself as Captain Marcantonio Piccinni of the forensic office, ostensibly to help his colleagues in the police force deal with the journalist's questions. The disguise initially consisted of a large moustache, an eye patch, and a wooden hand clothed in a brown leather glove. Later in the scene it transpires that the captain also has a wooden leg. In the course of the proceedings, his glass eye falls out, his hand comes apart, and Bertozzo removes his false leg, conveying through farcical means a visual representation of the literal deconstruction of power (Wing 1990:148). In Richards's text, the disguise is increased to include glasses, a wild wig, a crutch, and, during the run of the production, a parrot. Fo's carefully constructed semiotic point becomes an exaggerated comic gag (see Fo 1973:167; Richards 1989:50; Hirst 1989:50–52).

Susan Bassnett has pointed out that much of the language of translation is characterized by the notion of "loss," and it is tempting to see Richards's version of Fo's play in this light (1998:91). Despite the strong political commitment of the Belt and Braces Roadshow Company, it did not achieve what Fo saw as an essential element of his political theater, that is, that it should avoid catharsis and leave its audiences in a state of unrelieved anger (Fo 1973:189; Lorch 1997:29–30). It is important to remember, however, that Richards's version found a niche in British culture of the early 1980s that was not matched by the reception of Cumming and Supple's in the early 1990s, despite being closer to the Italian text and more authentically English, though not fulfilling the rash and impossible claim to see "Italy through a British filter and so to see both clearly" (1991:xxiv).

Some comparisons can be made between the North American and English experience of the play. *Accidental Death* played to full houses at the Eureka Theater in San Francisco in 1984, with comic actor and clown, Geoff Hoyle, in the role of the Madman. Like Alfred Molina, Hoyle found that taking the lead in the play had a positive influence on his future; he went on to make an impressive career in both theater and film (D'Aponte 1989:541). For the Arena Theater production in Washington, D.C., Douglas Wager cast the theater's popular actor Richard Bauer; when it moved to Broadway (Belasco Theater), as the English fringe production had moved to the West End, the British actor Jonathan Pryce took over the role in the short Broadway run. In each of these productions, the direction concentrated on the comedy and sought to adapt the play to the American context. But here the comparisons stop, for although there have been unpopular productions in North America (one, the U.S. premiere at the Mark Taper Forum in Los Angeles, in 1983, adapted by John Lahr, directed by Mel Shapiro, with Ned Beatty as the Fool; and another, the Canadian premiere by R. G. Davis at the Open Theatre, Toronto, 1979, with Allan Royal as the Fool), none have concentrated on making the political ideas accessible. No North American production presented the play with the left-wing commitment of the Belt and Braces Company (Davis 1986:315–18; D'Aponte 1989:541; Mitchell 1999:297–303).

I would suggest, however, that it is not possible to produce a version of this play that aims both to be faithful to the author's intentions of the period and to make of it a viable play for the English/American stage, whether fringe or mainstream. The gulf between the two political cultures is too great. Fo's play was presented to audiences in a country that boasted the largest Communist Party in Europe at a moment when a socialist revolution was believed to be possible. This is a situation not likely to be repeated in the foreseeable future, and it was definitely not what pertained in the United States and England at the beginning of the 1980s, the first years of Margaret Thatcher's long "reign." Nevertheless, Richards's version created a place for itself in the history of English theater that no other English or American production of this play is likely to challenge.

And it did so by adopting a particular style of presentation quite different from that of Fo and his Collettivo, as a comparison of the illustrations of the 1970–71 Italian production and this first English production reveal.[7] The pictures of the English production show a gang of undifferentiated policemen, a comic chorus of men with heavily accentuated eyebrows and Hitler moustaches; illustrations of the Maniac show him with his mouth wide open, aggressively shouting. Pictures of the first Italian production, on the other hand, show a relaxed, almost laconic Fo as a bishop with a pistol and a forensic officer with an eye patch; the only illustration with his mouth open is of him laughing genially during the telephone call to Bertozzo in part 1; and the policemen are all individualized. These illustrations indicate that the Italian production was played within the tradition of naturalism and that the English production owed its style to a form of expressionism, a kind of anglicized version of *commedia dell'arte* mentioned in the Belt and Braces

Roadshow program and in Billington's review (1991). The choice of acting style is at least as problematic as the political ideas for directors wishing to present this much-translated but transfer-resistant Italian play.

All unattributed translations are by the author.

Notes

I would like to thank those people who have shared their knowledge of theater and translation with me and answered specific queries: university colleagues Clive Barker, Susan Bassnett, Joe Farrell, and Tony Howard; librarians and archivists Lucy Bartlett of High Cross House, Totnes, Devon; Jonathan Gray of the Theater Museum, London; Caroline Hayman of Totnes Museum; and Richard Taylor of Dartington College. I would also like to draw the reader's attention to the updated and expanded version of Tony Mitchell's *Dario Fo: People's Court Jester*, which was published between the completion of this article and the arrival of the page proofs.

1. In a recent contribution to debates on translation studies, Susan Bassnett refers to theater translation as the "most problematic and neglected area of translation studies" (1998:90). It is the "added factor" of performance that renders the area so problematic.

2. One incident concerned the production of *Footfalls* in 1994, when director Deborah Warner was refused permission by the Beckett estate to direct Beckett's plays in the future because she had not adhered strictly enough to the stage directions in the play (Billington 1994). Another concerned Visconti's production of Pinter's play *Old Times*. An angry Pinter told a press conference: "I have never heard of or witnessed a production such as this that is totally indifferent to the intentions of the author or that introduces such grave and shocking distortions and that I consider a travesty." He went on to list liberties taken by the director with reference to the sexual subtext of the play and ended with: "All the acts I have referred to are not only inexpressibly vulgar in themselves but are totally against the spirit and intention [of the play]" (Billington 1996:237–40).

3. "In those cases where it was impossible to find even a remote English equivalent, I simply translated the text and explained the joke in a footnote" (Cowan 1979:11).

4. The *Internationale* is a proletarian song or hymn originally written by E. Pottier in the days of the French Commune and later set to music by P. Degueyter in 1888. It was used as the official song or hymn of the Soviet Union from 1917 to 1944.

5. For information about British alternative theater, see Craig 1980; Itzin 1980a, 1980b; MacLennan 1990; Mitchell 1999:248–70.

6. The name 7.84 reflects McGrath's Marxist commitment: "Seven percent of the population owns 84 percent of the wealth."

7. For illustrations of the Italian production, see Fo 1973:291–92; Cappa and Nepoti 1982:90–92. For illustrations for the Richards production, see Belt and Braces 1979:5; the cover to Richards 1980; *Dartington Hall News and South Devon Scene* 1979; Radin 1980; Tisdall 1980.

References

Barber, John. 1979. "Outrageous satire on police graft." *Daily Telegraph* (London), 17 October.

Bardsley, Barney. 1991. "Farce." *City Limits* (London), 3–10 January.

Bassnett, Susan. 1998. "Still Trapped in the Labyrinth: Further Reflections on Translation and Theater." In *Constructing Cultures*, ed. Susan Bassnett and André Lefevere, 90–108. Philadelphia: MultiLingual Matters.

Bassnett, Susan, and Jennifer Lorch. 1993. *Luigi Pirandello in the Theater. A Documentary Record*. Chur, Switzerland: Harwood Academic Publishers.

Bayley, Clare. 1991. "Dead Funny." *What's On* (London), 16 January.

Belt and Braces. 1979. "Accidental Death of an Anarchist." Belt and Braces Roadshow Company Ltd. Theater program.

Billington, Michael. 1979. "Accidental Death of an Anarchist." *Guardian* (London), 5 October.

———. 1980. "Accidental Death of an Anarchist." *Guardian* (London), 7 March.

———. 1991. "Farce Forfeit." *Guardian* (London), 9 January.

———. 1994. "Footfault." *Guardian* (London), 22 March.

———. 1996. *The Life and Work of Harold Pinter*. London: Faber and Faber.

Burnett, Andrew. 1990. "Rebirth of an Anarchist." *List* (Edinburgh), 26 October.

Burrows, Jill. 1981. "Quick Theater Guide: Half Moon." *Plays and Players* (November):70–71.

Cappa, Marina, and Roberto Nepoti. 1982. *Dario Fo*. Rome: Cremese Editore.

Cederna, Camilla. 1971. *Pinelli: Una finestra sulla strage*. Milan: Feltrinelli Editore.

Cowan, Suzanne, trans. 1979. "Accidental Death of an Anarchist." *Theater* 10.2 (Spring):13–46.

Craig, Sandy. 1980. "Unmasking the Lie: Political Theater." In *Dreams and Reconstructions: Alternative Theater in Britain*, ed. Sandy Craig, 30–48. Ambergate: Amber Lane Press.

Cumming, Alan, and Tim Supple, trans. 1991. *Accidental Death of an Anarchist*. London: Methuen Drama.

D'Aponte, Mimi. 1989. "From Italian Roots to American Relevance: The Remarkable Theater of Dario Fo." *Modern Drama* 32.4:522–44.

Dartington Hall News and South Devon Scene. 1979. 9 February.

Davis, R. G. 1986. "Seven Anarchists I Have Known: American Approaches to Dario Fo." *New Theatre Quarterly* 2.8:313–19.

Emery, Ed, trans. 1994 [1992]. *Accidental Death of an Anarchist*. In *Plays: One*, by Dario Fo, 123–206. London: Methuen Drama.

Fenton, James. 1981. "Theater." *Sunday Times* (London), 28 June.

Fitzpatrick, Tim, and Kzenia Sawszak. 1995. "Accidental Death of a Translator: The Difficult Case of Dario Fo." *About Performance: Working Papers of Center for Performance Studies* 1:15–34.

Fo, Dario. 1966–98. *Le commedie di Dario Fo*. 13 vols. to date. Turin: Einaudi.

———. 1972. *Morte accidentale di un anarchico*. Verona: Bertani.

———. 1973. *Morte accidentale di un anarchico*. In Collettivo Teatrale La Comune, *Compagni senza censura*, 2. Milan: Mazzotta.

———. 1974. *Morte accidentale di un anarchico*. In Fo 1966–98, Vol. 7, 3 83.

Hastings, Michael. 1979. "Glum Theater, or killing them with laughter." *Plays and Players* (September):12.

Hirst, David L. 1989. *Dario Fo and Franca Rame*. Basingstoke: Macmillan.

Hood, Stuart. 1989. "Open Texts: Some problems in the Editing and Translating of Dario Fo." In *The Commedia dell'Arte from the Renaissance to Dario Fo*, ed. Christopher Cairns, 336–49. Lewiston: Edwin Mellen.

Hoyle, Martin. 1990. "Accidental Death of an Anarchist." *Times* (London), 13 October.

Hutcheon, Hilary. 1991. "Accidental Death of an Anarchist" *Tribune* (London), 11 January.

Itzin, Catherine. 1980a. *Stages in the Revolution*. London: Methuen.

———. 1980b. *British Alternative Theater Directory*. Eastbourne: John Offord.

Lane, John Francis. 1973. "No Sex Please, I'm English." *Plays and Players* (July):19–21.

Lorch, Jennifer, ed. 1997. *Morte accidentale di un anarchico*. Manchester: Manchester UP.

MacLennan, Elizabeth. 1990. *The Moon Belongs to Everyone*. London: Methuen.

Mitchell, Tony. 1999. *Dario Fo: People's Court Jester*. 3rd ed. London, Methuen.

Morley, Sheridan. 1979. "Full Marx." *Punch* (London), 24 October.

Nelson, Richard, adapt. 1987. *Accidental Death of an Anarchist*. New York: Samuel French.

Pirandello, Luigi. 1993. "Illustrators, Actors, and Translators." In Bassnett and Lorch 1993.

Radin, Victoria. 1980. "Why the Fringe Has Gone West." *Observer* (London), 2 March.

Richards, Gavin. 1989 [1980]. *Accidental Death of an Anarchist*. (Adapted from a translation by Gillian Hanna.) London: Methuen.

Smith, Les. 1990. "Accidental Death of an Anarchist." *Guardian* (London), 23 October.

Tisdall, Carolin. 1980. "The Collective Explosion." *Guardian* (London), 1 March.

Venuti, Lawrence. 1995. *The Translator's Invisibility*. London: Routledge.

Wardle, Irving. 1980. "Accidental Death of an Anarchist." *Times* (London), 6 March.

Wing, Joylynn. 1990. "The Performance of Power and the Power of Performance: Rewriting the Police State in Dario Fo's *Accidental Death of an Anarchist*." *Modern Drama* 23:139–49.

Young, B. A. 1980. "Accidental Death of an Anarchist. *Financial Times* (London), 6 March.

CHAPTER 9

Parliamo di donne
Feminism and Politics in
the Theater of Franca Rame

SHARON WOOD

T he theater of Franca Rame has been held, and hailed, by some recent critics as the dramatic counterpart of the Italian feminist movement, a subversive and carnivalesque dissection, deconstruction, and re-creation of women's lives and the multiple potential of female subjectivity. Rame is seen to have made an essential contribution to the work of her lifelong partner and collaborator, Dario Fo, to have emerged from their political, dramatic, and personal alliance as feminism evolved out of, and away from, left-wing politics in the late 1960s and early 1970s. While early commentators made comparatively little mention of Rame, her powerful performances, the boldness and humor with which she articulates a feminist position from *Venticinque monologhi per una donna* (Twenty-five monologues for a woman)[1] onward, and her militant and economic involvement with women's groups have all led to a reassessment of Rame's contribution to the couple's work and to an attempt to regard her as a dramatist—as well as a performer—in her own right. The purpose of this chapter is to consider the extent to which Rame's feminism resonates with the broader women's movement in Italy; to examine the interface between political feminism and theatrical performance in Rame's work, between form and ideology; and to expand current definitions and understandings as to what constitutes "feminist" theater.

Conventional criteria are inadequate to deal with the Fo-Rame phenomenon. Theirs is never dramatic literature but, as has been well documented elsewhere, a process that ends, rather than begins, with a written script that, in its turn, is open to change and adaptation in subsequent performance or, notably, in translation. Texts are worked out on the stage rather than on the page, in rehearsal, and in a unique collaboration with audiences, whose comments and observations are frequently recorded by the company. The principal difficulty in assessing Rame's work then, other than onstage performance, is to identify a body of texts authored by her alone. The only texts that are indisputably hers are the 1977 *Lo stupro* (*The Rape*) and the most recent productions, the 1991 *L'eroina* (Heroin) and the 1992 *La donna grassa* (The fat lady). Yet even these are not radical new departures in terms of either content, ideology, or performance technique. The discussion of drugs in *L'eroina* was begun years previously in *La marijuana della mamma è la più bella* (Mother's marijuana is always the best), while the solitude and alienation explored in *La donna grassa* also figured in earlier plays.

Strictly literary and textual criteria of authorship leave us little further forward, as do recent attempts to define characteristic features of feminist theater. This is much more than the shock to feminist sensibilities in Britain and America of seeing Rame appear onstage in scanty negligées; while Italian feminists have never been as suspicious of fashion as their counterparts elsewhere, Rame makes a forceful critique of a culture that would have women instantly available to the male gaze.

Rame's working methods, the theatrical tradition from which she emerges, are far removed from the *fin-de siècle* dramatic forms developed by Ibsen, Shaw, Wilde, and Pinero that exposed the double standards and hypocrisy that compel women, and women's virtue, to serve as the cohesive social force that will both keep degeneracy within unspoken limits and make male degeneracy possible. Nor is her work comparable to the fringe counterculture of much feminist theater in Britain and the States, run on a shoestring by all-women companies, sometimes even playing to all-women audiences.

Rame's work emerges from the context of an almost unique collaboration with Fo, and demarcation lines are difficult to draw. If most of the plays carry his signature, they bear her imprint in both structure and performance. Similarly, her feminism, expressed through plays and monologues written by Fo and elaborated with him, is not the radical feminism that would banish men from the feminist stage but a political and politicized feminism that echoes the writing and thinking of a large part of the Italian feminist movement in the 1970s. The plays penned by Rame herself differ to the extent that they deal with the issues of femininity and, in particular, of female sexuality, within a context that is psychological and existential as well as political. While the 1980s and 1990s have seen the notorious *riflusso*, the generalized withdrawal from political and activist militancy, Rame has explored femininity in a rather different key either to earlier work or to the developments of feminism in its thinking on relationships between women or its sometimes tortured thinking on sexual difference. Rame's women do not break with heterosexuality, or with the enduring difficulties of family life. The humor, the complex and refined stagecraft, are still there. What has changed is the tone. The move away from politics and Brechtian agit-prop, while reflecting a wider social and intellectual shift, has made space for a sense of the tragic, a sense of the abyss that threatens to destroy women, and their alienation in the modern world. Other commentators have noted Rame's ability as a tragic as well as a comic actress. Earlier plays from the 1970s placed women's issues within a revolutionary political culture. The trenchant satire of farce loses its cutting edge when the focus of criticism is less reformable institutions, laws, and parties than a less tangible, existential state; depoliticization makes space for the darker notes of the tragic.

Tutta casa, letto e chiesa (All Bed, Board, and Church)

> What has always troubled Dario and me is the condition of women . . .
> for a theater like ours . . . to not connect with women's issues would
> really be serious. . . . The issue today is too important.
>
> —Franca Rame, quoted in Valentini 1977

The "play dealing with the condition of women, on the sexual servitude of women," was first performed at the Palazzina Liberty, Milan, in 1977, "in support of the feminist struggle" (Fo and Rame 1989f:5). As Rame specifies in her prologue, performances were organized throughout Italy by feminist groups; proceeds went to the feminist movement, to striking workers, to set up women's clinics. The monologues, performed by Rame alone on the stage, frequently with a minimum of props, are introduced by short prologues in which Rame addresses the audience in her own voice, speaking with the authority of three decades of work as actress on both stage and television, and as noted political activist on the left. Gillian Hanna, translator and performer of several of the pieces, comments on the difficulty faced by any other actress playing these parts:

> Whichever character [Rame] is playing, her audience recognizes her within all her characters. This is not to imply a lack of technical skill, to say that the actress somehow does not get inside the character she is playing. Quite the reverse, her virtuosity enables her to move seamlessly between herself and her characters. It enables her to speak to the audience through her characters. But her history means that she can speak directly to the audience with authority and without the mediating force of those characters. When she performs these plays, she starts the evening as herself. She challenges the audience head on saying, in so many words, look, you know who I am, I want you to think about the shitty way women get treated in this world and this is how I am going to make you deal with it. (Rame and Fo 1991:xvi)

In Rame's case, traditional, orthodox categories of voice, authorship, and performance are disrupted. The special relationship Rame has developed with her audiences breaks down the fourth wall, turning her audience into a fundamental part of the show, enabling her to slide between her own voice and that of her characters, between reality, fiction, and metafiction. This process explodes a traditionalist and essentialist vision of the female subject in a rearrangement of parts that embodies both the fragmentation of women's lives and the joyful, carnivalesque subversion of oppressive philosophical and sociopolitical casting.

In *Feminism and Theater*, Sue-Ellen Case distinguishes between a radical feminist theater and a theater of materialist feminism. While radical feminism holds that patriarchy is the primary cause of women's oppression, that male culture suppresses women of all classes and races, materialist feminism, by treating women as a class, can

> analyse women's underemployment, unemployment and wage inequities with revised notions of surplus value. Women are identified as a kind of surplus labor force necessary for the enforcement of general lower wages, strike-breaking tactics and other controls over labor that serve the cause of the owners, or profit-makers. By

extending this analysis into the domestic sphere, women as a free
labor force in housework and reproduction serve both the male
worker and the owner. The wife-mother reproduces the laborer in
two ways: by producing future laborers as babies and by preparing
the laborer for each day's work. Her unpaid labor represents money
in the pocket of the worker, grants him leisure-time and privileges
she does not herself enjoy, and provides the owners with laborers
at no extra cost. (1988:84)

Rame's monologues are firmly rooted within a Marxist-Leninist discourse of labor, profit, alienation, and ownership of the means of production. They function on two levels of ideology, the economic and the
sexual. The satire lies in the misapplication of discourse of one level of
ideology to the other, the failure of left-wing thinking to acknowledge,
even to recognize, the condition of women.

From the opening moments of *Una donna sola (A Woman Alone)*,
every object and every movement simultaneously stages a woman's life
and offers a critique of it. The multiple roles women are compelled to
fulfill are indicated by the overflowing piles of ironing and cleaning
equipment (domestic drudge), the first aid kit (nurse and carer), and the
low-cut negligée (sexual provider). The frenetic dance of the woman as
she begins to work recalls *La maestra di ballo: catena di montaggio* (The
dancing mistress: On the assembly line), in which the rhythm of production is literally ingrained into the female workers as in a keep-fit
class; the radio music, which provides the beat, is just one element of a
degraded culture that pours into the home (through radio, television,
cassettes) as an impoverished substitute for dialogue, exchange, and real
human contact. And as in *La maestra di ballo*, the woman in *Una
donna sola* has learned to be grateful for these meager comforts and
regard them as company rather than accomplices in her oppression. As
in comedy from time immemorial, misrecognition is the key here: Oppression disguises itself as light entertainment and is passed off as its
opposite, as surplus value. The woman comments to her new neighbor,
whose part is taken by the audience itself:

But you won't hear me complain. I'm fine here in my home. I've
got everything I need, my husband sees to it. Everything! God,
how many things I have . . . I've got a fridge! I know, everybody's
got one (putting on airs) but mine makes little balls of ice! I've got
a washing machine . . . 24 cycles . . . wash and dry . . . and how it
dries! Sometimes I have to dampen the clothes again in order to

iron them, they're so dry! (Fo and Rame 1989e:12; ellipses in the original)

Una donna sola is a grotesque rendition of woman as servicer of male needs and legitimate object of male fantasy, to be appropriated and manipulated in the same way as she wields her iron or her pots and pans. Motherhood, the sticking point for a century of thinking about woman's role in society for Right and Left alike, is quickly revealed to be small consolation. Her daughter offers little solidarity and is out with her friends; her baby son eats, sleeps, and snores. If her son is a typical male in the making, her brother-in-law, completely encased in plaster, requires the same attention as a child: "I was saying, don't worry, everyone has done a wee-wee" (Fo and Rame 1989e:14).

The play rapidly focuses on the woman as sexual object, legitimate prey for the peeping Tom in the flats opposite (and the suggestion that she is guilty of provocation, in her scanty clothes, clearly echoes social and legal judgments that women bring sexual aggression upon themselves and are responsible for their own violation), the man phoning continually to make abusive and obscene phone calls, the *reductio ad absurdum* of the brother-in-law, whose only movements are those of groping and masturbation. Even the woman's economic exploitation, her unpaid, unvalued, and unrecognized contribution to the domestic economy, are less catastrophic than this canceling of her own sexual autonomy and sexual pleasure. Subject to domestic violence and the social infantilization of woman, physical and sexual violence slip one into the other:

> He says he does it because he adores me! That I am still a child and he has to protect me . . . and to protect me it is better if he's the first to exploit me! He keeps me cooped up at home like a chicken, and he slaps me around . . . and then he wants to make love! That's right, love! And he couldn't care less if I'm not up for it or in the mood! I must always be ready, like Nescafe! Washed, perfumed, depilated, warm, relaxed, willing, but silent! (1989e:16; ellipses in the original)

The woman recounts an affair with a young boy in which for the first time she experienced pleasure and orgasm, and the discovery of which has led to her incarceration in her own home. The insufficient language

that circumscribes women's bodies and sexuality is a point to which
Rame repeatedly returns: "What a word! I never say it! Orgasm! Sounds
like some horrible monster . . . a cross between a monkey and an open
sandwich . . . Orangutan and smorgasbord" (1989e:16). Women's sexual
pleasure, Rame suggests, is unnameable, unspeakable, deemed not to
exist. The woman mistakenly confused sexual pleasure for love, as the
young boy reveals himself equally rapacious: Just like the brother-in-law,
we see only his arm as he attempts to grab the woman through the door
and have her masturbate him. In the manner of nightmare, farce, sexual
aggression, and hostility multiply dizzyingly and become increasingly
invasive, encroaching onto the minimal space left the woman. Her final
act of revenge, moving from attempted suicide to murder, taking a rifle
and awaiting her husband's return, is literally madness, no solution at
all. There may be a moment of catharsis, a "kill the bastards" pack men-
tality, but it might be more prudent to suggest that the woman's situation
turns her insane rather than homicidal.

The title of *Una donna sola* is clearly ironic, itself open to deconstruction. The woman is not alone: Half a dozen other characters are
constantly claiming her as the object of their attentions. Neither is she
alone in her experience, which is shared with large sections of Rame's
audience. The woman neighbor, in whom she confides, is located not in
the wings of the stage but, provocatively, in the audience; their conversation, in the guise of chat and gossip, has the function of consciousness-
raising sessions, of *autocoscienza*, in which the public share on a metatheatrical level; it is the neighbor who, tellingly, gives her language,
suggests that she is *manipolata*, and provides the word "orgasm," which
the woman cannot herself bring out.

Il risveglio (*Waking Up*) focuses the arguments of *Una donna sola*
within the leftist political context of the PCI (Italian Communist Party).
The play is a tour de force that stages a woman's life as a nightmare;
waking suddenly from a nightmare within the nightmare, in which the
machine on which she works slices off her fingers, the woman rushes
ineffectually to get herself and her baby ready to leave the house for the
crèche and for work, while her husband stays a little longer in bed. In
slapstick style, she puts grated cheese rather than powder on the baby's
bottom and sprays herself with radiator paint rather than deodorant. In
attempting to find her keys, she conjures up the previous evening's
events and conversations with her husband. With the final crushing re-
alization that it is, after all, Sunday, she returns to the matrimonial bed,

to a mirror image of the opening sequence, but where the apparent domestic tranquillity now comes with an enormous price tag.

In the evoked exchanges with the husband, the nature of the comedy shifts from the physical humor of lost and mistaken objects and the increasingly frenetic pace of activity as the woman attempts to make objects stay in their correct places. This may be a satire on women's supposed housewifely skills, but it also taps into a broader experience in which exhaustion and overwork leave women unable to control even their physical environment. That the husband stays on in bed needs no comment.

Il risveglio, then, is a demonstration of the *doppio lavoro* (double work); women's freedom to offer themselves in the marketplace does not unlock the chain that binds them to housework and child care. As she says to her husband, who complains about wasted time traveling to work:

> Besides working eight hours like an animal for him, I'll be your servant for free! For him, for the corporations! . . . The family, this sacred family, was invented so that those of you who've gone a little wacky from the stress of working like a beast, can find in us the all-purpose wife, the mattress upon which you can unburden yourself! . . . We'll regenerate you for him, for free! So that you're ready for tomorrow, nice and refreshed, to produce more efficiently for him, the corporations. (1989b:31)

What is striking here is that even while she provokes her husband to rage by attacking his obsession with football (the love of which is perhaps one of the most fundamental differences between men and women), the analysis of women's position is firmly tied to a class analysis, even while Luigi's own analytical orthodoxies exclude women's issues. The woman's free, unpaid labor profits neither her nor her husband, but the owners. The woman blames not the man but the system, but also the man for behaving in his turn like an owner. Relationships are linear rather than mutual: His problems are hers, hers are her own, in a denial of reciprocity and mutual concern and affection, which is the goal. The PCI is seen to have no response to this situation. Having failed to mollify his wife by persuading her to make love, the husband begins his self-criticism. It is a brilliant moment because with a simple verbal act, the physical displacements of farce are transferred to the ideological and discursive plane; the technical language of left-wing politics, the *auto-critica*, is grafted onto the low-cultural function of an emotional cathar-sis, like a good weepie, as her husband attempts to solve the crisis by edging her toward the bed:

> He pulls me into the house: "Come on, don't be like that, wait . . . "
> "Leave me alone!" "Let's talk first, then if you still want to leave
> fine, but let's talk first! We can have a dialogue, can't we?" . . . and
> he pushes me towards the (she sits on the bed) *dialogue*. He tells
> me that I was right, but that he was used to his MOTHER . . . and
> believed that I was like his MOTHER . . . that he was wrong, that
> he has to change. To cut a long story short, he became SELF-
> CRITICAL. But he did it so well, oh so well, that I was crying.
> And the more he criticized himself the more I cried and the more
> I cried the more he criticized himself. What a good cry I had last
> night! (1989b:32; ellipses and emphasis in the original)

The motionless husband, the dummy still in the bed, is left as mute, ironic comment on the purpose and consequence of the *autocritica* in the realm of domestic, gender, and sexual politics (let alone Luigi's ap-propriation of a political/Marxist strategy to accommodate his sexual desire), while the separation of female function into mother and sexual provider is all the more cutting for the ambiguous tension it continues to generate.

Franca Rame states unequivocally in her prologue that

> the supreme protagonist of this play on women is man. Better, it's
> his sex! It's not present in flesh and blood, but it's always here
> amongst us, large, huge, hanging, and it crushes us! . . . Socially
> we've made a little progress, but on sexual parity, forget it. We'll
> never be able to equal men in this. To hope for it is pure utopian
> fantasy, even if we try, it's just an anatomical fact. (1989f:5)

The women of these monologues give a clear account of lives circum-scribed and infantilized, and of the clear failure of the Left either to accommodate gender issues within a socialist credo or, more radically, to allow gender to become a structuring constituent part of socialist thinking or discourse. This was the dilemma that led many radical woman in Italy to break with orthodox politics in the 1970s to set up a separate women's movement or, for those who chose to remain within the Communist Party, to adopt a strategy of *doppia militanza* (double militancy) in an attempt to place sexual politics on the Communist agenda. The hegemony of the Catholic Church in private and domestic spheres, unchallenged since the Lateran Pacts of 1929,[2] was deemed largely outside the remit of the revolutionary struggle. The "confession" of the woman in *La mamma fricchettona* (The freak mother) reveals both the church's failure even to hear women's voices (giving rise to much humor as the woman tries to catch, and keep, the attention of the priest) and its collusion with a dominant, repressive order as the priest finally gives her up to the carabinieri who have pursued her into the church.

Once again Fo-Rame address women as mothers. In her attempt to protect her son, now involved in far-left politics and terrorist activity, the *mamma* of the title herself abandons her traditional role as wife and mother, adopting the clothes, music, and habits of the student youth whose confidence she gains to the point of becoming a feminist icon, cheered by the crowds when she is released from police custody. The orthodox politics of the Left (she and her husband are both members of the PCI, *militanti osservanti*) are unable either to engage her son or to disengage her from the *doppio lavoro* already explored in previous monologues. Women's entry into the paid work market has merely led to double exploitation, a consequence of which the women's movement should have been aware: "Fine women's lib that is! By getting married I got two jobs!" (1989c:42).

The internal dynamic of this monologue springs from the subtext, a discursive analysis of motherhood in the social and political arena and a textual gesturing toward another conception of femininity. The traditional view of womanhood fostered by patriarchy, in which women's humanity is a function of her reproductive rather than productive powers ("What is a woman if she's not a mother? She's not even a woman, she's just a female!" [1989c:42]), is displaced as the woman becomes *mamma* to a group of disaffected youth, leaving her domestic walls. Yet, there is a curious ambiguity here. The youngsters are initially suspicious of this older woman come to look for her son: "No one would tell me anything! Get it? I was a mother! Symbol of repression: code of silence" (1989c:43). Again the woman is betrayed by language, as by the social pact that constrains her: Cast as the ultimate symbol of oppression, she is herself the most repressed. While she subverts the maternal role to an extent, the youth movement, playing at politics as it plays at life choices, offers no radical change. That it is no more than an adolescent phase, whereas for the woman it is a matter of identity and survival, is poignantly shown when she rediscovers her son in a dapper suit and neat haircut. The woman is left with nowhere else to go: The PCI silences the paradoxes of its analyses in the sphere of gender and the "private" realm, while the youth and protest movements do not take her position as woman/mother into account in their ideological games.

To this extent, the monologues clearly resonate with the debates taking place within the Italian women's movement in Italy. A more original contribution lies in their distillation of the complex philosophical question of women as speaking subject in a language governed by patriarchy. A recurrent theme of these monologues is the betrayal of woman by language, by discursive practice, by ideological formulation. Women's speech is constantly cut off, truncated, silenced; their language is deemed inappropriate. It is a nice irony that while a solo actress commands the stage, what is dramatized is women's lack of access to language, their distance and exclusion from it. *Una donna sola* reveals the distortion of language to persuade women to accept their lot: Talking to her husband on the telephone, she yells, "'I'm happy, Aldo, I'm very happy. *(More and more nervously)* I was here ironing and laughing. *(Screaming)* I'm happy'" (1989e:14). In *La mamma fricchettona*, the woman's perception of her own experience, her response to it, is censored by the priest as she is constantly admonished to mind her language: "What an asshole I was! Oh sorry Father, I meant to say what a shithead . . . In any case, you get the idea" (1989c:42; ellipses in the original). In *Abbiamo tutte la stessa storia (Same Old Story)*, language becomes a means of keeping women in their rightful places, on their backs, in the service of men and party. Rame provocatively mimes a woman who, when making love, asks for a little warmth and emotion to accompany the sexual act and is quickly defined, and dismissed, as a bourgeois romantic:

> Why is it that when a woman doesn't immediately get into the position—slip up, knickers down, legs spread—she's immediately labeled as having a complex, with the prudery of a reactionary-imperialist-capitalist-masonic-conformist-repressed upbringing? I'm uppity, right? And conceited women are ball-breakers. Better play the dumb bimbo with the sexy giggle. (1989a:49)

Fo and Rame dramatically stage a woman's absence from her own desire, the impossible contradiction of a woman speaking as sexual desiring subject. The *donna sola* confesses to her new neighbor her "inability to reach . . . ":

> That's it . . . that word! And what a word! What a word!! I never
> say it! Orgasm! It sounds like the name of a disgusting beast . . . a
> cross between a mandrill and an organ. I seem to read it in large
> print in the newspapers: "Adult Orgasm Escapes from the Ameri-
> can Circus!" "Nun Attacked at the Zoo by a Crazed Orgasm."
> (1989e:16; ellipses in the original)

The point is expanded by Rame in *Manuale minimo dell'attore* (The actor's mini-manual, published in English as *Tricks of the Trade*). The language of phallocracy and of patriarchy are indistinguishable:

> I was saying that men have always graced their own sex with lofty
> anatomical names. Listen to how they ring: Phallus! Prepuce!
> Prepuce could be anything but what it actually is: "What a splen-
> did preacher who, from the perch of his prepuce, harangues throngs
> of faithful!" Glands seem like the name of an exotic flower: "Here,
> take this bouquet of fragrant glands, hold them close to your
> breast!" . . . On the other hand, with the terminology they stuck us
> with, we can't evoke such images. They chose horrible terms for
> us: "vagina." The most you could do is slip on one: "I slipped on
> a vagina peel and cracked my shin! See?!" Worse yet is uterus. God
> what a word! It sounds like an insult or a blunt object. "I'll smash
> you with this uterus and break your head!" (Fo 1987:311–12)

To control language is to control the world, our expression and experience of it. If men experience pleasure, women are left with orgasm, objects rather than subjects of sexual pleasure and desire. *Monologo della puttana in manicomio* (Monologue of a prostitute in an asylum) juxtaposes women's censored language with the canceling of their sexual autonomy and leaves them as objects for consumption. *Lo stupro* is the most harrowing of these monologues in its recounting of a gang rape, unmediated by satire or farce, and in the lack of redress available to the woman, for whom to report the rape to the police would lead only to further violation by both individual unbelieving policemen and by the judicial process itself.

With *La Medea*, derived from an Italian dialect version of the story as well as from Euripides, the tone shifts from satire and denunciation to pure tragedy. In *Manuale minimo*, Rame challenges feminist readings of Euripides' tragedy *Alcestis*, all too often seen as a classic statement of the imperative for women to sacrifice themselves for their children and husband, for the wider social good. For Rame, Euripides' own feminist credentials discredit such a reading of a play, which she herself sees as an attack on hypocrisy and individual egotism rather than the male sex. Her interpretation of *La Medea* is similarly independent. While Pasolini adopted the story of Medea as a parable of colonialism, of an intra- and inter-cultural collision, Rame's Medea embodies the enforced divide between woman as sexual being and woman as mother. Medea's experience of being abandoned for a younger woman is, her handmaids tell her, common enough; they, too, have wept tears as their husbands left them. They appeal to her motherly love, encouraging her to comply with the requirement to give up both Jason and her children, for this is the law of nature:

> You should be worrying about your children instead of yourself! They'll be much better off after this wedding. They'll wear much finer clothes. . . . For the love you bear them, Medea, you must sacrifice yourself! Your thoughts must be those of a worthy mother, not of a proud woman! (1989d:71)

Refusing the role of self-sacrificing mother, Medea resolves to murder her children so that she herself will not be canceled out, annihilated, by this law that favors men alone. Hers is not an act of individual madness or even revenge but an assertion of her own subjective identity and being. It is a political act that defies the assimilation of femininity to motherhood, that refuses to contemplate women as both mothers and sexual beings (the same dilemma addressed by Sibilla Aleramo, Natalia Ginzburg, Dacia Maraini, and numerous other writers over the past century). Hers is a symbolic act that has little to do with the notion of the "symbolic mother" in the *affidamento* (entrustment) of Italian feminist thinking, which would have younger, less experienced women turn to another woman for guidance and affirmation. Motherhood for Rame is not cerebral or hypothetical but visceral and emotional. Medea's anguish is evident, but the murder is a profoundly political act intent on breaking the chain of servitude that the patriarchal ideology of motherhood has foisted on women:

> Man is not a traitor if he exchanges his woman. And a woman must be happy to be a Mother, which is in itself great reward! And in

this cage you have imprisoned us, chaining us with our children, like a yoke on an ox, the better to keep us subjugated and tame, the better to milk us, the better to mount us. (1989d:74)

Medea becomes a revolutionary, seeking what has never before been seen: woman as subject. Even as she stages the desperate murder of her children, she will cry out, "Die, die! And let a new woman be born!" (1989d:75).

Rame is clearly not inciting her audience to murder. Mothers feature regularly throughout Fo and Rame's work, including the feminist monologues of *Tutta casa*. Yet *La Medea*, with its compelling tragic tone, remains the most profound excursus into the tragedy of a woman alienated from herself, erased and expunged by tyrannical laws not of her own making. The multiplicity of voices, as the actress adopts numerous parts, both refracts Medea's experience (just as Aleramo's *Una donna* becomes all women) and politicizes her action.

If Rame rejects feminist thinking on *affidamento* and the maternal, she also rejects a simplistic, ritualistic feminism that is forever anti-male, whose rhetoric is no closer to the truth than the blunt and feebleminded slogans shouted by the *sessantottini* ('68ers):

> Certain exasperating forms of hysterical extremism have dissolved: After a time of great fervor, you can see many women—some of whom used to dance, like witches in the name of emancipation, with a final ritual honoring male castration—who have returned to the ranks of the happily married, even if a bit jaded. Who can explain why, in every struggle, the hotheads always rush on ahead? Even recently I've clashed with groups of feminists, the most radical—they're still around—on the subject of how better to understand the crucial relationship with men. Some of them remind me of certain political groups in '68 who would go at everything with a hatchet: The bourgeois is an untrustworthy, exploitative bastard, while the proletariat is always a clean, intelligent revolutionary. (Fo 1987:308–9)

Rame refuses the separatism of much feminist thinking and its emphasis on sexual difference. As a practitioner of the theater, she is a pragmatist rather than a philosopher, firmly heterosexual in personal and artistic orientation, and continues the attempt to "understand the crucial relationship with men." *Coppia aperta, quasi spalancata (Open Couple)*,[3] one of the most successful Fo/Rame productions of the 1980s, offers a different solution to Medea's problem as the woman, too, takes a lover. The game playing, the deadly double standards and hypocrisies of the "open couple" (a notorious experiment tried unsuccessfully by numerous couples, Fo/Rame included, in the 1980s), are brought dramatically and economically into focus by the structure of the play, its circularity, its constant shifts between fiction and metafiction. Levels of deception, lying, and desperate vaunting, the chain of disruptive and disrupting relationships engendered by the dissolution of the monogamous couple, are figured in the slippage of scenic space: When the man threatens to throw himself from the window, he is at one moment dealing with death and the next reminded that he is, after all, only on the stage. The woman's attempt to control the fiction of dramatic conventions mirrors her attempt to restore order and equity to her marriage. If Pirandello shattered theatrical illusion to make a profound philosophical point about the epistemology of "truth," Fo and Rame adopt a similar device in order to emphasize the Sicilian playwright's profoundly humane point about the need for an irreducible human bond.

Rame never wavers from her ideal of the primary heterosexual fusion of the monogamous couple. Relationships between women, so consistently explored by Italian feminism either as political lesbianism, the subjective affirmation of *affidamento*, or simply the warmth and solidarity of sisterhood, cannot for her compare with the mutuality of affection and commitment over time. In her extensive lecture on sex, published as an appendix to *Lo Zen e l'arte di scopare* (Zen and the art of screwing) by her son Jacopo Fo, the anatomy and dynamics of the sexual act defer to the gentle tenderness of affection and closeness. Her hypothetical couple's hilarious sexual acrobatics give way to an understanding that "love is maintained by renewing tenderness. The fascinating thing is for man and woman to discover together new and different ways to offer each other gentle emotions" (Fo 1995:147).

Throughout the 1980s, short plays by Fo and Rame continued to explore issues that related to women's lives. Moves to undermine the hard-won abortion law (the one issue that really united the fragmentary women's movement in Italy) were countered by the 1988 *L'uomo incinto* (The pregnant man). The hypocrisy of the *bienpensant* ruling classes, happy to foist repeated pregnancies on women reluctant for reasons either personal or medical, is caricatured when the husband unexpectedly finds himself pregnant and suffering all the attendant cravings and nausea, demanding an immediate abortion. The 1988 *Ho fatto la plastica* (I had a nose job) is similarly grotesque in its condemnation of the beauty myth that distorts women's lives and bodies. Italy's lack of regulation and standing committees to assess the ethical implications of scientific and medical advances in reproductive technology, which led, for example, to the notorious and internationally reported cases of postmenopausal women having babies, is spotlighted in the 1988 *La nonna incinta* (The pregnant grandmother), in which a woman carries her daughter's fetus. Hypocrisy rather than technology is the target here: The real reason for the surrogate pregnancy, we discover, has to do less with physiology than with style, a way of avoiding the inevitable physical consequences of pregnancy in a culture that values appearance above all else. The struggle to put on the statute books a law against the continuing physical and sexual violence that is the reality of so many women's lives is given implicit support in the bitter parody *Previsioni meteorologiche movimento di stupro in Italia* (Meteorological forecasting of the rape movement in Italy), in which the appalling violence evoked in *Lo stupro* is refracted and multiplied in the disturbingly banal guise of a weather forecast.

    L'eroina and *La donna grassa*, written and performed by Rame and directed by Fo,[4] take up from where their 1986 play, *Una giornata qualunque (An Ordinary Day)*, left off. The earlier play, like the 1977 monologue *Una donna sola*, has a single character onstage, with a variety of electronic media and voices off, ranging from telephone callers to neighbors shouting, fighting, arguing, making love, and protesting at the consequent noise. Giulia, center stage, yet another woman abandoned by her husband, attempts to videotape her final message to him before she commits suicide. Again we see the refraction and multiplication of a defining experience in a woman's life, as telephone callers believe her number to be that of a therapist. Techniques of theater and film montage are adopted to bring about a tragic farce as Giulia—in a destiny common to so many women in Fo and Rame's repertoire—is finally taken to the asylum even as she attempts a spontaneous act of assistance to one of her women callers. There is a deeper note of pessimism in this play, as years of feminism and political activism are seen to have brought women no closer together as women are abandoned to their perpetual loneliness. Stage tricks and the paraphernalia of farce here barely conceal a deeper note of despair.

    The 1991 *L'eroina* and the 1992 *La donna grassa* (banned from a

number of venues on tour) are even darker in tone. In *L'eroina*, with its
ambiguous wordplay on "heroin" and "heroine," Mater Tossicorum, former teacher of Latin, has turned to dealing in porno videos, dummy
telephones, condoms of all shapes, sizes, and flavors, and all the degraded detritus of modern living. She also deals in drugs, in order to
guarantee a safe supply of heroin for her daughter Anna. Having lost one
son to AIDS and another to an overdose, she herself injects her remaining child, who is kept tied to her bed. With the profits from the sale of
her shoddy goods, she plans to take her daughter to a drug rehabilitation
project in Liverpool.

The atmosphere of *L'eroina* is a cross between Samuel Beckett's *Fin
de partie* and Ridley Scott's *Bladerunner*. In the persistent downpour in
which the action takes place, a tide of rubbish generated by technologi-
cal advances swills about the stage, like the drifting humanity it threatens to engulf. Flashes of thunder and lightning are taken by Carla, the
Mater, to be the scornful laughter of an indifferent god. Characters drift
more or less silently, more or less meaningfully, across the stage: the
"blind man," the "deaf-mute," the "peddlar," and other passersby. Gun-
shots, police, and ambulance sirens are heard offstage as well as on; the
radio reports a fight at the football stadium even though the match has
been canceled; a loudspeaker intermittently announces a meeting on
the theme of "the existence of God"; the railway station has disappeared.
The parameters of people's lives have shrunk to domestic and sexual
violence, to drugs and the vast crime wave it spawns, to AIDS and its
three daily victims. The frantic activity of the police as they burst in like
the Keystone Cops looking for drug pushers and il Colombia, who lies
literally gutted on the floor, the technical seamlessness as Carla's vision
of Mary is revealed as nothing but a dream, together with the sacks of
money suddenly thrust into her hands, do little to dispel the play's core
of static loneliness, of individual solitude, in which the only act of gen-
erosity, toward the drug addict, ends as he attempts to steal from her.

The figure of Mater Tossicorum, while recalling *La marijuana*, offers a far more radical and desperate subversion of the maternal role. If
Rosetta in the earlier play posed as a drug dealer in order to teach her
son a lesson, the highly ambiguous Mater Tossicorum deals in drugs and
imprisons her daughter to prevent a worse occurrence. She is a mixture
of Brecht's Mother Courage and the mater dolorosa (stage directions
indicate a Stabat mater soundtrack) in her desperate attempt to stem the
tide and save her own child. Carla is still the wise-cracking, fast-talking

type we would expect from a character played by Rame. The "pale girl" reproaches her for her language and her irony, which are "revolting": In this play, language has lost its satirical edge and become a way to stave off the final cataclysm. This is a harshly angry play denouncing not addicts but those who put drugs into circulation and who tolerate the decimation of young people through drugs and disease, governments that turn a blind eye to the social and family disintegration it brings in its wake, the human and social wasteland.

Language stripped of its content and of its real human emotion, opens *La donna grassa*, companion piece to *L'eroina*. Mattea, weighing 123 kilos, abandoned by her husband, awakens to the tape recorder's seductive voice, speaking in caressing tones of love. She phones the magazine *Grassa è bello* (Fat is beautiful), which claims to cater for larger women while supplying their surplus flesh for pornographic films. The magazine title, with its oblique reference to the gender-bending feminist slogan of the 1970s, *Donna è bello*, is a mute intimation of the little distance women have traveled in the last twenty years. Rather than *dare nell'occhio* (stand up and be seen), as earlier feminists wished to do, Mattea, paradoxically and comically, wishes to remain invisible. When she finally admits the man who has come to her door in search of reconciliation with his own abandoned wife, Mattea goes through elaborate contortions to avoid his gaze: "Besides being decisively closed to all relationships, I'm arid, apolitical, egocentric. I exist neither as a person nor as a woman, despite being obvious" (Rame 1992:76). His attempts to catch sight of her, convinced that she cannot be of the proportions she claims, meet a tragicomic rebuff: "Get out or I'll take my clothes off!" Finally glimpsing her substantial person, the man runs for the door.

With the arrival of Mattea's daughter Anna, typical designer-clad, university-educated woman of the 1980s and 1990s, women's unhappiness, their desperate loneliness, is more securely pinned to women's own actions, not those of their philandering men. This is the point with which Rame sought to challenge old ideas of radical and political sisterhood, newer ideas of *affidamento*, and the struggle to find new ways for women to be together. As Anna recounts her latest unhappy love affair with yet another married man, she is rounded on as the architect of her own pathetic misery:

We prattle on about solidarity and sisterhood! Really?! Are we sisters, united in the great struggles, abortion, divorce, after fifty years? In everyday life, we are hyenas. Then again, no, hyenas rest every now and then. We are insatiable! You know what? After so many years of personal experience and experience of women I know, I have a great doubt. There will always be competition, but I have a strong notion that in certain situations women's worst enemies are women themselves. (1992:102)

Rame reveals her distaste for the new division of public and private that leaves women free to wreak damage on each other while mouthing platitudes learned from the hard struggles of the 1970s. Her bold denunciation of women's personal ethics is tightly linked with her perennial concern with the fragility and supremacy of monogamy. In these days of political quietude, Rame challenges women once more to make their personal and their sexual lives subject to a broader ethical, if not political, base.

Mattea differs from other female characters insofar as she has set up business, marketing the products of her own loneliness with astonishing success—the seductive alarm-calls are her own invention, snapped up by "all the lonely people" of the Beatles song she plays. But the satisfactions of work and success are not for her. Learning that her husband is about to remarry, and more fundamentally that her role as mother has been usurped by his new wife, who is carrying his child, she expresses her own bitterness and grief. Liberation is the last thing she wants:

This is my fantasy: I finally succeed in overcoming this idiotic guilt complex about breaking up the family. I'm free! I'm a successful woman. I'm signing contracts for a lot of money. Finally I can realize myself. Finally I find myself alone! Alone with myself! And that's what makes me want to vomit. (1992:104–5)

Fo and Rame's plays on women, and Rame's own work, gradually part company with the dominant concerns of Italian feminist thinking in the 1980s and 1990s. While the materialist feminism of the early monologues performed by Rame resonated with the struggles for abortion, for recognition of the *doppio lavoro* and the campaign for salaries for housewives, for *autocoscienza*, for legislation against sexual violence, the theoretical abstractions of the symbolic mother, the elaboration of theories of sexual difference, and the aspirations of *affidamento* remain outside their sphere of interest. Rame's principal concern is the heterosexual, monogamous relationship, which is women's best hope for happiness, and she persists in seeking the emotional understanding that sustains a relationship over the years. If this is not radical feminism, it is perhaps all the more humane.

Translations are by the author and Antonio Scuderi.

Notes

1. The collection *Venticinque monologhi per una donna* is subdivided into five groups of monologues. The first group, *Tutta casa, letto e chiesa (All Bed, Board, and Church)*, includes *Una donna sola (A Woman Alone)*, *Il risveglio (Waking Up)*, *La mamma fricchettona* (The freak mother), *Abbiamo tutte la stessa storia (Same Old Story)*, and *La Medea*, which are mentioned in this essay. The second group, *Altre storie* (Other stories), includes *La maestra di ballo: catena di montaggio* (The dancing mistress: On the assembly line), *Lo stupro (The Rape)*, and *Monologo della puttana in manicomio* (Monologue of a prostitute in an asylum), also mentioned in this essay (editor's note).

2. The Lateran Pacts, signed by Mussolini and Cardinal Gasparri, defined the relationship between church and state and recognized Catholicism as the state religion.

3. *Coppia aperta, quasi spalancata* is the title of the collection that includes the plays *Coppia aperta*, *L'uomo incinto* (The pregnant man), *Ho fatto la plastica* (I had a nose job), *La nonna incinta* (The pregnant grandmother), *Previsioni meteorologiche movimento di stupro in Italia* (Meteorological forecasting of the rape movement in Italy), and *Una giornata qualunque (An Ordinary Day)*, which are mentioned in this essay.

4. The two one-act plays, *L'eroina* and *La donna grassa* (The fat lady), make up the collection *Parliamo di donne* (Let's talk about women).

References

Case, Sue-Ellen. 1988. *Feminism and Theatre*. London: Methuen.

Fo, Dario. 1987. *Manuale minimo dell'attore*. Ed. Franca Rame. Turin: Einaudi.

Fo, Dario, and Franca Rame. 1989a. *Abbiamo tutte la stessa storia*. In Fo and Rame 1989, 49–57.

———. 1989b. *Il risveglio*. In Fo and Rame 1989, 27–35.

———. 1989c. *La mamma fricchettona*. In Fo and Rame 1989, 37–47.

———. 1989d. *La Medea*. In Fo and Rame 1989, 67–75.

———. 1989e. *Una donna sola*. In Fo and Rame 1989, 11–26.

———. 1989f. *Venticinque monologhi per una donna*. Turin: Einaudi.

———. 1991. *Coppia aperta, quasi spalancata*. Turin: Einaudi.

Fo, Jacopo. 1995. *Lo Zen e l'arte di scopare*. Verona: Demetra.

Hanna, Gillian. 1991. Introduction in Rame and Fo 1991.

Rame, Franca. 1992. *La donna grassa*. In *Parliamo di donne*. Milan: Kaos, 61–105.

Rame, Franca, and Dario Fo. 1991. *A Woman Alone and Other Plays*. Tr. Gillian Hanna. London: Methuen.

Valentini, Chiara. 1977. *La storia di Dario Fo*. Milan: Feltrinelli.

CHAPTER 10

Tradition, Traditions, and Dario Fo

PAOLO PUPPA

O ccasionally, Dario Fo takes his stand on the stage, all alone. Egalitarianism, collectives, and group spirit notwithstanding, Fo is driven by the impulse to isolate himself, to give free rein to his artistic narcissism, and I have to say that it suits him very well. Indeed, these monologues are the performances of his that, for various reasons, I most prefer, particularly because I find in this occasional solitude traces of earlier times. It is not just a matter of the far-off *giullare* style but of a more recent tradition. I am referring to codes that date from the nineteenth-century *soirée d'honneur*, to the performer who freed himself from his subordinate colleagues to allow himself to shine in well-honed, personal pieces. In the same way, Fo, having left aside the other actors with whom he stages plays—which too frequently show signs of having been put together in haste or of having been snatched from the political headlines of the day and from current debates on manners and morals—can finally enchant audiences by offering us tried-and-true tales and by displaying to the full his own expertise, which is considerable. Here he is as the high priest of mime, all outrageous contortions and mocking routines, tracing figures and stories in the void (painting is his *violon d'Ingres*), pouring out sniggering pho-nemes in suggestive, joyous blasphemies and in the broadest of double entendres. His body, even now when an examination of his birth cer-tificate suggests that it must be well beyond its prime, displays, if com-pared with his massive physical bulk, a scandalous and paradoxical light-ness that defies the law of gravity. This may well be due to his acrobatic apprenticeship in the mime school of Jacques Lecoq. Anyone who has been personally present at those sessions when the tales comes tum-bling out will be able to recall the masses of adoring and grateful faces, crowded at his feet like waves in a turbulent sea, among which he moves as the shaman-narrator. And, following a well-tested routine, latecomers will be brought forward and settled on the stage, as though they were the outpost of the stalls, sucked into the opening of the evening's business.

Nonetheless, to take the longer perspective, the perspective less in-volved with ideological polemics, one can glimpse behind this soli-tary Fo the nineteenth-century figure of the "great actor." It could be Gustavo Modena (1803–61), the sublime Romantic declaimer of Dante's verses, the Republican agitator in the grips of some feverish, civil, or patriotic passion; or perhaps Tommaso Salvini (1829–1916), the awesome Othello who scared the wits out of a refined, relaxed critic like Henry James; or perhaps Ernesto Rossi (1827–96), the languid, sonorous Ham-let who set the hearts of generations of lady spectators aflutter. Or it might be more apropos to summon back those actresses who gave a social dimension to their performances, none more so than the great Giacinta Pezzana (1841–1919), the Piedmontese follower of Mazzini, who played Hamlet in the latter part of the nineteenth century. However far removed he may be from the classical "young lover," Fo, with what-ever purely personal twist, can still recall the figure of the *brillante*, who was the origin of the neurotic and cerebral *raisonneur*, the mouthpiece of Pirandello's witty words. That beetling tall physique of Fo's could also stand in the grotesque shadow of the versatile Ermete Novelli (1851–1919). In any case, Fo is most strongly reminiscent not of the director, who by preference never displays his own body, but of the romantic, charismatic star, the actor who is heedless of the success of the company as a whole, and who will never, in any production, accord the script priority. This is not to ignore the fact that often in recent years, Fo has taken on the role of director, not only of his own texts but also of the scripts of other writers, from Stravinsky at La Scala in Milan in 1978 to Rossini in 1987 and Molière at the Comédie Française in 1990.

Still we are not done, because among the predecessors of Fo the
monologist must be numbered the figure most opposed to the sublime
"great actor," even if one no less exaggerated in his own way. I have in
mind the figure who emerged from the suspect breeding grounds of the
variété, the *café chantant* or the *avanspettacolo*.[1] The supreme example
is the Roman vaudevillian Ettore Petrolini,[2] whose death occurred in
1936, the same year as Pirandello's. If we were to apply Freud's division of wit into the aggressive and masculine on the one hand and the
sophisticated, elegant, and intellectual on the other, Petrolini would
emerge as the authentic source of the caustic and virile comic spirit of
Fo, while the earlier archetype, the "great actor," would have to be
placed in the second category. The popular performer, the Petrolini
type, never still as he treads the boards, cannot merely face the audience
in statuesque poses from downstage. No, he tends to come down into
the stalls with an attitude of some ferocity, giving no quarter to his spectators, squaring up for a primitive combat in which anyone who holds
back knows he is done for. The impact of Franca Rame on Fo in this
context has been intense: Rame his partner in life and in theater, Rame
the soubrette and *figlia d'arte*, Rame the wife who brought as her dowry
the whole legacy of the coarse traveling folk, the strolling players, and,
in particular, the craft's command of perfect comic timing.

We could identify the two above-mentioned models, the romantic "great actor" and the popular entertainer, in the extraordinary range
of sounds that issue from Fo. These could, in spite of the extreme polyphony of his means of expression, be summed up in two antithetical
and complementary notes. It is worth listening, or relistening, to his
standard pieces, those which he uses for personal appearances—from
the 1969 *Mistero buffo* (Comic Mystery), the 1979 *Storia della tigre*
(Tale of the Tiger), the 1982 *Fabulazzo osceno (Obscene Fables)*, and the
1991 *Johan Padan a la descoverta de le Americhe (Johan Padan—The Dis-*
covery of the Americas) to the 1995 *Fo recita Ruzzante* (Fo performs Ruzzante). Whatever he does onstage, whether he sets himself the ambitious
task of giving life to an inexhaustible multiplicity of characters, without
losing himself in the differentiation of their voices, or whether he limits
himself to a few hints, such as moving from one corner of the stage to
another or giving the merest movement of his upper body, his acting
devices, a kind of performance synecdoche, may constitute a presentation in the epic style but do not conceal the fact that what distinguishes
his day-to-day style as an actor are its poetic high points. It would not

be out of place to compare, in this context, the grand gestures of Fo, which rise to a fortissimo at such moments of lyricism, with the liberated body that was the goal of the Living Theater (it should not be forgotten that it was Fo who in 1967 had the American company's *Antigone* invited to the Parma festival), or with orientalist notions of the liberated body upheld by the Grotowski/Barba laboratory (in 1969, Fo was guest of the Odin Teatret), so as to identify an individual point of contact with, or a secular response to, the physical mysticism of those groups.

A brief parenthesis might be of value at this point. I say Brechtian epic style because of the constant use by Fo of procedures of alienation and of a lowering of tension by parody. This has been so ever since the days of his earliest incursions into cabaret in the Milanese piano bars of Franco Nebbia and Gino Negri, where life was enlivened by the songs of Enzo Jannacci and by the presence of *outré*, flamboyant actors such as Giustino Durano and Franco Parenti. This period produced such works as the 1952 *Poer nano* (Poor wretch), the 1953 *Il dito nell'occhio* (*A Finger in the Eye*), and the 1954 *I sani da legare* (A madhouse for the sane). In later stages, there was no lack of borrowings from the German dramatist, with such works as the 1981 *L'opera dello sghignazzo (The Opera of the Sneering Laugh)*, the freest of adaptations of the *Threepenny Opera*. These are *giullarate* pressed into service as counterhistories, whose aim is to compensate the victims of official history, that history that pays no heed to the anonymous masses after having, it may be, seen them shed their blood on the glorious trails left by victors. This backward look, not substantially different from the Manzonian precedent, toward the past aims to allow the forgotten to speak for themselves and to give new life to cultures that have undergone acts of violence and abuse. These acts may be located in the most remote corners of the globe and in the most forgotten ages in history, may involve peoples such as the Cathars or the lower clergy of the Middle Ages, while not forgetting the Palestinians of today, Maoist peasants, the partisans of the Resistance, and anarchists mysteriously "suicided."

The whole of *Mistero buffo*, with its much vaunted use of the apocryphal gospels, seems written by a Borges overwhelmed by the inebriation of a social palingenesis and is made to seem an offense against the manuals of official history, to use Walter Benjamin's expression. It is, in other words, a history written in direct contradiction to the version produced by authority. This is the explanation of the dialect epic, which could have been patched together from the Fescennines, from *lazzi* and

burlesque puns, leaving the usual protagonists, the famous, to be rele- gated to walk-on parts. But the term "epic" is to be seen in a sense
purified of all Brechtian overtones since it must be accepted that the
enhanced, incantatory function produced by a use of space aims not to
keep people at a distance—to use Blanchot's polemical terminology—
but rather to bring the audience closer, in a tighter and tighter embrace
with this man alone onstage.[3]

■

Tradition,
Traditions,
and
Dario Fo

It would be worth reconsidering certain plays that can now be
also analyzed on videocassette. There is no need to go beyond *Mistero
buffo*—with its effeminate angels and its drunken peasants, its sorrowful
Mary Magdalens and blustering popes, its furious Christs, its cynical
soldiers and troubled thieves, its roistering paradises and its bountiful
Infernos—in order to grasp the emotional temperature, the will to com-
motion that rises and falls between the actor and the stalls. But let us go
back to my attempt at classification. It can be easily seen how, in spite
of the transparent polyphony, three voices emerge from this too noisy
solitude, to paraphrase the great novel of Bohumil Hrabal, three voices
that correspond to three separate profiles. There is in the first place the
voice of the lecturer, the speaker of the preface, who begins calmly as
though he wished to save his breath. Those long historical preambles,
the examples that point toward present-day topics, are a sure means of
disarming the audience, of sidling up to them, of stunning them and
thus of preparing for the sucker punch, the comic stroke, the surprise.
The body follows this discourse with a style that I would like to define
as *sermo cotidianus*, that is, a discourse produced by a Fo steeped in
reality, ready to wax indignant when the comic context permits it, a Fo,
in other words, who is cultural popularizer and political commentator.
His body here is that of a good-hearted tribune, totally determined to
provide the complicit spectator with counterinformation and enquiries
from the grassroots, coaxing the spectator to get into the habit of reject-
ing those imperious invitations to collaborate that emanate from the ar-
rogance of power. However, no sooner is the sketch underway than the
long introduction begins to slide, in a style that is close to the ad-lib,
into the performed section, and it is here that the essential diversity lies.

I have identified two moments, while being fully aware that it is
scarcely possible to halt the action of the unstoppable impromptu and
that it is scarcely correct to categorize and separate two qualities that
are, in fact, mixed and mingled in a thousand wild combinations. But
the voice undergoes its own undoubted metamorphosis and with it the

body itself. At this point, without warning, the spectator becomes aware of the frenzied activity, of the process of aging or of infantile regression, of a descent to the level of the beast, of an adenoidal palpitation, of the throat opened wide to emit groans and snorts, of the protruding mouth with lower lip stretching forward as though to bite. The face, then, enlarges, dominated as it is by that great wind-cheater of a nose, the ears flap like sails in the wind through a very excess of excitement, and the neck swells up as though it belonged to some bulbous frog. This is a body that wants to eat, defecate, belch, in other words, the body of the *zanni*, in touch with both stage and ground. And meanwhile the arms are lowered, the arms of an ape in heat, while the legs are raised as though they were an erection or an extension of some enormous phallus, and the eyes come to resemble rotating balls, rolling in demented, menacing glances. This is the register of the *sermo rusticus*, of the body that seems to curl up like a fetus, to infect, to tempt, to soil. The explosive energy unleashed on the stage by a metamorphosis of this kind permits Fo to hurl himself into unrestrained enumerations, into vertiginous and delirious verbal lists. This linguistic excess, this thick web of syllogisms that seems to be spinning out of control even if the speaker never loses command of his own phonic instruments, is often based on popular bestiaries, on human-animal grafts that would have delighted a Rabelais, and becomes — most particularly in *Mistero buffo, Storia della tigre*, and *Johan Padan* — a grotesque parody of a child's Noah's arc.

There is yet another voice, a light, ballerina's voice in which the pyrotechnics of the other voices are toned down to produce a white sound like that of a child whimpering and to create a kind of passive and humble feminization, that of the victim who weeps and wishes to lay his or her head on your lap. Then the arms are raised, the body seems to levitate, twisting round in an attempt at flight toward some unseen heights, and the legs appear on the point of leaping and jumping without restraint. The teeth protrude out and above, like some banner, and the eyes diminish to the dimensions of tiny holes, in an attempt at some fatuous, pander's smile, conveying the suggestion that the fool is more than ever a medieval charlatan. This is the *sermo elatus* in the Punch-and-Judy, popular sense of the term rather than in some pseudosublime, aristocratic sense, inasmuch as behind this defensive attitude can be glimpsed the underhand ways of the "peasant" who is what he has always been and who would gladly deliver a stab in the back. Indeed, this voice could be seen as a praise of cowardice, an indirect hymn on the Ruzantian

or Brechtian model, from works such as *La bilora (The Weasel)* or
Schweyk,[4] to remain with Fo's favorite theatrical predecessors, in other
words, as the saga of the antihero. If the preceding voice was obviously
a voice that rose from the depth, from the innards, this latter is a nasal
voice. Here once again the force of a tradition can be felt. In my opinion,
in the person of Fo, the ancient clash between the first and second *zanni*,
or between the two clowns, the Auguste and the White clown, is given
new life and is reconciled.

Voices, as is well known, disappear from the memory. They leave
behind them no document of any sort, just as bodies, no matter how
exciting and desirable, inexorably decay with time. For Fo, this process
was assisted by the decisions of RAI to destroy the radio tapes of the
1940s and 1950s, considering the actors of that time to be worthless as
indications of the age. They may remain in commentaries, in exclama-
tions, in adjectives that are, alas, defective and insufficient. The voices
of actors are not written words. They are air; they are physical signs en-
trusted to distracted and voracious senses. And yet, some chromosomes
are passed on by some physiological or cultural descent. Thus, in the
alternation between black and white sound, between the earthy and the
volatile, the nonacademic *phoné* returns miraculously to life, that *phoné*
that was not programmed by the Silvio D'Amico college of dramatic art,
the academic institution set up in 1935 to bring some unity to the voices
of our actors. There is no "Tuscan-centric" diction in Fo, no trace of
that pronunciation with an overlay of "hen's arse" (as it was put, somewhat biliously, by the nonconformist critic Alberto Savinio),[5] that pronunciation that has contributed in no small way to deepening the gulf
that separates stage and stalls. "Correct" diction represents a translation
of an overwritten, indeed "exclusively" written, theater, of a theater that
"smacks of lead," as it was put by another minority voice in twentieth-
century Italian theater, Anton Giulio Bragaglia.[6]

On the contrary, the voices produced by Fo exclude every head
sound, have no trace of the buskined voice, of that rhythmic bourgeois axis that smacks of the humdrum-realist verisimilitude of the well-
heeled, the dum-de-dum of conversation in the most elegant, dandi-
fied salons, and that recalls, at the same time, the starched, anemic
sound of the likes of Gualtiero Tumiati, Ruggero Ruggeri, Renzo Ricci,
Memo Benassi, voices that reach their climax in the hendecasyllables
declaimed by Vittorio Gassman, in the syllable-by-syllable warblings of
Paola Borboni, in the sugary-sweet, melodic line that, by way of the

silvery falsettos and the youthful irony of Ruggero Ruggeri, descends to the depth of an arpeggio with Carmelo Bene.[7] The voices of Fo themselves struggle to conceal an impulse toward song, but here it is the panting, asymmetric song of work, of exhaustion and of struggle, or the slaver that dribbles from the famished throats of country workers; it is the sound that, interwoven with the dialects of *commedia dell'arte*, makes itself heard through the liberating belches of the impudent and noisy *zanni*. The 1966 and 1996 *Ci ragiono e canto* (I think things out and sing about them) bring tendencies of this sort out into the open. There appears to emerge from Fo's mouth a whole piazza of traveling salesmen, of charlatans and gypsies, of rope makers and circus freaks, a whole throbbing, picturesque, and sardonic undergrowth, compelled by atavistic appetites to speak, invited to pretend, to charm with rhetorical tropes that invent a mirage and then transform it into reality. Between the stench and the sweat of the ring, between the yell and the guffaw, between the impotent invective and the unheard prayer, the voice seems to vindicate its own right to be rude and coarse, in the widest and most joyful sense of these terms.

In the midst of this babel of voices, a delightfully dirty word can emerge, as can a whole vocabulary taken from literary byways, both quite out of keeping with the official, academic dictionary of high culture. Fo, through the agency of the Padan dialect, brings to life a mixed language, a rich mixture of elegance and peasant force, particularly from *Mistero buffo* onward. With the dialect, the whole carnivalization of the world, as Bakhtin would have it, comes into play, with all the preeminence of the body and scatology of the lower aspects of life that that involves. This effect has been strengthened by the elaboration over time of an open koinè, devised, refined, and reinvented with the assistance of the famous *grammelot*, that is, mime speech, the use of abstract phonemes spoken in such a way as to bypass obstacles erected by censorship. In this case, too, however, there is no lack of illustrious predecessors who each made full use of this lexical babel. Predecessors could include the *Scapigliatura*[8] movement in nineteenth-century Lombardy, as well as later Lombards or Venetians, including Carlo Emilio Gadda, Giovanni Testori, and Luigi Meneghello.[9] The actor Franco Parenti, for whom Testori created his blackest texts, emerged, as has been said already, from the cabaret experience of Fo. Strangely, in his actorly solitude, Fo has become a fertile master and has given birth to a substantial school of direct and indirect descendants who today are to be found in the most exciting sections of Italian theater. People such as Paolo Rossi in comedy, Moni Ovadia in yiddish-musical theater, and Marco Paolini in straight theater are the most engrossing and uninhibited monologists, the most pleasing and unpredictable entertainers, and are all in one way or another indebted to the magisterial lessons imparted by Fo.

Voice, gesture, and word do not of themselves provide adequate equipment for a reassessment of Fo. His uniqueness of the panorama of Italian theater lies in the fact that from a certain point of his development, Fo has incarnated an amalgam of various traditions and brought them together in an equilibrium, however precarious and contradictory. What is the nature of these (other) traditions? Here it is essential to proceed with care. I am tempted to put forward, as the decisive element, the memory of the audience, as I have attempted to show on other occasions.[10] Fo, by the very act of production, establishes, in the most concrete way, the primacy of the circuit, in the sense that the recipient becomes the privileged motivator of his writing, the objective of his repertoire, and the standard of all possible interpretations. In this case, the impulse is at precisely the opposite end of the scale from that which persuades him to take the stage as solo performer. Fo, even before he was swept along by the so-called cultural revolution of the years 1967–68, when he grew tired of operating, in his own words, as a *digestif* for the bourgeoisie in the theaters of central Milan, was always conscious of the "other," of the spectator whom he set out to involve in a complex series of ways, for example, by his stubborn quest for the contemporary. A meticulously individualized audience becomes a part of the corpus of his dramatic work as, virtually, coprotagonist of that work. For Fo, the theater is, more than anything else, a contemporary dialogue with people physically present, and this was so even in the lighter phase of apparent noncommitment, at the time of his *boulevardier* output.

Everything must have as principal aim the maintenance of an immediate contact with the audience. Both partners in this relationship must each remain totally conscious of their proximity to the other. If by some chance the stalls grow distracted, if they immerse themselves too deeply in the fiction, the performer will immediately make it his or her business, with digressions and counterattacks, to bring them back to the urgency of the front page of that day's newspaper, because theater of this sort must be, in some way, converted into a newspaper, a living agit-prop newspaper, of the kind familiar in the Weimar Republic in the 1920s or

America in the 1930s. In consequence, the writing aims at the creation of a chorus, with an imagined legion of actors on the set. Feminism and piecework, drugs and proletarian expropriation, prison conditions and AIDS are recurrent themes in the headlines. All are grist for the mills of the actor-dramatist and inspiration for the works performed by his partner, Rame, and his various groups.

It is in this sense that we should examine his career, regarding it as a progressive shift of audience, an unceasing invention of new users on the ideological, if not the social, plane. In other words, the progress through cabaret, revue, television, and the more opulent Milanese theaters on to the *case del popolo* and ARCI (the Communist-leaning cultural and recreation circles), at the time when he was closest to the Italian Communist Party, the Palazzina Liberty, and La Comune, during his extraparliamentary period, involve continual adjustments both in montage and the topics themselves.[11] Once the theater and its audience have been identified, it becomes a matter of creating with it a dialectical relationship, made up of moments of agreement and moments of provocation. Even during the time of his television stardom of 1962, with his brief appearance on some episodes of *Canzonissima*, in a television medium then dominated by the Christian Democratic party, Fo could still, behind the forced cheer of the advertising sketch, be seen to choose a recognizable and relaxing form so as to make undigested content acceptable. However, during that brief idyll, he set his aim too high and attracted in return complaints over a sketch featuring deaths at work in the building industry, for which he was rewarded with excommunication and expulsion from television screens for the next fifteen years. The same attitude was responsible for the crisis that brought to an end the collaboration between ARCI and Nuova Scena, his own theater company, in 1969–70. The cause of these disputes was the debate he inspired over the activities of the "Red Cooperatives," anticipating by several years the Milan magistrates' *mani pulite* (clean hands) anticorruption drive of the 1990s.

In this case, the denunciation was also based on gaps between the private behavior and the political beliefs of Communist activists who were authoritarian bosses and exploiters in their own homes, as well as on the position of Russia on the international stage. The model chosen by Fo was inspired by the registers of the medieval discussion play, and by an apologia of the morality play type, as can be seen most clearly in two intriguing works: *L'operaio conosce trecento parole il padrone mille per questo lui è il padrone* (The worker knows three hundred words, the boss one thousand, that's why he's the boss) and *Legami pure che tanto io spacco tutto lo stesso* (Tie me up but I'll still smash everything). Both of these 1969 plays were constructed by putting together enquiries at grassroots level and local interviews, that is, by transforming debates undertaken in the community into stage works. On each occasion, Fo sought out the roots of any conflict not for reasons of mere self-promotion but to make productive use of persecution and ostracism. Fo will have no truck with routine relationships, with the amorphous silence of anonymous acceptance, preferring in their stead full-frontal conflict, with the theater at the very heart of civil and political reporting. Indeed, it could be said, that his aim is to have the theater at the heart of the city. Fo's theater takes on the role of a university chair, even if, it must be emphasized, of a purely popular type. Undoubtedly, Fo is guilty of extreme oversimplification and of choosing extreme examples, which will never be to the taste of academic specialists in that field, whatever their ideological leanings.

Normally, in Fo's scripts, a binary, explicitly Manichean opposition is set up between pairs—Christian Democratic power versus liberal satire; capitalism versus socialism; revisionism versus revolutionary communism; traitors of the masses versus the people themselves, not to mention a deeper alternation between a debunking parody of the enemy and a liturgical celebration of friends and of the group themselves. Plainly, given the rigid division between good and bad, innocent and guilty, victims and executioners, with no scope for doubt left to the audience, this is not a scientific dialectic so much as a militant approach, aiming not at analytical research into the past but at its coincidence with an *engagé* present. In keeping with this approach, the plot generally requires the figure of an irresistible buffoon hero, often of a peasant background. This humble being, who could have emerged from some secular gospel, will be made into the perhaps unconscious representative of the persecuted. Fortunately, at this point, magical or fairy-tale motifs, surreal flights of fantasy, or wildly imaginative metaphors overwrite and nullify the banalization of politics and raise the work to the dream dimension. The omnipotence enjoyed by this strange, *faux naif* clown is the same as the power of a harlequin who is enabled to undermine power, to create an upside-down world in which the villain is forced to confess his misdeeds in public, as occurs in Fo's highly successful 1970 *Morte accidentale di un anarchico (Accidental Death of an Anarchist)*, or in the 1975 *Fanfani rapito (Fanfani Kidnapped)*.

The twin poles of Fo's writing in this period of widespread mobilization could be summarized as being, on the one hand, the poetic metaphor or the ambiguity of sign and, on the other, the downplaying of the stage, now made identical with the slogan. The fundamental risk in an itinerary of this kind lies in the possibility of the death of theater. Since he was at this time fully involved in social and political struggles, Fo's aim was to give heart to the recipient, who is the audience-protagonist, but this brings with it risk of the disappearance, or the extreme undervaluing, of production values, of aesthetic considerations in themselves. This is the phase that precedes and overlaps with the dark years of the 1970s, the years of terrorism and the historic compromise. No one should ignore the personal torments of Fo himself, who appeared, in the reports of struggles, almost to waver between apprehension and joy at the prospect of disappearing from sight. Then, once the ideological tension had evaporated and the danger of the elimination of the theater had been overcome, the support given by the public at large began to wane. A sea change occurred between the late 1960s and the 1980s and 1990s. The utopian outlook that had been reinforced by the best and most necessary efforts of the actor appears today, at the millennium, to have been dulled by disenchantment and leaden cynicism. Today, the enthusiastic masses of other times, those crowds who readily lent their support, who were pursued and assembled at the time of the occupation of the Palazzina Liberty, flock more readily and more willingly to rock concerts, to gatherings promoted by singer-songwriters and by homespun *raissoneurs*, such as Giorgio Gaber, Grillo, and Luigi Proietti. These have the advantage of an organizational and distributive system better able to guarantee an audience, and one that will be more easily electrified and involved. Finally, in 1997, came the Nobel Prize for Literature, and, thus, the discussion must be, at least in part, opened up all over again.

In any discussion of Fo's practice, it is essential not to neglect another tradition, the tradition that is dominant in him, the tradition of the actor-author. Here, the solo performer and the militant journalist, the monologue and the chorus, the metaphor and the sermon, the elaboration and the improvisation, the self and the other find some kind of agreement. The performer who has the scripts made to measure, so that writing and performance merge, is a professional figure typical of the highest moments of the history of theater. Once again, there is no need to go as far back as the productive system of the stock characters of *commedia dell'arte*, since nineteenth-century romanticism and naturalism lend their aid with their own great models. There is, to quote only one emblematic case, the example of the celebrated actress Adelaide Ristori (1882–1906), who commissioned melodramatic arrangements from Paolo Giacometti and Giulio Carcano. The divine Eleonora Duse,[12] with her Shakespearean relationship with Arrigo Boito,[13] followed the same path. In short, the entire drama of nineteenth-century Italy, considered at first sight lacking in authors, is in fact overflowing with authorial talents, provided one switches the emphasis from the conventional image of the writer at his or her table to an onstage collaboration between the "great actor/actress" and the on-duty script-writer. The whole regional and dialect front draws its success from synergies of this kind, particularly so in the case of the Neapolitan theater from Eduardo Scarpetta (1853–1925) to Raffaele Viviani (1888–1950) right down to the more recent Eduardo De Filippo (1900–1984).

Fo is a master of do-it-yourself, in the sense that he composes with his own body, on his own body, on the set. For this reason, he exploits everything that will be of value to him, always. In the early years, with the disorder of an unusually receptive casual worker, his output drew from all sources. Indeed, if the song-and-dance and escapist comedies of the late 1950s and the early 1960s are analyzed, those in the period from the 1958 *Ladri, manichini e donne nude* (Thieves, mannequins, and naked women) to the 1965 *La colpa è sempre del diavolo* (Always blame the devil), it can be seen that the keyboard that produces his music contains a mixture of registers that include *commedia dell'arte*, *lazzi*, calques from American silent cinema, farce or cabaret routines, parodies of thriller-detective literature, eternal triangles worthy of the French *pochade*, not to mention the remains of the futurist avant-garde, the whole shaken and stirred with a weird surrealism inspired by Achille Campanile[14] and the overflow of the absurd styled on French plays of that time, especially those by Ionesco or Anouilh. The whole period finds its apex in the songs, those near nursery rhymes that provide a rhyming, rhythmic satire of modes and morals.

Denunciation takes place in the shadow of an over-the-top game of substitutions, of recognitions, disguises, knockabout, death and resurrection, but yet in the 1964 *Settimo: ruba un po' meno (Seventh Commandment: Steal a Bit Less)*, Fo's theater, astonishingly, gives us a police charge with policemen firing on the workers! From the time of the 1967 *La signora è da buttare (Toss the Lady Out)*, an allegory on the United States and on the Kennedy years, the writing, assisted by a change of performance spaces and of circuits, swerves between jumbled, circus-style inventiveness, pop language, and the use of hand and string puppets. During this period, a typical Fo stage would be filled with images of gigantic beastly figures that might have been borrowed from street theater, as is the case with, for example, the 1968 *Grande pantomima con bandiere e pupazzi piccoli e medi* (Grand pantomime with flags and small and medium-sized puppets). Here Fo draws inspiration from such American groups as *Bread and Puppet* to launch himself into a new style of stage design, making use of audio-visual aids, almost in homage to the long dead Piscator. By the same token, the partisan narratives presented in the 1970 *Vorrei morire anche stasera se dovessi pensare che non è servito a niente* (I would like to die this very evening if I thought it was all useless) seem to make use of neorealist sequences from the cinema of Rossellini. This is nothing less than an act of plunder or expropriation, because everything can now be of service to the body writing onstage, although the results are at times light and at others more prolix. The underlying notion of writing is essentially functional, serial, lay, a kind of blotting paper laid on the world.

To conclude this piece on Fo and on the interweaving of various traditions that he represents, it might be worthwhile to wonder about the longevity of his writing when separated from the greatness of the actor, even if the two aspects are not easily separable.[15] Fo has not been able to put together a stable company; he has never trained working companions who have remained with him, if one makes an exception for the radiant support of Rame, often his equal in overall responsibility for the play. There are disciples, but they are dispersed and distant. Perhaps when removed from their militant context, and without the audiences that had helped prepare these dishes at the right temperature, or these "roadshow" scripts, the plays will be seen to work only with their author onstage. Without Fo, the words risk becoming ponderous, as though the scripts themselves were being deflated bit by bit, or as though the great light in his magnetic voice were being slowly extinguished. On the other hand, abroad, his words, once translated, can acquire again a strange strength and can be reinvented for the comic rhythm of other struggles.

Translated from Italian by Joseph Farrell.

Notes

1. The *variété*, *café chantant*, and *avanspettacolo* are forms of popular and variety entertainment.

2. Petrolini began as an entertainer in a *café chantant*. He rose to international fame, touring Europe and America and performing in the Comédie Française.

3. Maurice Blanchot wonders whether the Brechtian theory and practice of alienation, linked to a movement of distancing from the audience, is not paradoxically transformed into a surplus of fascination (1966).

4. *La bilora* is a play by Ruzzante. *Schweyk* is Brecht's adaptation of the novel *The Good Soldier* by Czech author Jaroslav Hasek.

5. Alberto Savinio (1891–1952), essayist, novelist, playwright, and director, was the brother of painter Giorgio de Chirico.

6. Anton Giulio Bragaglia (1890–1960) is associated in his youth with the Futurists. As a theater director, he was concerned with reducing the importance of the word in favor of physical theater. He wrote several books on the history of masks in theater.

7. Of the actors mentioned here, it is worth noting that Ruggero Ruggeri (1871–1953) was a leading man in Pirandello's company; Vittorio Gassman (1922–2000) was one of Italy's leading stage and film actors; and Carmelo Bene (b. 1937) is also known for his experimental approach as a film director.

8. The *Scapigliatura* was a nineteenth-century, avant-garde, bohemian literary movement, centered in Milan in postunification Italy.

9. Carlo Emilio Gadda (1893–1973) was a novelist known for his quasi-Joycean linguistic experimentation. Giovanni Testori (1925–93) was a Catholic playwright. Luigi Meneghello (b. 1922) is a novelist who uses his native Vicenza dialect in his books.

10. I refer the reader to my various other studies on Fo, in particular Puppa 1972, 1976, 1978, 1990:211–14, 1992. These pieces are different in nature, some being occasional writings, others more systematic and organic. It would be possible to trace a shift in the evaluation of Fo, as though he had obliged me, over the course of time, to continually modify and alter my stance. What has remained unchanged, if I may be permitted a personal note, is my admiration for the actor and my affection for the man.

11. The *case del popolo* were the local meeting and activity centers run by the Italian Communist Party. The Palazzina Liberty was an abandoned building in Milan. Around 1970, Fo, Rame, and their alternative company occupied it and made it their theater; in 1982, they were forced to abandon it.

12. Eleonora Duse (1858–1924) was one of the greatest actresses of her age. She was much admired by Chekhov, played Verga, Ibsen, and D'Annunzio, with whom she had a long relationship.

13. Arrigo Boito (1842–1918) was a writer of melodramatic tales and a librettist for, among others, Giuseppe Verdi.

14. Achille Campanile (1900–76) was a humorist and an author of plays and film scripts.

15. Every discussion of Fo runs the risk of being overwhelmed by recognition of the charisma of the actor and must also resist the temptation of hagiography. Among the analyses that I consider of enduring value, I would like to mention those of Meldolesi (1980), Holm (1980), Pizza (1996), and Nepoli and Cappa (1997).

References

Blanchot, Maurice. 1966. "Brecht e il disgusto per il teatro." *Nuova corrente* nos. 38–40:14–19.

Holm, Bent. 1980. *Dario Fo e la fantasia popolare*. Stockholm: Drama.

Meldolesi, Claudio. 1980. *Su un comico in rivolta: Dario Fo, il bufalo, il bambino*. Rome: Bulzoni.

Nepoli, Roberto, and Marina Cappa. 1997. *Dario Fo*. 2d ed. Rome: Cremese.

Pizza, Marisa. 1996. *Il gesto, la parola, l'azione: drammaturgia e storia dei monologhi di Dario Fo*. Rome: Bulzoni.

Puppa, Paolo. 1972. "Tutti insieme! Tutti insieme! Ma scusa, quello non è Dario Fo?" *L'erba voglio* no. 4 (April):5–15.

———. 1976. "Ruzante e le piste nere." *Biblioteca teatrale* no. 17:43–54.

———. 1978. *Il teatro di Dario Fo: dalla scena all piazza*. Venice: Marsilio.

———. 1990. *Teatro e spettacolo nel secondo novecento*. Rome: Laterza.

———. 1992. "L'America scoperta dai Padani." *L'indice* no. 4 (April):7–8.

CHAPTER 11

The Actor Who Writes
Dario Fo and the Nobel Prize

JOSEPH FARRELL

The September 1959 issue of *Sipario*, Italy's most prestigious theatrical periodical, carried the text of Dario Fo's first three-act play, *Gli arcangeli non giocano a flipper (Archangels Don't Play Pinball)*. In a brief, but generous and enthusiastic, introductory note, a journalist who signed himself G.D.C. raised a question that was to haunt Fo throughout his career. He pointed to the idiosyncratic nature of Fo's farces, which—since they existed on fringes that "may be tiny but are real and are all that our age leaves to the irrational"—he defined as "more than examples of purely escapist theater." He went on:

> In any calculation [of the value of the plays], there is no reason to exclude—and why should there be?—the physical, I might almost say, biological presence of Fo the actor. In terms of the typically Italian phenomenon of the actor-author symbiosis, the question is bound to arise of the worth of the literary creations of Fo, if they are considered separately from the acting. (G.D.C. 1959:37)

The same question of the connection between Fo's acting and writing was raised again in the August 1963 issue of the same periodical.

It should be stated that *Sipario* was in no way hostile to Fo's work or style of theater and, indeed, had followed him with interest ever since his debut in Milan with his cabaret performances in the company of Franco Parenti and Giustino Durano. *Sipario* had shown some enthusiasm for Fo's subsequent two programs of one-act farces, the 1958 *Ladri, manichini e donne nude* (Thieves, mannequins, and naked women) and *Comica finale*, and had already published five of his plays. The script it carried in the August 1963 issue, *Isabella, tre caravelle e un cacciaballe (Isabella, Three Sailing Ships, and a Con Man)*, represented another milestone in Fo's burgeoning career, being the first of his plays accepted for publication in book form. In his introduction to the magazine version, the critic Ettore Capriolo wrote that there was a special problem to the appreciation of Fo's plays in their printed form:

> In this style of understanding theater, the script, that is, the words, constitute only one of the components of the discourse that is to be integrated with the movement and the gestures. . . . Each is inseparable from an imagined whole. To read a script by Fo as a thing in itself, in other words, to make a judgment of the playwright separately from the actor and the director means gaining a somewhat incomplete idea of the script itself. (1963:39)

Isabella had already been an enormous success on the stage, enjoying a protracted run of over sixty performances at Milan's Odeon Theater and ranking very highly in the official ministerial accounts of the takings of that year's productions. The following issue of *Sipario* carried a brief report on the official book launch. Although not referring explicitly to Capriolo's remarks, Fo used the occasion to issue an implicit reply to his strictures on the inadequacy of the text. The words were subdued, but even at a distance of years, the annoyance is clear. Fo took the fact that his play had been judged worthy of publication as a refutation of the accusation that it was an indifferent work in itself, or at best one that acquired value only when performed, much less only when performed by Fo himself. Fo believed he merited appreciation as a writer and not only as a performer.

This writer-versus-performer polemic was the first installment of a dispute that was to dog the critical assessment of Fo's work throughout his life, most especially in Italy. It partially explains the curmudgeonly response in certain quarters to the award of the Nobel Prize for

Literature in 1997. The *querelle* has been variously formulated. Is a written text by Fo merely a pretext, and often a very flimsy pretext, for a display of the bravura of the actor? Have the scripts he produced any depth and vitality independent of his onstage presence, or are they a fraud perpetrated on a gullible theater public but easily exposed by the more alert reading public? Is Fo an actor who writes rather than a writer who acts? The defense case can be simply stated: Those who are convinced that Fo's comedies are intrinsically lifeless until given oxygen by his performance magic are required to account for the enormous success of his plays overseas, where Fo is, obviously, absent. In its most basic form, the question is, How good is Fo as a writer? The question has been given added focus by the award of the Nobel Prize for Literature.

The official, fulsome citation by the Swedish Academy provides essentially ethical reasons for the attribution of the prize. Fo, it stated, "emulates the jesters of the Middle Ages in scourging authority and upholding the dignity of the downtrodden" (1997). The Vatican daily, *L'Osservatore Romano*, agreed with the description of Fo as the jester (*giullare*) but added the spice of condescending patrician *hauteur* to the term fulsomely employed by the Swedish Academy: "Fo is Italy's sixth Nobel Prize winner after Carducci, Deledda, Pirandello, Quasimodo, and Montale; after such good sense, a jester," it wrote (Vatican 1997:82). It was not a compliment.

The citation by the Swedish Academy also identified the "noninstitutional tradition" as vital to his development and added that apart from medieval jesters and the *commedia dell'arte* tradition, such "twentieth century writers as Mayakovsky and Brecht had provided Fo with important impulses." The statement concluded by focusing squarely and uncompromisingly on the abilities of Fo as writer:

> Fo's strength is in the creation of texts that simultaneously amuse, engage and provide perspectives. As in *commedia dell'arte*, they are always open for additions and dislocations, continually encouraging the actors to improvise, which means that the audience is activated in a remarkable way. His is an oeuvre of impressive artistic vitality and range. (Swedish Academy 1997)

Not everyone in Italy was able to detect the "vitality and range" that so impressed the "Immortals of the Royal Academy in Stockholm." The critic Carlo Bo proclaimed himself "as surprised as Fo" and wondered about the gulf between Fo and Italy's last Noble laureate, Eugenio Montale (1997:19); the historian and essayist Giuseppe Galasso declared himself "terrified" by the award (1997:20); and the veteran critic Geno Pampaloni stated that the award was a "joke—there are several more poetic poets with a better claim to the prize" (1997:20). Giulio Ferroni, author of the much admired *History of Italian Literature*, was left perplexed and returned to a familiar refrain: "I have a high regard for Fo the actor, but where is the literature?" (1997:15).

Although Fo enjoyed the support of such prestigious figures as the novelists Dacia Maraini and Vincenzo Consolo, the only writer of any prominence prepared to state unequivocally that the prize had gone to Fo in recognition of his literary talents was Umberto Eco:

> I am delighted by the fact that they gave the prize to an author who does not belong to the traditional academic world. What I find impressive is his enormous popularity abroad. For us in Italy it is very difficult to separate the power of Fo as a theatrical character from the scripts he writes. We are mistaken if we allow ourselves to be conditioned by the character, great as he is. His plays are of great importance in our literature. (1997:15)

In the ensuing public fracas, Fo himself seemed for a time to desert the field, leaving his defense team to assert his merits as a writer while he advanced the thesis that the award was a vindication of the acting profession. The term "vindication" recurred in his interviews and articles. It was not Fo alone who was being vindicated but generations of actors, or the whole lineage of stage writers. "I am pleased about this prize because it represents the vindication of the actor, because it goes to an actor and not only to a writer, to the jester and not to the man of letters. It will be the first time an actor has shaken a king's hand" (Fo 1997d:19). It was not his last word on the subject. When one journalist put to him the apocalyptic scenario, voiced by some critics, that the award to Fo marked the end of literature as such, Fo couched his reply in terms of the demands of theater, not literature. Traditional theater, he said, had never relied entirely on the written text.

> Improvisation has always been important, and then there is what we could call the lesson of Molière. From those times onwards, the actor who wrote was always taken as a fool. In the case of Molière,

the word was put about that he couldn't have written his own works. This prize is a vindication of poor Molière as well. (1997d:13)

With the authoritative backing of the Swedish Academy, Fo could now reiterate his most deeply held conviction that theater writing, and not only his style of theater writing, is an independent genre, to be judged on terms that are different from those applied to other genres of literature. Now the debate about the value of his own scripts could and should be rephrased so that it is not a writing-versus-performance dispute but a recognition that writing-plus-performance, or writing with a view to performance, provides the only standards by which theater can be judged. The qualities required of the playwright are not to be compared to those exhibited by novelist or poet. In upholding this tenet, Fo insisted that he was not a radical dissident but part of the mainstream tradition of Western dramaturgy. This positioning of himself in a tradition is invariably of primary importance to Fo. Radical though he may be in his politics, in matters theatrical he is a blue-blooded conservative and has not wished to adopt positions that are not sanctioned by illustrious predecessors. When Chiara Valentini, author of a biography of Fo, put to him the frequently made point that he was an excellent actor but that playwrights are something else again, he replied:

> Those who reason in this way show that they have never understood what theater is. These gentlemen who go into ecstasies over the reading of Shakespeare forget that his scripts too were *canovacci*. "The word is the theater," said Shakespeare. And I believe that this Nobel Prize is indeed a recognition of the value of the word on the stage. The word can become written only after it has been used, after it has been chewed many times on the set. That's the way it was for many famous authors. Half of what we know of Ruzzante was printed only after his death. The scripts of Molière were *canovacci* until some traditional authors encouraged him to have them published. (1997b:80)

Shakespeare would have known that a *canovaccio* was the outline script employed by actors in the *commedia dell'arte* tradition, but I have no idea where Shakespeare used the phrase Fo attributes to him, and I doubt if a computer search would yield any enlightenment. Fo's quotations are taken from a library in his head, and while that library is magnificently stocked after years of meticulous research into all aspects of theater and theater history, many of the volumes are forgeries. That is less important than the light this "quote," like others of the same sort, casts on Fo's thinking. For him, theater is indeed the word made flesh. One of the most important aspects of his break with conventional theater in 1968 was, he said, the liberation from the slavery of the script. As he said to Chiara Valentini: "We rejected the law according to which 'the script is theater'; we put a bomb under its butt" (Fo 1997b:79).

The instruments employed both in the academies and in newspaper reviews to judge a playwright are, Fo suggests, inadequate. No one would respect a critic who based his assessment of a lyric poem on meaning alone, without paying heed to meter, scansion, rhyme, imagery, and music and without being at least aware of some haunting emotional appeal that transcends these technical factors. Nor would anyone be impressed by an exercise that set out to prove that Dickens was a better writer than Virgil, or the reverse. And any critic who, in all seriousness, attempted to establish such a hierarchy would leave himself open to scornful accusations of unintelligent incompetence. In Fo's case, however, a snare of this sort lies waiting for even the best prepared and most sympathetic of reviewers or critics. Fo follows what were conventionally considered the lesser trodden and minor paths of the Western tradition. Farce, his favorite medium, is viewed as being of lesser moment than comedy and of virtually no standing if set beside tragedy. The critical tools for assessing farce and theater writing of the Fo type are lacking, and the consequence is that many critics have perpetrated the equivalent of judging Dickens by the standards applied to Virgil.

Fo insists on the discipline and professionalism intrinsic to the trade. Theater writing could not afford to be fey and meandering; any verbal magic has to be subordinate to action and incorporated in a vivid whole. Ambiguity is an effete indulgence and, in spite of what critics might imply, not necessarily a value in itself. Cooperation with actors is of the essence, and action and immediate impact are what theater has to aim for. Those who wish to tease out new depths and to subject a work to successive reinterpretations are free to do so, but the surface visual and scenic qualities of the production are always of prime importance, especially for one who worked in the popular tradition. Farce merits equality of consideration with tragedy.

Fo has made these and other points about his theater on various occasions, but his official Nobel Prize lecture constitutes the fullest statement of his own poetics. This observation may seem like a bizarre, harlequin's joke. To the consternation of the official committee, there was no written text to be translated and issued in advance but only a semi-improvised monologue delivered on the basis of a series of sketches, scrawls, cartoons, and images Fo had prepared in Milan to act as prompts for himself. They were sufficient. Fo disarmed his listeners with the wit and exuberance of his delivery, but those who saw beyond the extravagance and hilarity of the performance would have noticed a similarity of objective with other acceptance speeches in the same venue. Malraux, Camus, Shaw, and Beckett had used the occasion to issue a manifesto detailing the meaning of writing and literature for them. Fo was engaged on the same task. The subject was comic theater, and as ever with Fo, the medium and the message were at one. The harlequin behaved as a harlequin to proclaim the mission of the harlequin, but the speech represented an article of faith, a statement of the seriousness of the theatrical vocation, and as such it can rank alongside Brecht's *Short Organum for the Theater*.

Coming as it did toward the end of his career, the statement was a compendium of established belief and practice, rather than a revolutionary pronunciamento. The lecture had an imposing Latin title, *Contra Jogulatores Obloquentes* (Against jesters of irreverent speech), which, according to Fo, was taken from the official title of a law passed in 1221 by the Holy Roman Emperor and king of Sicily, Frederick II. This edict permitted citizens of the empire to insult, barrack, throw missiles at, assault, and even assassinate strolling players, without the need of any further sanction from courts. It is worth underlining that in the very title, Fo identified himself with actors, not writers, and that in his speech, he spoke once again of theater practitioners not of his own time but from the past. The secretary of the academy, Sture Allen, quoted from the commendation of Bernard Shaw when the Nobel Prize was conferred on him. That document had made reference to Shaw's idealism, humanity, and stimulating satire, and Allen suggested that Fo and Shaw were kindred spirits. Fo did not respond on this point. His admiration for Shaw is the dutiful respect paid to the elders of the tribe, not a living force. During his stay in Stockholm, he paid a fulsome tribute to Strindberg, probably the only time he has felt the need to praise a playwright he otherwise consigned to a lonely fate in the circles of lower hell reserved for writers who have dedicated themselves to analyzing bourgeois angst. Even so, the acclamation of Strindberg was of a limited

Sketch by Dario Fo for his Nobel Prize acceptance speech. (Courtesy C.T.F.R.).

sort. Fo had discovered that Strindberg had been held in contempt by the Establishment of his day and had been on occasions obliged to appear onstage in his own work. Strindberg was given honorary, if temporary, membership of the elite club of troublesome actor-dramatists.

Fo's speech was a carefully structured venture in literary autobiography. The ingredients were familiar—a heretical examination of passages

from history, an act of homage to acknowledged masters, known and
unknown, who had contributed to his formation as writer, and then a
switch of key to denounce injustices perpetrated in his own day. The
recipe was the same as in many of his plays: laughter with anger, farce
with denunciation, history and topicality, and always theater as the universal fulcrum. Fo had always asserted that he had learned the art of
storytelling from the *fabulatori* (storytellers) who visited his home village on the shores of Lake Maggiore, although on this occasion he spe-
cified that many such were not traveling performers but fishermen and
glassblowers who worked in a local factory. The need to tell the story in
the moments while drawing breath between successive puffs at the mol-
ten glass imposed a rhythm of its own. In his recital of popular song, *Ci
ragiono e canto* (I think things out and sing about them), Fo had insisted
on the twinning between musical rhythm and rhythms of work. The
essence of the *fabulatore*'s art did not consist only in the use of suspense,
the creation of atmosphere, or the skilled retelling of well-plotted narratives but also in the interweaving of elements of fantasy, of irony, of
the grotesque, and of wayward truths. From them, Fo learned an approach he used in all his theater, a style that combined disparate elements with the savor of tragedy and comedy. As he explained in his acceptance speech: "We laughed, but we stopped to appreciate the irony"
(1997a).

Fo retold their tale of the village of Caldè, a mythical, thriving community on a spur of rock overhanging the lake. The only drawback to
life there was that each day the village slipped a little closer to the water,
but in spite of pleas from people in surroundings townships, the inhabitants of Caldè refused to move, regarding all such advice as an unscrupulous effort to make them abandon their homes and their possessions.
They carried on working, ploughing the land, fishing, marrying, and
giving in marriage until the day the entire village tumbled into the
water. The lake was deep at that point, so the village, houses, church,
belfry, and town hall were all totally submerged. Even then, the inhabitants refused to flee. Some said it was nothing, merely a minor incon-
venience, nothing more than a bit of settlement, even if they all agreed
conditions were somewhat uncomfortably damp. When they saw fish
before their eyes, they were only moved to express mild surprise that fish
had learned to fly. The glassblowers concluded by telling the listening
boys that if they were to go to the rock during a storm, when the light-
ening was flashing, they would still see the people of Caldè going about

The
Actor Who
Writes

their business unabashed, driving to church, visiting friends, buying and selling, doing what they had always done, "because there are people who would prefer to sink into an abyss rather than recognize a truth" (Fo 1997a).

Fo has never been adequately appreciated as a teller of tales, but throughout all the various vicissitudes of his dramatic career, that element has remained constant. Perhaps the great discovery he made with *Mistero buffo* (Comic mystery) was that he could be successful by merely being himself and allowing people to become engrossed in the tales he tells. Fo has been celebrated as a satirist, a monologist, an exponent of the popular viewpoint, and a man whose vision is imbued with irony, but his roots lie in the popular tradition of storytelling. He began his performance career on the radio telling grotesque tales that were later staged and published as *Poer nano* (Poor soul), and he returned to this unvarnished, solo style with such major works as *Mistero buffo, Storia della tigre (The Tale of the Tiger)*, and *Johan Padan a la descoverta de le Americhe (Johan Padan—The Discovery of the Americas)*.

Fo's development as a man of theater shows in the clearest way his indebtedness to the predecessors he has chosen as exemplars. Fo's work is created inside a cultural tradition, and in his speech, he paid homage to those predecessors, not Brecht and Shaw but Ruzzante and Molière. "Ruzzante remains too little known, but this man who lived seventy years before Shakespeare is the greatest playwright of the Italian Renaissance. Together with Molière, he is my master" (1997a). Both Fo and Ruzzante were actor-authors, both were producers of their own work, and both were insulted by the court poets because they took their themes from ordinary life and spoke out against violence. To further irritate their critics, they had the knack Fo admired of being able to treat serious subjects through laughter. Fo gave Ruzzante credit for having devised many of the techniques he himself exploited, particularly the use of dialect and of *grammelot*. In the course of his speech, Fo performed an extract from Ruzzante and a poem by Mayakovsky. He somewhat spoiled the effect the following day by admitting that he had made up the poem on the spot but suggested that Mayakovsky would have been pleased with it.

Fo rounded off his exposition of his vision of theater with the consideration of two topics: the nature of the political and moral commitment required in theater and the role of laughter. All theatrical activity is portrayed by him as a vocation, whose mission consists not of providing a celebration of living but of spreading awareness of social reality.

There has been no shortage of theatrical gurus this century, men like Jerzy Grotowsky and Eugenio Barba, who have expressed a quasi-mystical view of the nature of theater and its capacity to implement a change of minds and values, and who have demanded near monastic commitment of their actors, or acolytes. Fo has no ambition to set himself up as the father-abbot of a theatrical monastery, but he is as demanding as Barba or Grotowsky, and even if he is by temperament uninterested in any transcendental vision, his beliefs are inspired by the same ferocity of passion. To win his approval, the actor or writer must not allow himself to become a mere professional or a master of technique, capable of arousing any reaction by acquired skill, nor can he allow himself the indulgence of objectivity. His obligation is to temper his capacity to arouse indignation, hilarity, or rage by convictions that compel him to direct these emotions toward a cause that is worthwhile. The luxury of moral neutrality cannot be justified in the actor or writer.

For this reason, Fo has found himself at odds with the master of mime, Jacques Lecoq. Already, in his 1987 *Manuale minimo dell'attore* (The actor's mini-manual, published in English in 1991 as *Tricks of the Trade*), Fo had expressed his friendship and esteem for Lecoq, but also his profound disagreement with his exclusive concern with technique.

> "In my school, I [Lecoq] offer the pupils the entire repertoire needed for physical and gestural expression. It is up to each individual to apply it as he sees fit." "No," I [Fo] reply, "it is a grave mistake to separate technique from its ideological, moral and theatrical context." (1991:148)

In a workshop in the Drammaten in Stockholm during his visit to receive the prize, Fo reiterated the same charge: "Lecoq teaches his actors to walk, stand, use their hands, impersonate, hold their breath and deliver a joke, to talk endlessly but to say nothing" (1997e). Lecoq's method encourages performers to exist in a historical vacuum, to take no responsibility for the effects they create. For Fo, the impact created by performance and writing is central. Makers of theater, in Fo's terms, need to be conscious of the hierarchy of values underlying their work, to be aware of how performance determines content, to refuse to be bewitched by notions of pure art or pure professionalism, and to be in touch with their own times. At times, Fo talks of theater with the wary moralism Einstein employed when discussing the duties of scientists.

Since his is comic theater, Fo discusses laughter with the same seriousness as Henri Bergson in his celebrated treatise. Once when participating in a debate after a show during a tour with his company, La Comune, Fo told a questioner that the laughter was of no importance, that it could be put in or left out, since the vital element was the political point to be made. This was not his final position. Even in those days of militant theater, he never denied the value of laughter as relaxation, entertainment, or enjoyment to which weary spectators, be they middle or working class, were entitled, but he came to see laughter in more transcendental terms. In the course of the same wide-ranging talk in the Drammaten, he said:

> The ancients regarded the moment when man comes to awareness of his own humanity. In the South of Italy, during a baby's first forty days, everyone speaks in funny, clowning voices so as to make it laugh. A baby's first smile is viewed as the birth of intelligence, or even as the moment of the infusion of the soul. Laughter is sacred. (1997e)

For the political playwright, laughter is the enemy of catharsis. Laughter prevents a purging of the emotions occurring inside the theater and enables the playwright to encourage the spectator to focus on a topic raised in grotesque or comic terms. The title he used for three successive shows, *Ci ragiono e canto*, could be a wider metaphor for the best of his theater. Laughing, or singing, is to be accompanied by a demand for reasoning.

Fo then provided in Stockholm the poetics by which he would have his work assessed. His poetics may be rejected, but that is a different matter. To say that his genre is popular theater is only to erect a signpost, but one that will proclaim that Fo is bound to make a strange bedmate for Luigi Pirandello, Bernard Shaw, Eugene O'Neill, Samuel Beckett, or previous Nobel Prize-winning playwrights. He will also present an awkward intellectual problem for critics whose standards have been honed on dramatists of that type. Fo himself was, at one time, aware of this. He was nominated for the Nobel Prize in 1975 and used the opportunity for satire on the bourgeois establishment that makes such awards. "I do not run any risk of winning anything, and this for two precise reasons," he said then. The first was related to the political overtones of the Nobel Prize, but the other, as he reiterated to *Il foglio*, was that "my theater is not made to pass into history. I write and perform satire linked to daily news. They are scripts that immediately burn up their contents"

(1997c:1). Further, at the beginning of a book-length dialogue with
Erminia Artese, he rejected any parallel between himself and Pirandello. The questioner drew his attention to a book that had been recently published by Franca Angelini entitled *The Italian Theater in the
Twentieth Century from Pirandello to Fo* (1976). Fo replied that he simply could not see how anyone could put Pirandello's name and his at
opposite ends of the same book (1977:2). Their aims and means belonged to different worlds. In Fo's world, the distinction between dramatic literature and theater remains of prime importance. On this
point, the contrasts, discussed in the introduction, between Fo and Pier
Paolo Pasolini, are instructive. The aridity of intellectual debating theater, including Pasolini's, was not for Fo. In his more overtly Marxist period, he dismissed the central tradition of European theater as "bourgeois," including in that all-embracing category writers of the stature of
Chekhov and Pirandello. (On Pirandello, in particular, he expressed the
most diverse views on various occasions). Being a man with roots in tradition, Fo has little contact with modern theater, or with the psychic
wounds or moral dilemmas that that theater probes. No man has less
interest in any avant-garde. The image—totally accurate—of Fo as the
overthrower of the temples and altars where the powerful worship represents only one side of his ideology; Fo himself gambles and plays in
the amphitheaters where the Atellan farceurs, the medieval *giullari*, or
the late Renaissance harlequins performed. Although he deals with his
own times in his plays, other aspects of Fo's written and performed theater can be appreciated only if seen robustly "out of context," out of the
context created by his contemporaries.

He has no interest in investigating fractured psyches, in portraying
the plight of the human animal in a world made barren by the death of
God, or in delving into the inadequacies of language for the communication of emotional or intellectual dilemmas. There is no value in ap-
proaching Fo with a postmodern primer of deconstructionism, post-
structuralism, or reception aesthetics. There is rarely any subtext to be
uncovered or any hidden ambiguities to be revealed and never any deli-
cate psychology of character to be probed, curiosities of flawed personality to be dissected, or alternative world of the fantasy to be contem-
plated. Further, he does not construct a philosophy to compare with
Pirandellismo, or offer a portrait of a bourgeoisie in thrall to a claustro-
phobic malaise, as does Ibsen, or of a regime in terminal decline, as does
Chekhov. Critics will search in vain for the metaphysical dimension

constructed by fellow farceurs such as Beckett or Ionesco. Nor does his theater display, unlike that of Artaud or early Strindberg, symptoms of some neurosis of the creative mind, which could be taken as providing warped enlightenment of the world in which men and women have their daily being. The working class, and the popular theater addressed to them, had, in Fo's view, more concrete concerns, such as survival, employment, and prosperity.

In his complaints of critical misreadings, Fo has a case. His theater should no more be compared with that of Chekhov than Conan Doyle with Dostoevsky. It is odd and inconsistent that the harlequin of times past is now an object of reverential study but that a harlequin of today such as Fo is treated with condescension. Fo's real success can be gauged by the way he made theater dangerous again. His Stockholm speech touched on the perils faced by performers in other times, but he too was the object of official harassment and persecution. He was hounded by the censors and, when they were abolished, by magistrates. He faced twenty-two trials and was once imprisoned, in Sassari. Only the alertness of collaborators in locating dynamite around performing spaces prevented worse catastrophes. It is now, as a result of the investigations of the judge Guido Salvini, known that the kidnap, assault, and rape of Franca Rame in 1973 was ordered by elements within the carabinieri.

Fo fashioned a theater as a public arena where values, mainly but not exclusively political values, were aired and discussed. He was the first to attempt to weld this seriousness of purpose onto the supposedly lightweight genre that is farce. He is not to blame if a series of followers caused his style of theater to degenerate into pedestrian, didactic farce. His comedy, or farce, has an underlay of a seriousness that tragedy cannot attain, or at least cannot attain for a contemporary audience. Like Molière and Ruzzante, Fo lacks refinement of taste and has no urge to conform to the canons of aesthetics sanctioned by the elegant, voguish salons of the day. Like them, his wish is to create an upside-down world in which to flay the practices of those who wield power in the hope that these practices will be shown as preposterous, executed by people who, whatever status they have arrogated to themselves, are themselves preposterous.

The fact that a work depicts a purely contemporary dilemma does not mean that it will have nothing to say to posterity. *Gulliver's Travels* was conceived as a satire on British politics in the eighteenth century, but its inventiveness, its fantasy, its wry observation of human foibles have preserved its appeal. Fo's theater, like his comic world, is set in an indefinite area between the wasteland and wonderland. It might seem reasonable to expect that the plays most firmly anchored to a contemporary wasteland will fade but that those that depict a wonderland will endure, but these areas overlap in Fo. His theater, unlike Swift's novel, can never be reduced to mere whimsy. The paradox is that some plays, most notably *Morte accidentale di un anarchico (Accidental Death of an Anarchist)*, tell of events that could have been perpetrated by the March Hare of Wonderland, but Fo's skill as a playwright is to employ those techniques to make spectators focus unswervingly on matters that were an offense to the civil conscience. The explanation of the success of that play among people who never heard of the anarchist Giuseppe Pinelli or of the police officer Luigi Calabresi lies in the fact that the situation, always the prime element in Fo's theater, is so strongly imagined and seemingly whimsical. The skill in devising situations is likely to be sufficient to guarantee that the writer will be remembered when the performer has faded from memory.

All translations are by the author.

References

Angelini, Franca. 1976. *Il teatro del Novecento da Pirandello a Fo*. Bari: Laterza.

Bergson, Henri. 1900. *Le Rire: essai sur la signification du comique*. Paris: Gallimard.

Bo, Carlo. 1997. Reaction to the Nobel Prize. *Liberazione*, 10 October.

Capriolo, Ettore. 1963. Introduction to *Isabella, tre caravelle e un cacciaballe*, by Dario Fo. *Sipario* (August).

Eco, Umberto. 1997. Reaction to the Nobel Prize. *La Repubblica* (Rome), 10 October.

Ferroni, Giulio. 1997. Reaction to the Nobel Prize. *La Repubblica* (Rome), 10 October.

Fo, Dario. 1977. *Dario Fo parla di Dario Fo*. Interview by Erminia Artese. Cosenza: Lerici.

———. 1991. *The Tricks of the Trade. (Manuale minimo dell'attore)*. Tr. Joseph Farrell. Ed. Stuart Hood. New York: Routledge.

———. 1997a. "Contra Jogulatores Obloquentes." Nobel Prize acceptance speech.

———. 1997b. Interview. *Espresso* (23 October).

———. 1997c. Reaction to the Nobel Prize. *Il Foglio*, 10 October.

———. 1997d. Reaction to the Nobel Prize. *La Repubblica* (Rome), 10 October.

———. 1997e. Workshop held in the Drammaten. Stockholm.

Galasso, Giuseppe. 1997. Reaction to the Nobel Prize. *La Stampa* (Turin), 10 October.

G.D.C. 1959. Introduction to *Gli arcangeli non giocano a flipper*, by Dario Fo. *Sipario* (September).

Pampaloni, Geno. 1997. Reaction to the Nobel Prize. *La Stampa* (Turin), 10 October.

Swedish Academy. 1997. Official press release.

Vatican. 1997. Reaction to the Nobel Prize. *L'Osservatore Romano*, quoted in *Espresso*, 23 October.

CONTRIBUTORS
INDEX

Contributors

JOSEPH FARRELL is a senior lecturer in Italian studies at the University of Strathclyde, Glasgow. He has translated plays by Dario Fo, Eduardo De Filippo, Carlo Goldoni, and Alessandro Baricco. He is the author of a book on Leonardo Sciascia and has edited an anthology of writings on the Mafia and a volume of essays on Carlo Goldoni. He broadcasts regularly for BBC arts programs.

BENT HOLM teaches drama at the University of Copenhagen. He has published works on the *commedia dell'arte* and a monograph on Dario Fo entitled *Den omvendte verden. Dario Fo og den folkelige fantasi*. He has edited twelve annotated volumes of works by Dario Fo and translated works by Fo, Eduardo De Filippo, and Carlo Goldoni.

RON JENKINS is a professor of theater at Wesleyan University, Connecticut. He is the author of *Subversive Laughter: The Liberating Power of Comedy*. His collaboration with Dario Fo began in 1986 with the support of a Sheldon Post-Doctoral Fellowship from Harvard University. His research on Fo will continue with a Guggenheim Fellowship.

JENNIFER LORCH is an honorary senior lecturer in Italian at the University of Warwick. Her publications include an edition of Dario Fo's *Morte accidentale di un anarchico*. She has coauthored *Luigi Pirandello in the Theatre: A Documentary Record* and is preparing a history of the productions of Pirandello's *Sei personaggi in cerca d'autore*. She is also the author of *Mary Wollstonecraft: The Making of a Radical Feminist*.

COSTANTINO MAEDER is the head of the Center for Italian Studies at the Université Catholique de Louvain, Belgium, where he teaches Italian literature and linguistics. He has published on various topics dealing with Italian literature and theater, including Metastasio, Carlo Goldoni, Cesare Pavese, Arrigo Boito, Leonardo Sciascia, and Dario Fo.

TONY MITCHELL is a senior lecturer in writing and cultural studies at the University of Technology, Sydney. He is the author of the first book on Dario Fo to appear in English, *Dario Fo: People's Court Jester*, and the compilation

File on Dario Fo. His translations of plays by Fo, Franca Rame, and Dacia Maraini have been performed in various countries around the world. Mitchell is also the chairperson of the International Association for the Study of Popular Music (IASPM).

PAOLO PUPPA is a professor of theater history at the University of Venice. His works on Dario Fo include *Il teatro di Dario Fo.* He has published books on Pirandello, Ibsen, and Rosso di San Secondo, and several works on twentieth-century stagecraft. Puppa is also the author of two novels and several plays, including *Le parole al buio* and *Svevo a Venezia*, which have been performed in the leading theaters of Italy.

ANTONIO SCUDERI is an assistant professor of Italian at Truman State University, Missouri. His work on Dario Fo in the context of folklore studies and the oral tradition includes various articles and the book *Dario Fo and Popular Performance.* He has published various works on the Sicilian poet and playwright Nino Martoglio, including *The Dialect Poetry of Nino Martoglio: Sociolinguistic Issues in a Literary Context.*

WALTER VALERI is the author of several successful plays and collections of poems, including *Ora settima.* He has coedited a standard sourcebook on Dario Fo, *Fabulazzo*, and is a regular contributor to the Italian theater journal *Sipario.* From 1980 to 1996 he worked with Dario Fo, serving as his personal assistant and as organizer for his tours abroad. He now serves as the representative of Fo and Rame in North America.

SHARON WOOD is a reader in Italian literature at the University of Strathclyde, Glasgow. She is the author of *Woman as Object: Language and Gender in Alberto Moravia* and *Italian Women's Writing, 1860–1994* and the coeditor of *History of Women Writers in Italy.* She is currently preparing a book on Elsa Morante.

Index

Illustrations are indicated by italicized locators.